NEW SCHOLARSHIP FROM
BFI RESEARCH

Edited by
Colin MacCabe and Duncan Petrie

BFI PUBLISHING

First published in 1996 by the
British Film Institute
21 Stephen Street
London W1P 2LN

The British Film Institute exists to promote appreciation,
enjoyment, protection and development of moving image
culture in and throughout the whole of the United Kingdom.
Its activities include the National Film and Television
Archive; the National Film Theatre; the Museum of the
Moving Image; the London Film Festival; the production and
distribution of film and video; funding and support for
regional activities; Library and Information Services; Stills,
Posters and Designs; Research; Publishing and Education;
and the monthly *Sight and Sound* magazine.

British Library Cataloguing-in-Publication Data.
A catalogue record for this book is available from the
British Library.

ISBN 0–85170–520–0

Typeset in 10 on 11.5pt Sabon by
Fakenham Photosetting Ltd, Fakenham, Norfolk
Printed in Great Britain by
St Edmundsbury Press Ltd, Bury St Edmunds, Suffolk

CONTENTS

BFI WORKING PAPERS

Executive Editor: Colin MacCabe

BFI Working Papers are intended to make theoretical and practical contributions to debate and reflect the wide range of research activities and interests undertaken by the BFI.

Already published:

1. *Screening Europe:*
   Image and Identity in Contemporary European Cinema

2. *New Questions of British Cinema*

3. *Cinema and the Realms of Enchantment:*
   Lectures, Seminars and Essays by Marina Warner and Others

4. *Television and the Household:*
   Reports from the BFI's Audience Tracking Study

NOTES ON CONTRIBUTORS

Mary Scott Albert has worked as a film-maker and is currently working as a researcher for BFI TV's world-wide series *The Century of Cinema*, in addition to writing a doctoral thesis on slow motion.

Sue Dinsmore is a freelance lecturer in film history and theory. She is currently conducting research in the Media and Communications Department of Goldsmiths' College, University of London. She organised the *Real People on Television* conference at the National Film Theatre in May 1994.

Daniel Frampton has studied both philosophy and film and is currently writing a complete Filmosophy as a doctoral thesis at the BFI and Birkbeck College.

Patrizia Lombardo is Professor of French at the University of Geneva. Her publications include *Edgar Allan Poe et la modernité: Breton, Barthes, Derrida, Blanchot*; *The Three Paradoxes of Roland Barthes*. She has also written articles on architecture, art and literature.

Colin MacCabe is Head of Research and Education at the British Film Institute and Professor of English at the University of Pittsburgh. He has written on Joyce and Godard and is currently working on how to understand audiences in relation to both literary and audiovisual texts.

Claire Monk is a freelance film and cultural critic turned academic researcher. She is currently researching the British 'heritage film' in relation to questions of gender, audience and culture at Middlesex University. An article on this topic, 'The British Heritage Film and its Critics', has been published in *Critical Survey*. She is also a regular contributor to *Sight and Sound*.

Duncan Petrie is Director of the Bill Douglas Centre for the History of Cinema and Popular Culture at the University of Exeter. In addition to editing all four of the previous Working Papers volumes he is also co-editor of *Bill Douglas: A Lanternist's Account* and is currently completing a history of British cinematography.

Janet Thumim lectures in film and television at the University of Bristol. Her publications include *Celluloid Sisters: Women and Popular Cinema* and the collections (co-edited with Pat Kirkham) *You Tarzan: Masculinity, Movies and Men* and *Me Jane: Masculinity, Movies and Women*.

Linda Williams teaches film and women's studies at the University of California, Irvine. Her publications include *Figures of Desire: A Theory and Analysis of the Surrealist Film, Hard Core: Power, Pleasure and the Frenzy of the Visible* and two essays in the BFI collection *Dirty Looks: Women, Power, Pornography*, edited by Pamela Church Gibson and Roma Gibson. She was a BFI visiting fellow in 1993.

Maria Wyke is a lecturer in classics at the University of Reading. She has published in the field of gender studies in antiquity and undertaken research on 'the Classical Tradition'. Her book on the representation of ancient Rome in Italian and American cinema will be published by Routledge.

INTRODUCTION

Colin MacCabe

Some five years ago under the then newly appointed director, Wilf Stevenson, the British Film Institute formed a Research and Education Division. This not only provided a way in which the BFI's existing publishing, magazine and educational activities could be brought together with new focus and efficiency; it was also intended to increase the Institute's own research capabilities and, perhaps most importantly, to directly involve the Institute in postgraduate education. This initial programme is largely completed. *Sight and Sound* has been relaunched and last month sold more than 25,000 copies for the first time. BFI Publishing has increased its output from 8 to 30 volumes a year and has embarked on a major programme of reference publishing. The Media Education and Research Department is undertaking major research on television audiences and the structure of the industry and has also mounted a very successful campaign around the need for media studies in the national curriculum. The postgraduate programme is also well underway with the Institute's MA in its third year and a new PhD to be taught with the Architectural Association, Birkbeck College and the Tate Gallery taking its first students in October 1995.

The Institute's decision to involve itself directly in research and postgraduate education may be considered the third stage of a process begun under Paddy Whannel in the late 1960s. The first, which focused on the Society for Education in Film and Television (SEFT) and its magazines *Screen* and *Screen Education*, played a crucial role in establishing film and television studies as part of the university curriculum, while the second, concentrating on teachers, advisers and the secondary curriculum, was a very significant element in the widespread adoption of media studies in the schools.

Despite the undoubted successes of the previous twenty years, the situation in the late 1980s was anything but sanguine. While there were ever more undergraduate courses in media studies, and even a proliferation of masters' degrees, the study of the moving image remained absolutely peripheral to fundamental research – whether this

1

was calculated from an intellectual or an administrative perspective. Perhaps equally serious, the development of the subject often seemed over-theoretical. If earlier generations had wished to distance themselves from an overemphasis on technical proficiency or a fetishisation of production, the extent to which academic discussion of the moving image seemed to have completely removed itself from the concerns and discourses of practitioners suggested that media studies had succumbed to the worst and most traditional of university vices. From the perspective of primary and secondary education there was a similar desire to promote and support those elements of teaching and the curriculum which placed production (or more precisely editing) at the very centre of the subject.

It would be more than economical with the truth to claim that the BFI's decision to engage directly with postgraduate education was greeted with enthusiasm by the universities. Some were neutral or vaguely encouraging, but most were alarmed by what they saw as the emergence of a new competitor in an environment characterised by ever-diminishing resources. This reaction may be partially explained by the general climate in which the universities found themselves at the end of the 1980s, when morale and expectations in all subjects seemed to hit an all-time low. More specifically, the study of the moving image – caught inevitably between the humanities and the social sciences – was chronically underfunded. The implications of this second factor meant that in its initial phase the Institute's efforts had to be supported by sponsorship lest it monopolise (or, equally bad but more realistic, was thought to monopolise) the very scarce resources available.

One can hope that much of this initial alarm has now dissipated. In general the universities seem to have achieved greater stability and the chief funding councils, the British Academy and the ESRC, have both taken their responsibilities for the study of the moving image much more seriously. If there are some who would still argue that media studies need their own research council, this is a view overwhelmingly rejected by the universities themselves. Perhaps most significant of all, it is clear that the demand by qualified students for graduate-level study in the moving image continues to outpace supply.

The Working Papers were conceived as an integral part of the new research initiative and the four volumes published to date have drawn on different aspects of that initiative. From the very first it was clear that questions of identity and image – the ways in which we recognise ourselves in and through images – were central to the Division's project. Most important, how could one talk of British or European images (the common themes of arguments about film subsidy or public service television) in ways that recognised the current cultural realities of British and European societies? This question underlay the 1991 conference, Screening Europe, the proceedings of which were published as the first volume of the Working Papers.

It is one of the paradoxes of the last twenty years that while British cinema staggers from economic crisis to economic crisis the films of the recent past are among the most interesting produced in Europe. It was this paradox which was the focus of an early seminar which was subsequently published as the second volume of the series, *New Questions of British Cinema*.

As part of an attempt to re-engage the analysis of the moving image with the most vital currents of contemporary thought, the Institute has invited a visiting research fellow annually since 1989. In addition to the work that they undertake on their visit, it is always intended that their ideas should reach wider audiences not only through lectures and seasons at the National Film Theatre but also through subsequent publications. The third volume of the Working Papers, *Cinema and the Realms of Enchantment*, grew out of Marina Warner's extremely successful tenure of such a fellowship.

Over and above conferences, seminars and fellows, the Research Division has initiated several long-term projects looking at both the relations between creativity and organisational structures within the industry and the constitutions of audiences in relation to the moving image. The most developed of these stretches back to 1988 and the 20,000 diaries which were so successful a part of *One Day in the Life of Television*. A proportion of those diarists have subsequently contributed to a five-year longitudinal study of the development of the television audience in the cable and satellite age, the first fruits of which were published as the fourth volume, *Television and the Household*.

If the development of active research into the moving image can be seen as a long-term concern of the Institute – of which the funding of *Screen*, in the 1970s and the development of the Broadcast Research Unit, in the 1980s, were precursors – the direct teaching of students through the establishment of the MA in 1992 and the PhD in 1995 marks a new departure. Of course, the BFI's engagement with adult education is long-standing, and indeed the very foundation of the Institute in the 1930s is inconceivable without that rich tradition. However, the establishment of a graduate course, in collaboration with Birkbeck College, within the Institute marks a significant new departure.

There were pressing internal reasons for the development of such a course. The BFI, which in institutional terms is a relatively young organisation, has not developed any way of reproducing its own internal knowledge and skills. The wealth of wisdom accumulated within the archive, the library and the National Film Theatre risks being dissipated with the death or retirement of those of the post-war generation who built the Institute. What makes this wisdom so precious is that it is the product of that mixture of practice and theory which is part and parcel of so much of the Institute's work – where the practical aspects of producing, distributing, exhibiting and curating are constantly inflected and determined by the concern to generate historical and generic accounts of the moving image. The MA thus finds its fundamental rationale in the second part of the course where, following an engagement with the history of film and television and before producing a dissertation, the students undertake a four-month research placement in one of the departments of the Institute. (It is worth noting that this necessarily limits the number of places available to about twelve each year.)

This fifth volume of the Working Papers is consequently devoted to the first fruits of the MA. Five of the papers are versions of either dissertations or placement reports from the first two years of the course. These are supplemented by Patrizia Lombardo's essay on the photographic image, which grew out of a course taught in the first year of the MA in November 1992; a seminar by Linda Williams on *Uncle Tom* which was part of her very successful visiting fellowship in the summer of 1993; and an article by Janet Thumim, who was the winner of a prize that the BFI awarded in the same year for the best dissertation submitted in 1992.

It would be idle to claim some specious unity for the articles collected here. The aim of the Working Papers is to provide a space in which the wide range of research generated by the Institute can reach an academic audience. But three emphases are worth noting.

The first is the importance of history. Whether delving back into the 19th century to trace the history of the photographic image in general, or the specific image of *Uncle Tom's Cabin* in particular, or casting back no further than 1990 to begin considering the history of video diaries, almost all these pieces are fundamentally informed by a commitment to historical understanding. But in the past decade the appeal to history in film studies has often embraced an explicit call to abandon more general social or cultural analysis. This call would urge film studies to get on with the scholarly task of establishing a tradition and ignore the siren voices of theory or politics which would beckon it to understand this tradition in a wider intellectual context. It is to these wider contexts that the new developments in the BFI are fundamentally committed and it is hoped that one feature which does unite the work presented here is its intellectual ambition.

Finally, and much more obvious in the essays by Monk and Dinsmore than in the others, the new work at the BFI is determined to develop in relation to audiences. Monk's research on African television is a prelude to an exhibition strand in Africa '95, while Dinsmore's work on video diaries was intimately linked to a conference on factual programming at the NFT. In the long run the research undertaken at the BFI must be constantly inflected by and addressed to audiences wider than the academic community. This is the only way that such work will make a really original contribution to that community.

COLIN MACCABE
March 1995

TOWARDS A THEORY OF SLOW MOTION

Mary Scott Albert

Introduction

Film history begins with the systematic, scientific, experimental study of time and motion. We all know the story of Eadweard Muybridge's 1872 sequential photographs of Leland Stanford's racehorses, whose galloping hooves were too swift for the eye to see. The desire to capture motion as an image and then slow that image down to an analysable rate prompted the development of cinematography. A horse cannot gallop slowly, but a horse projected in slow motion can. Since then, film-makers all over the world have employed slow motion in infinitely varied circumstances: narrative and non-narrative, silent and sound films, musicals, television commercials, feature films, sporting events, music videos, nature films, home movies, news reports, and documentaries. It is as prevalent as the close-up, parallel editing or a tracking shot.

The elements of slow motion include rhythm, repetition, simultaneity, subjectivity, duration, and speed. Slow motion does not simply slow down a filmed action; it actually depicts more of an action by taking, say, 48 exposures in a second instead of 24. It is associated with memory, dream, and heightened awareness. It can elevate an image to the status of metaphor, extend the suspense of a thriller, or examine in detail an unseeable event. It spans the most practical and the most abstract extremes of film language.

In an effort to widen the methods of analysing film in general, this paper attempts to uncover the often glossed-over effects of slow motion in the cinema. Tracing its technological history, it is clear that the related technical and aesthetic qualities of slow motion were recognised from an early stage. It is important to look at film theory from the 1910s and 1920s, before narrative film-making became the norm. Slow motion and other expressionistic techniques were widely used, and the notion of cinema in general, new and exciting, was almost indistinguishable from them. In the 1930s, Sergei Eisenstein and, to a lesser extent, V. I. Pudovkin put forward theories which addressed the aesthetic issues posed by the use of slow motion. A careful reading of these works provides a context in which to examine the device and to read later essays on time and the cinema by Andrei Tarkovsky. Many describers of slow motion cannot help but apply musical terminology to its visual and psychological effects. A musical analysis on a more fundamental level is called for, and, in comparing the two on a structural level, a useful analytical tool is produced. Finally, a close analysis of slow motion sequences in various films, especially *The Thin Blue Line* (Erroll Morris 1988) and *Raging Bull* (Martin Scorsese 1980), is made, using the tools and theories assembled.

Technical Origins and Some Early Theory

In the early days of cinema, camera and projector rates were fluid and flexible, and the concept of slow motion as we know it did not exist. We understand it as a variant from the standard frame rate of 24 frames per second; a shooting speed of higher than this produces slow motion when projected at the standard rate. Before the advent of sound (which demanded synchronous shooting and sound-recording speeds), there was no standard frame rate, because cameras and projectors were hand-cranked, and speed variations in either shooting or projecting, whether intentional or accidental, were inevitable. Film audiences must have taken for granted slight oscillations of temporality when unintended, and no doubt fully appreciated full-blown spectacles of manipulated time when carefully constructed by the filmmakers. In fact, Tom Gunning, in defining his theory of the cinema of attractions, sees slow motion as one of the forms of cinematic manipulation used by early cinema showmen which 'directly solicit[ed] spectator attention, inciting visual curiosity, and supplying pleasure through an exciting spectacle'.[1]

Gunning sees films made before 1906 (or so) as defined by this exhibitionist quality: an 'enthusiasm for this new medium and its possibilities ... this fascination with the *potential* ... its ability to *show* something' dominated the cinema until narrative conventions overtook, but did not eliminate, it.[2] The use of slow motion in this context must have been fairly common. Certainly, filmgoers were, from the beginning, familiar with the device; just as the cinema allowed viewers to travel the world over, it allowed them to witness 'impossible' movement.

Many of the early slow-motion techniques and equipment were developed within the context of science. At the Marey Institute in Paris as early as 1904, M. Lucien Bell experimented with flying insects and developed electric spark cinematography which allowed him to expose more than 100 frames per second with a camera which had no intermittent movements.[3] The resulting film images were silhouettes. Subsequently, Dr C. Cranz in Germany made similar images of the flight

8

of bullets at the rate of 500 exposures in a tenth of a second.[4]

These devices were based on the concept of an intermittent view of moving objects through a spinning slotted disc, a technique which can create the illusion of slow motion.[5] Developed to replace the disc with pulsing light, stroboscopic technology had scientific implications, but, when perfected to produce actual photographs and motion pictures instead of silhouettes, it became a descendant of Gunning's early cinema of attractions. Dr Harold Edgerton invented stroboscopic cinematography at the engineering department of the Massachusetts Institute of Technology in 1931, and reached exposure times of up to a millionth of a second. He produced a film called *Seeing the Unseen*, which included images of humming birds in flight, guns being fired, sports equipment in use and liquids splashing.[6]

The aesthetic implications of these techniques were explored by French critics from an early stage. They grappled with new concepts such as the idea of *photogénie*, which, in general, referred to the expressive camera techniques and *mise en scène* which made ordinary objects unusual or visible in a new way for the first time. And precisely because the use of such techniques, including slow motion, flourished during the silent period of the avant-garde, it is important to consider the ways in which the film-makers, critics, and theoreticians from this period defined and interpreted the device.

In 1911, Ricciotto Canudo described the cinema as modern and mechanical, full of velocity and potential. Speed was not experienced as a result of fast-motion, rapid editing, or even as a product of editing at all. The idea of travelling to faraway places – of, say, climbing a mountain in ten minutes – had nothing to do with technique but rather with the medium itself. Before the cinema, the only way to experience distant places was to go there physically. Now, for the first time, cinemagoers felt a kind of velocity, a 'symbolic destruction of distances',[7] which we take for granted. Canudo saw the potential of cinema in its ability to evoke artistically rather than imitate theatrically, to show the *essence* rather than the *appearance* of contemporary life:

The arrival of cinema heralds the renovation of all modes of artistic creations, of all means of arresting the fleeting, conquering the ephemeral. What it can already show us – for example, in slow motion studies of plant growth – is an affirmation of its stupendous capacity to renew the representation of life itself. Cinema gives us the visual analysis of such precise evidence that it cannot but vastly enrich the poetic and painterly imagination.[8]

In 1919 Jean Cocteau, who saw a new cinematic form emerging in

America predicated on certain of the experiments with technology, implored artists to invent new conventions by exploiting the unknown worlds of 'perspective, slow motion, fast motion, [and] reverse motion ... as a new means of expression',[9] while the power to express inner states of being was also addressed, in 1924, by Paul Ramain, who examined the relationship between dreams and the cinema, citing the parallel impulses at work in both.

All the expressive and visual processes of the cinema are found in dream ...
The simultaneity of actions, soft-focus images, dissolves, superimpositions, distortions, the doubling of images, slow motion, movement in silence – are these not *the soul of dream and daydream?*[10]

Jean Epstein, during the 1920s, went a long way toward defining the expressionistic predispositions and potentialities of the cinema:

Astonishing abridgements in temporal perspective are permitted by the cinema – notably in those amazing glimpses into the life of plants and crystals – but these have never yet been put to dramatic purpose ... cinema composed without taking temporal perspective into account is not cinematic.[11]

In 1928 Epstein described the techniques developed to compensate for natural gestures in actors which were too fast or too illegible at normal speeds. 'Only filming at thirty or forty frames per second can do away with this basically untruthful quality in an actor's performance.'[12] This use of slow motion as a subtle, perhaps undetectable enhancement of the image is confirmed by leading Soviet cinematographer Andrei Moskvin, who in 1927 asserted that 'part of the task of the cameraman is, together with the director, to combine the general laws of surface composition with the laws of movement across the frame and with the calculation and layout of the movement in time'.[13] He also stressed the need, when shooting separate elements of a sequence, to keep in mind the temporal qualities of the surrounding shots. Similarly, F. H. Richardson's 1912 *Handbook of Projection* instructs projectionists to 'vary his speed to suit the subject being projected'.[14] This flexibility of temporalities, perhaps to a greater degree than we can judge today, helped characterise early cinema.

Pudovkin, Eisenstein and Tarkovsky

In 1931, V. I. Pudovkin wrote an essay entitled 'Close-Ups in Time', which puts forward a use of slow motion that goes beyond what he sees as its common and long-practised use. 'All the directors who have exploited retardation of movement have ... failed to incorporate the retarded movement in the editing construction as a whole – in the general rhythmical flow of the film.'[15] Instead of editing together shots of different temporal qualities representing one action or sequence of actions, they inserted an entire action shot in slow motion 'almost as a "dragged in" sequence'.[16] For Pudovkin, the proper use of slow motion is:

> the incorporation of various degrees of retarded speed of movement integrally in the construction of a given editing phrase. A short-length shot in 'slow motion' can be placed between two longer normal-speeded shots, concentrating the attention of the spectator at the desired point for a moment. 'Slow motion' in editing is not a *distortion* of an actual process. It is a portrayal more profound and precise, a *conscious guidance* of the attention of the spectator.[17]

He gives as an example the blow of a fist on a table. As the fist hits the table in real time, a glass on the table 'slowly jumps, rocks and falls. By this conjunction of rapid and slow shots was produced an almost audible, exceptionally sharply sensed impression of a violent blow [which] ... seem endowed with a rhythm particular to themselves.'[18]

Pudovkin begins his essay with descriptions of two events: a summer rain shower and a man working with a scythe in a field of wet grass. Neither of these presents images too rapid for the eye to perceive them. Pudovkin's conclusion that the way to represent these events cinematically through the use of rhythmically edited slow motion is based on the resultant 'deepened ... remarkably enriched sense of the process portrayed'.[19] It is not an analytical or a psychological representation, but rather an almost physiological effect. After viewing his man-with-scythe sequence, spectators 'confessed to having experienced an almost physical sense of moisture, weight and force'[20] without even recognising the technique which had been used. For Pudovkin, this technique is above all else a method for accurately representing physical/visual experience.[21]

In developing his theory of montage, Eisenstein includes slow motion as a form of conflict within a shot.[22] He defines slow motion, or *Zeitlupe*, as the conflict between an event and its temporal nature (not simply a conflict of tempo, which is another category), and compares the use of slow motion in cinema with the 'decomposed acting' of Kabuki theatre, where motion is fragmented but also slowed 'to a degree that is unknown in [Russian] theatre'.[23]

Expanding his theory of montage from the conflicts *between* shots to include the conflicts *within* a shot, he recognises slow motion as a decomposition of the process of movement, as opposed to the decomposition of the links between movements. For Eisenstein, the only compositionally meaningful use of *Zeitlupe* is to present altered versions of 'normally acted states of mind, which ... produces unusual emotional tension'. He stresses that simply shooting in slow motion will not produce the specific effect he has in mind. Used improperly it produces only 'visual effects, dreams, formal trifles and pointless mischief'.[24] Once again he compares the device to Kabuki acting methods:

> If you bear in mind that the attraction exerted by the actor's performance on the audience is based on the audience's identification with it, you can easily attribute both examples to one and the same causal explanation. The intensity of our perception increases because the process of identification is easier when the movement is decomposed.[25]

Eisenstein's interest in identifying precedents for cinematic experience in other media, both contemporary and historical, has a twofold effect. First, it allows him to borrow terminology with which to describe the phenomena he was theorising, and, second, it allows him to build up a general, far-reaching tradition of artistic expression, the culmination of which was the cinema, specifically montage.[26] A reading of Eisenstein presents not only a theory of montage but also a history of montage, and includes examples from architecture, epic poetry, literature, haiku, sculpture, hieroglyphics, theatre, and painting, to name a few.[27] It is not surprising, therefore, to find within his work precedents for slow motion and high-speed photography as disparate as the Kabuki acting style, Tolstoy's *Boyhood, Childhood, Youth* (the description of a lightning storm), and a painting by Tintoretto, where within one figure the position of the limbs describes movement by virtue of the fact that the body segments reflect temporally sequential phases.

Eisenstein's conclusion from this type of analysis foresees one of the modern uses of slow motion:

> This [breakdown of movement into phases] being the method for the artistic representation of a 'self-contained' movement – i.e. gesture – it is also the logical tradition for depicting *the sequential nature of big, complex series of actions*.[28]

The notion of simultaneity is inherent in this kind of description. Eisenstein gives as an example a medieval miniature painting by Memling which shows all the phases of the events of Holy Week in Jerusalem. This notion of simultaneity, 'this comprehension and perception of the *unity* of simultaneity and sequentiality',[29] describes an essential element of the perception of slow motion. We can see slow motion as a kind of montage of temporality, where the conflict is not only between an event and its temporal nature but between differing/ simultaneous temporalities. It 'assumes the function of conducting the action ... by incorporating in its compositional resolution that intersection of past and future'.[30]

In his discussion of conflict within a shot, Eisenstein explains the ways in which a 'depiction' becomes an 'image' – in other words, how a shot can become a metaphor. In his story of the pretzel-shaped shop sign in 'Montage 1937', he describes how, by altering the composition of a drawing of a barricaded street, the depiction of a barricade becomes an image which signifies struggle. The elements which together produce this effect are the intersection of planes, the acute angles, the jagged lines, and, most important, the placement of the pretzel-shaped shop sign. For Eisenstein, the

> ultimate in metaphor is attained in the placing of the shop sign. . . . Here, what is normally seen above us is brought downward ... not by showing the baker's shop sign as lying physically beneath the barricade, but by purely *compositional* means. The distinction between these two examples lies in the fact that in the first sketch, the shop sign cannot be interpreted on any other than a naturalistic level, whereas the subtextual meaning of the second pretzel sign reads not as 'a sign thrown down' but as 'an overthrow': that which was above is now below. And we are made to adopt this metaphorical reading by the fact that the removal of the sign has not been brought about physically, but compositionally, i.e. by the viewpoint from which the event is observed.[31]

In other words, a distortion of the depiction, a different viewpoint, a decomposition and altered reconstruction can produce an image which functions as a metaphor. Slow motion is just such an altered reconstruction. The decomposition is not fragmentary and sequential, but is predetermined and presented whole, within the shot, as a single image. The process of breaking down the depiction and building up the image occurs in the shooting or pre-shooting stage of film-making, not in post-production (except in cases where a shot is altered by laboratory techniques), and does not eliminate the original depictive strategy of the shot.

Eisenstein asserts that the second version of the pretzel-shaped shop sign sketch 'repeats the depictive aspect, [it] in no way upsets the naturalistic, depictive integrity of the phenomenon as such'.[32] This is important because it underscores the notion of tension as an element of montage within a shot. The juxtaposition of elements, the simultaneous presence of depiction and image, of recognisable object and altered representation, of the pretzel-shaped shop sign and its expressionist placement in the frame, creates the potential for metaphor that Eisenstein describes.

Although Eisenstein never offers distorted temporality as a means of elevating a depiction to an image, clearly the 'compositional means' he refers to can be extended to include slow motion, which can elevate a shot 'beyond the limits of depiction to the super structure, expressive, spatial-compositional disposition of objects depicted (or colour, or space, or so on)'.[33]

Eisenstein further develops the idea of depiction→image→metaphor by introducing the element of rhythm – that is, the rhythm created by editing. From the juxtaposition of shots emerges 'a pure expression of the *dynamics* of the subject matter, through the rhythm of its articulation'. It is a 'maximally generalised depiction of a *process* within the subject matter, a graph of the changing phrases of contradiction within its unity'.[34] Again, the underlying process at work is one of tension, of conflicting elements whose differences form an oscillating and dynamic pattern.

Eisenstein also introduces the notion of repetition in relation to slow motion. Repetition is another essential element of the perception of slow motion. It is inherent to its temporal deviation that there is an original form which spawned it: 'The very term "slowed-down" … presumes the existence in our mind of a normative tempo from which the movement has deviated.'[35] It is impossible to see an event simultaneously live and in slow motion. Eisenstein sees this implied normative tempo as the reason that speeded-up motion can be funny; it is the discrepancy between our expectations or extra-textual knowledge and the action which deviated from these preconceptions in a silly way. More interestingly, Eisenstein notes that 'for the same reason, [speeded-up movements] are *not funny* when they occur, for example, in some episode of *heightened activity* in a crowd scene, i.e. where the visual distortion of plain reality is *imaginatively* more in keeping with the theme than straightforward, literal depiction would be'.[36] The degree of humour attached to a distortion of time may, it seems, be relative to the degree to which that distortion is in keeping with the theme. Speedy distortion tends to make light of a subject, and slowing tends to add weight, but speedy motion does not in itself cause humour.

The concept of the slow-motion image being at once identical (a repetition) and deviant, at once the same image of an event but placed in abnormal conditions, and also another, different image of the event points out the contrasting elements inherent in the device, and the notion of repetition and variation (deviation) as the essential components of pattern and rhythm. Repetition can also be interpreted in the context of thought process and memory. Because we can't possibly be watching a slow-motion event live, it must be in the past, a memory; and, because memory is subjective, the image is only one version of many possible variants – it becomes more specific. Slow-motion images are more specific than those shot at 24 frames per second because we literally see more of the action, but also because of this subjective quality linked to time and memory.

Decades later, another Russian film-maker theorised another conception of time and rhythm in cinema which is also useful for studying slow motion along these lines. Andrei Tarkovsky saw rhythm as the dominant factor in film – rhythm, that is, which exists as 'time-pressure' and expresses the course of time within a shot. For Tarkovsky, rhythm is not the result of editing: 'Time courses through the picture despite editing rather than because of it ... rhythm is determined not by the length of the edited pieces but by the pressure of the time that runs through them.'[37] Time-pressure may relate to movement, duration and speed, but not to a systematic juxtaposition of these elements. Rather, it is the flowing, 'coursing', overlapping nature of time and its relationship with consciousness which interests Tarkovsky, especially in relation to memory, dream, and the way that 'constant movement and change allows everyone to interpret and feel each separate moment in his own way'.[38] To represent these states faithfully is essential to Tarkovsky's aesthetic; 'for the cinema image is essentially the observation of a phenomenon passing through time [and] the basic element of cinema, running through to its tiniest cells, is observation'.[39] Tarkovsky understands any phenomenon, at any level of consciousness, as reality, and it is the time-pressure of a particular phenomenon which reflects rhythmically its true nature. The idea that 'facts and aesthetic structures existing and changing within time [constitute] ... a faithful record, a true chronicle'[40] is central to Tarkovsky's thinking, but this chronicle includes – indeed, is defined by – a subjective sense of what is real. Slow motion, then, on one level is not a distortion of time and motion at all, but a precise and accurate observation of a specific reality, and the rhythm produced by the movement is the time-pressure of the shot.

Rhythm in cinema is conveyed by the life of the object visibly recorded in the frame. Just as from the quivering of a reed you can tell what sort of current, what pressure there is in a river, in the same way we know the movement of time from the flow of the life process reproduced in the shot.[41]

Tarkovsky regards slow motion as a means of giving time a rhythmic expression, a rhythmic design, but only in the context of a flowing, organic joining of shots. Differing time-pressures can and must be introduced, but only 'in response to an endogenous development', working together organically as would a 'brook, spate, river, waterfall, and ocean'.[42] Equally, the time-pressure of a shot must be an accurate record of an event: 'Breaking off contact with fact and with time realism ... makes for preciousness and affectation.'[43]

In spite of the differences between Tarkovsky's ideas and those of Eisenstein, a close reading reveals that they both considered the image in its ultimate form to be transcendent. Indeed, Tarkovsky's description is remarkably close to Eisenstein's: 'What you see in the frame is not limited to its visual depiction, but is a pointer to something stretching out beyond the frame.'[44] Their disagreement is in the meaning of the images – Eisenstein looks for metaphorical, coded, intellectual meanings, while for Tarkovsky the pointer he refers to stretches out to infinity and to life. Pure observation and facts preclude the presence of any kind of symbol, verbal meaning or 'other such figures – that is, things that have nothing to do with the imagery natural to the cinema'.[45] However, the means of achieving transcendence are common to both, including the manipulation of time as an expressive device, and the importance of rhythm giving a shape to time and motion.

Music Theory and Slow Motion
The theories analysed so far have all embraced musical terminology in connection with the use of slow motion in film. Indeed, the relationship between film and music, on both a structural level and a level of reception, has been cited since the beginning of cinema. Canudo, for example, described cinema as a combination of the rhythm of space (plastic arts) and the rhythm of time (music and poetry); Vuillermoz, as an orchestration of images, a musical score of vision and memory through measure and rhythm; Faure, as living rhythm and its repetition in time, movements and cadences which unroll in musical space; Henri Chomette, as a visual symphony. For Ramain, music was an audible dream, and the cinema perfected an almost holy trinity of dream, music and cinema – and the greatest of these was cinema.

Epstein asserted that all movements – living and mechanical – have a rhythm, a frequency, a cadence which can at times converge together in a musical pattern. For him, to see is to idealise; to abstract and

16

extract, to transform. As a repetition of events, cinema becomes a multiplication of vision. In this way, *photogénie* is indefinable, like the taste of something or a musical phrase. The power of the cinema is its ability to generalise and define in terms of metaphor, to present not 'an evening', but 'evening'.[46] The elements of repetition, duration, rhythm, all intrinsic to slow motion, are present in Epstein's poetic descriptions.[47]

Musical analysis can relate to a wide variety of filmic phenomena,[48] but my purpose here is to examine briefly some musical concepts which are applicable to the use of slow motion in the cinema, and try to uncover the ways in which these concepts operate.

The general areas of interest in this respect include the basic concepts of *form, process,* and *implication,* as well as *conformant relationships* and *hierarchic structures.* Their meanings and uses as outlined here are based on a series of lectures given by Leonard B. Meyer at Berkeley in 1971, compiled in his book *Explaining Music.*[49]

In music theory, *form* refers to the pattern structures which make up elements of a composition, such as a motif, a phrase, a theme, or a movement, whose various 'parts are related in a functional, syntactic way'.[50] Similarly in film we recognise shots, sequences, scenes and other part–whole relationships. A structure is said to *be formal* if it establishes points of relative stability or closure. *Process,* on the other hand, refers to the mobile interaction among the various parameters of music – melody, harmony, rhythm, pitch, and so on – and their various states of stability and instability.

Form and process work together to create patterns; both must be present. Repetition, varied or exact, of all or of part of an element is necessary to pattern-making. As Meyer notes: 'The existence of both similarity and difference between ... events is a necessary condition for patterning of any sort.'[51] Exact repetition without variation is purely formal; like the ticking of a clock, or waves crashing on rocks, it is not disordered, but rather unordered. Similarly, uniform change is purely processive if the elements do not group themselves into differentiated, endable units. It is the tension between similarity and difference which produces patterns. In this way, a pattern is inherent within a single slow-motion shot – the presence of both similarity to the original action and difference from it, its status as an already repeated element – whereas more conventional parameters may take longer to establish compelling patterns.

Meyer defines *implication* as occurring when an event is 'patterned in such a way that reasonable inferences can be made both about its connections with preceding events and about how the event itself might be continued and perhaps reach closure and stability'.[52] An implicative pattern can be seen as a sign pointing to possible future events, as yet undefined. To use Meyer's example, thunder and dark clouds suggest it will rain. Implications can be more or less compelling, but the outcome of an event – whether it rains or doesn't rain – does not diminish the fact of implication, which in any case affects our understanding of both events. Antecedent phrases, described below, are strongly implicative.

Meyer sees this weighing of alternatives, of being aware of the contingency of temporal events, as a deep human habit tied to the ability to envisage alternative courses of action.[53] Perhaps for this reason:

> Understanding implicative relationships is an activity of our whole being, not just that artificial abstraction, the mind. The many facets of the human nervous system, physiological changes and adjustments, motor behaviour and the like, all are involved. For this reason, implicative relationships may be experienced as kinetic tension and resolution – that is, feeling and affect.[54]

Just as film suspense solicits a physical response from viewers subjected to deeply compelling implicative structures, the ways that slow motion in certain contexts produces emotional and physical effects can be tied to its use in implicative structures.

Conformant relationships are based on similarity. It is the 'sameness' of musical events within one or more of a number of pattern-forming parameters, such as pitch or rhythm. Think of the first two phrases of *Happy Birthday to You*: the rhythms are identical; the pitches are similar; the events are conformant. Pattern-forming parameters are found in film as well. Two shots can be linked by the depiction of similar or identical diegetic space, as in the case of shots alternating between people interacting in the same room, or by diegetic time, as in the case of shots alternating between people having a conversation over the telephone, or cross-cutting between parallel action. Theme can act as a parameter, as in a montage of disparate views of a city to establish place. Music or voice-over narration can link wholly dissimilar shots into a sequence. Similarly, character can act as a parameter, as when we follow the sequential actions of a person which are not necessarily linked by time or space. Point-of-view can link the image of a character with images he sees or perceives. A subcategory of point-of-view would be what Edward Branigan calls perception, where the use of distinct cinematic technique relates to the subjective state of a character.[55]

Slow motion can act as a parameter when, in a sequence, disparate images are connected by similar frame rates (two or more shots of disparate images all in slow motion), or when, in a sequence, the presence of slow-motion shots intercut with real time links all the shots in a pattern. Related to Branigan's perception shot, slow motion can link a character's point of view with a subjective state.

Conformant parametric relationships also occur *within* musical phrases, themselves patterns, where, in our example of *Happy Birthday to You*, the relationship between the individual disparate notes is linked by intervallic coherence (they're in the same key) and consistent tempo, thus forming a pattern. In film, the parameters within a shot form patterns similarly where, as in a long shot of a street scene, the disparate actions are linked by space, or, in a cross-cut sequence, they are linked by time. In a similar way in the case of a slow-motion shot, the frame rate informs our reading of the objects depicted.

Music can be analysed as *hierarchic structure*, which refers to the comparison of forms in successively more encompassing arrangements. For example, on a low level, two motifs can be compared with each other, and, depending on the parameters at work, one may be defined stable, the other unstable. At the next level, these two motifs may make a phrase which, compared with another phrase, has another formal relationship. In general, elements which on one level are formal, on the next become processive and vice versa. For instance, the processive note-to-note relationship of the first motif of *Happy Birthday to You* becomes on the next level formal – a phrase which is compared with other phrases at that level.

In a similar way, repetition plays a role in the analysis of hierarchic structures. 'On the level where repetition is immediate, it tends to separate events. But on the *next* level – where similar events are grouped together as part of some larger unit – repetition tends to create coherence.'[56] In other words, difference is stressed in repeated elements occurring close together, but similarity is stressed if they occur far apart. This will become important in the analysis of *Raging Bull* below.

A common result of hierarchic analysis is the identification of antecedent/consequent structures, where the antecedent is the open, unstable, processive phrase (the first half of the entire *Happy Birthday* song), and the consequent is the element of closure, the formal element (the last half of the entire *Happy Birthday*). The antecedent element is implicative. On the next hierarchic level, these two together become a formal element (in the case of *Happy Birthday*, a complete song; in longer compositions, closure would not be present in all the parameters of the consequent, thus allowing the song to continue).

In film, this type of structure can be seen in shot/reaction shot structures, and in point-of-view structures, where the object shot is the unstable, processive shot given closure by the resulting character or reaction shot, and, on a higher level, when a processive sequence or scene is resolved by a subsequent element of closure. While on its own a slow-motion shot can be seen as a formal patterned unit, in a sequence it can become an open, processive element which implies some sort of consequent closure. Similarly, a sequence defined by the use of intercut slow-motion shots is in itself a formal pattern, while on a higher hierarchic level it can be seen as a mobile, unstable implicative element.

Rhythm is a comparison. Musical rhythm only acquires definition when it is set against a constant metre. In the same way, an internal rhythm is defined in slow-motion shots by setting the shooting speed against the projected speed, the slowed action against our experience of real time. Similarly, slow-motion shots intercut with real time define a rhythm which compares the two temporalities. It is not dependent on the regular beats we associate with musical rhythm (although this element can exist as well). The most important aspect is, rather, the contrast between and parallel continuance of the individual patterns and the contrast between them. The better defined the patterns, the more established and evident the sense of rhythm in a sequence or scene.

Because of their strongly patterned sense of rhythm, slow-motion sequences produce a sensation in the spectator of suspended attention, of a moving, dynamic and ordered sense of time being carried from one moment to the next, a sensation which can be similarly produced by music. We physically experience waves of time as they move through the film. Each moment, each shot, implies the next, just as each note in a tune, while not determining the next note, strongly implies that there will be a next one. When we watch slow-motion sequences, our muscles tense and we hold our breath, not only as a result of the action portrayed, but because of the structure of the shots – their order, duration, and rhythm.

Film Analysis
Adequate and appropriate tools have now been assembled with which to dismantle the structure of slow-motion shots and sequences and to understand their use and effect. Early film forms used slow motion in the context of the cinema of attractions, as an avant-garde expressionist device, and as a subtle smoothing device. These continue through the history of cinema, but the dominant narrative force of Hollywood classical cinema limited such use in most contexts (and in America almost altogether), in that classical film form depends on invisible editing, spatial and temporal verisimilitude, and concealing the techniques of film-making.[57]

Of course there were exceptions. The epiphanous moment in Jean Vigo's *Zéro de conduite* (1933) is defined by the use of slow motion in the pillow fight and procession in the dormitory. Alberto Cavalcanti, in *Went the Day Well* (1942), included a single shot of slow motion when an English villager shoots her boyfriend, whom she realises is a German in disguise. Orson Welles uses slow motion to depict the advancing soldiers disguised as a forest in Macbeth's point-of-view shots in his 1948 *Macbeth*. In David Lean's *Oliver Twist* (1948) Nancy's outburst against Fagin and Bill Sykes ends as she throws herself against them and is thrown to the floor in slow motion. The amorous boys of François Truffaut's first film *Les Mistons* (1957), having worshipped their teacher on her bicycle from afar, lean over in slow motion to smell the bike's saddle as it leans against a tree. Tarkovsky, who would later use slow motion extensively, included just one shot in *Ivan's Childhood* (1962), although the film is built around dream and memory just as his later films are. Water is thrown in slow motion over Ivan's mother as she lies by the well in which Ivan hides.

Alfred Hitchcock, whose films defined and yet never quite follow the rules of the classic period, used slow motion in several films. The first time we see Grace Kelly in *Rear Window* (1954) she is leaning in to a giant slow-motion close-up kiss with Jimmy Stewart. Their heads in profile fill the entire screen, and slow motion occurs only in the one shot. It can be seen as an attraction for an audience eager to see Grace Kelly and to get the love story going; Hitchcock himself claimed he 'wanted to get right to the important part without wasting any time. It's the surprise kiss [as opposed to the suspense kiss].'[58] His terminology underscores the tension created in the shot. Neither expected nor implied, a surprise, compared with suspense, is something fast. An effect of stretching the moment of the kiss, then, is to heighten this tension between the action and the spectators' expectations in a rhythmic comparison, while gratifying their desire to see the star. Hitchcock similarly uses slow motion for single shots of kisses in *Spellbound* (1945) and *To Catch a Thief* (1955), while for *Psycho*'s famous shower scene (1960), he recounts to François Truffaut that slow-motion shots of the knife and the stand-in's torso were 'inserted in the montage so as to give the impression of normal speed'.[59]

In *Strangers on a Train* (1951), as Farley Granger walks up a flight of stairs a huge dog on the landing growls down at him. Since it isn't his house and it's the middle of the night, he's nervous, and this is reflected in the point-of-view structure of the shots, alternating between Granger and the dog as he climbs the stairs. The suspense builds until, after a close-up profile of the dog's head which breaks the point-of-view sequence, we see the dog licking Granger's hand in slow motion. The shot begins at normal speed and then switches to slow motion mid-shot.[60] The slow motion extends the suspense created by the parallel edit montage. It also makes the dog licking the hand look creepy, and so works to keep the dog scary for the audience even though he's shown himself to be harmless. It keeps the tension going and doesn't let the audience breathe too deeply; we're still worried about what's at the top of the stairs.

Following the classical Hollywood period, independent and semi-independent film-makers, influenced by European and Japanese cinemas as well as by American avant-garde film-making, began to build a new vocabulary which brought to the foreground the elements of cinema. Consequently, slow motion became a useful tool for film-makers more interested in exploring internal, subjective experience more overtly than their Hollywood predecessors.

In 1967, two films mark the post-classical resurgence of the use of slow motion in American cinema: Arthur Penn's *Bonnie and Clyde* and John Boorman's *Point Blank*. At the end of *Bonnie and Clyde* (itself a homage to the *nouvelle vague*, and, in fact, written specifically with François Truffaut in mind as director), the outlaws die in slow motion, ripped apart by machine-gun fire. The only other instance of slow motion in the film occurs much earlier, at a picnic with Bonnie's family, where there develops an unspoken sense that they won't see Bonnie again. A young boy who has been play-acting an outlaw fakes a falling, rolling death in slow motion, foreshadowing the end of the film and telegraphing the characters' sense of foreboding.

The British director John Boorman's first American film, *Point Blank*, depicts the highly subjective experiences of a single man. Sequences consist of shots which only relate in Lee Marvin's mind, when, for instance, the way a woman lies on a bed reminds him of another woman on another bed some time in the past. Boorman cuts the images directly together without explanation, and, as this stream-of-consciousness narrative runs throughout the film, slow-motion shots, singly and in edited sequences, help create the subjective elements.

But the first dedicated and extensive use of slow motion in this period can be found in the work of director Sam Peckinpah. Peckinpah experimented with the device while directing for television in the early 1960s, but did not fully develop his technique until 1969 with *The Wild Bunch*. Forever linked with the portrayal of violence, Peckinpah used slow motion to heighten the impact of violent gunfights. For him, the expressionistic device made the action more real: it made injury look painful, and death look immutable.

Peckinpah's use of slow motion fulfils Pudovkin's ideal of incorporating various degrees of speed of movement integrally in the construction of a given editing phrase.[61] The compelling feature of his technique is the way he intercuts slow-motion footage with normal-speed shots. For example, in a complicated gunfight near the beginning of *The Wild Bunch* there is a slow-motion shot of a man falling from a rooftop in the Texas town of Starbuck. In the film, this shot is intercut three times with normal-speed action. Conventional, classical editing techniques would demand that when we return to the shot of the man falling he should be closer to the ground than when we left him to show something else happening simultaneously. But Peckinpah brings us back to the very next frame: we see the entire action, *plus* parallel action. This sequential method of portraying simultaneity recalls Eisenstein, who, remember, foresaw the use of juxtaposed simultaneity and sequentiality in depicting complex action.[62]

A key element for Peckinpah in this respect is establishing the diegesis very clearly, so that the disorienting effect of the rapid cuts, fragmented images and simultaneous action occurs within a predefined space. It allows him to cut back to these previously seen viewpoints for fractions of seconds, giving the audience the overall view of simultaneous action. In the gunfight in Starbuck, for which multiple cameras running at different speeds were used to film the action, we are given substantial information from many angles about the geometry of the space and the spatial relationships of all the important participants (the Bunch, the bounty hunters and the marching, hymn-singing members of the Temperance Union), in a scene which primarily functions to create the tension leading up to the battle. Music is important to the building of tension in the lead-up to the battle, but, once it begins, the music drops out and the gunfire takes over as a rhythmic element. The patterns created by the various intercut temporalities as well as the soundtrack form the rhythm of the sequence and the slow-motion shots themselves heighten our perception. Peckinpah used these techniques in most of his subsequent films, including *The Getaway* (1972), *Cross of Iron* (1977), *Bring Me the Head of Alfredo Garcia* (1974), *The Killer Elite* (1975), and *Osterman Weekend* (1983).

The impact of Peckinpah's depiction of violence was far-reaching and continues today; it is not overstating matters to claim him as the major influence on the film portrayal of violence since *The Wild Bunch*.[63] The many examples of this tradition include *The Long Riders* (1980), *Born on the Fourth of July* (1989), *Die Hard* (1988), and the *Terminator* films (1984, 1991). However, most action pictures even now limit their use of slow motion to the ultimate or penultimate moment of suspense or violence, as the climaxing shot of a parallel edit montage, where suspense builds between two alternating elements. When the elements finally come together, the moment is prolonged by the use of slow motion, or, in a variation of this method, the moment preceding the union of the elements is delayed even

23

further by the use of slow motion, thus extending the suspense. Slow motion is almost obligatory for the standard moment of victory for the good guy and death for the bad guy, or for big expensive stunts usually involving plate-glass windows and motorcycles.

To date, the most exciting example of the Peckinpah legacy is seen in the Hong Kong action films directed by John Woo, including *A Better Tomorrow* (1985), *The Killer* (1989), *Bullet in the Head* (1990), *Once a Thief* (1991), and *Hard-boiled* (1992). Like Peckinpah, Woo uses multiple cameras and usually edits or closely supervises the editing of all his films. In an interview at the National Film Theatre in London on 1 October 1993, Woo described his technique as intuitive; for him the rhythm of the action develops in the editing room, and is based on musical feelings. He does not storyboard or plan sequences. Instead, Woo says that during editing he places himself in the mind of his characters and imagines how they will get themselves through an action sequence. This combination of rhythm and subjectivity is a potent context for the use of slow motion. By extending even further the duration of the slow-motion action sequences and including slow-motion shots in the build-up to the action as well as the action itself, Woo has widened the Peckinpah vocabulary.

Woo uses shots which in themselves change speed, and he also uses slow motion for key narrative moments, as in *Once a Thief*, when Cherie waits anxiously at the airport for Joe and Jim to arrive, and then as Jim walks toward her with the news of the Joe's death. The image of Jim in slow motion from Cherie's point of view works as a predicted memory: this is the moment she will look back on; it will signify Joe's death for her. In addition, Woo manipulates his audience by playing on the conventions of slow motion. Knowing the expectations that slow motion creates, he uses it to build up false alarms, as in the tearoom scene at the beginning of *Hard-boiled*. The fact that slow-motion action sequences constitute most of the films' duration points to the resurgence of a cinema of attractions in the 1980s.[64]

In Peckinpah and in all the action pictures which derive from his model, the conception, developed earlier in the discussion of rhythm, of slow motion as a comparison works to signify the immediacy of the danger for the characters involved. Slow motion acts like a shot of adrenalin: the chemical reaction in the brain heightens perception and quickens the metabolism so that the surrounding environment seems relatively slowed down, and personal, mental time speeds up. The combination of fast action and slow depiction sets up rhythmic comparisons of agitation with calmness, acceleration with deceleration, frenetic with hypnotic, action with contemplation, mobility with stillness, and, ultimately, life with death. For the characters, the depicted action is the extended split second where life is most present and death is most imminent.

Post-classical use of slow motion is certainly not limited to the depiction of action, however. Kubrick uses it in the famous shot in *2001* (1968) of the bone thrown in the air, as well as in *The Shining* (1980), as the blood pours out of the closed elevator doors. The transcendent moment of *Star Wars* (George Lucas, 1977), when Obiwan Kanobi becomes one with the Force, is the only slow-motion shot in the film, and its effect on Luke Skywalker propels the rest of the narrative. In a similar way, Brad Pitt's character in *A River Runs Through It* (Robert Redford, 1992) enters a state of grace as his father and brother watch him fly-fish in slow motion, which also places the moment as a crucial memory in the mind of the brother. David Lynch used it to undermine the image of small-town America with the fire engine driving by a picket-fenced street in *Blue Velvet* (1986), while Federico Fellini (whose early films had no slow motion, although their highly subjective nature undoubtedly influenced its resurgence) combined beautifully all of the elements of the technique in *E la nave va* (1983). In a short sequence which follows the ship's waiters from the kitchen to the dining room, Fellini uses fast motion in the kitchen and slow motion in the dining room. The movements of the kitchen staff follow patterns created by the well timed workings of the kitchen, and are underscored by the fast motion. Similarly, Fellini imposes a rhythm and pattern on the dining room with diegetic music which changes tempo as the image slows down, and by choreographing the movements of the diners so that they all raise their soup spoons to their mouths at the same time, in slow-motion time to the waltz being played just off screen. Fellini succeeds in creating the subjective experience of the waiters moving between the opposite and juxtaposed environments by building a complex pattern of rhythm and speed.

The Thin Blue Line

The Thin Blue Line[65] opens with a thematically linked sequence. We see four close-up views of the Dallas skyline – the tops of buildings and groups of buildings against a darkling sky. Also linking these shots is the presence of glowing red circular lights – signals to aircraft which blink on and off. In the successive shots, these flashing red lights create a rhyming pattern, a conformant relationship, and, in addition, link retroactively to the opening titles in which the four words are written in white and then the word 'BLUE' switches to red. Randall Adams's voice-over comes in over the third shot, and we see him in the fifth shot. As he continues to speak, the sixth shot brings back the rhyme in the form of a fat red circle – a big close-up of a slowly spinning flashing red light of a police car.

Throughout the film this rhyming element (not exact repetition) continues, with the addition of red car tail-lights, both moving and stationary; a red flashing light in the recreated interrogation room; red flashing police lights in close-up as well as wide shots which include varying amounts of the car; and as the flashing illumination bathing the re-creations of the crime scene in a pulsating red glow. If the metaphor for the prosecution in the Randall Adams case is the 'thin blue line' of police which separates society from anarchy, the introduction of red circles as the film opens is a metaphorical assault on the methods used by the police and the conclusions reached by them. The use of slow motion provides similar key metaphors for the defence in this cinematic trial.

The sense of 'past' inherent in slow motion defines the re-enacted scenes in the film. The use of slow motion underscores an inaccessibility to the facts. Noting these and other conformant relationships, we can break the film into a number of formal elements, including interviews, existing material from the past (such as police reports, newspaper accounts, photographs, and legal documents), and re-enactments. Within the re-creations of the crime, conformant relationships based on similarity of theme (objects such as a flashlight, a milkshake, a firing gun, and actions such as a car driving away, a policewoman shooting after the car driving away, the policeman's feet approaching the car) and similarity of frame rate (slow motion) build patterns which at a higher hierarchic level develop the conflicting memory/multiple point-of-view structure of the narrative. The slow-motion shots become signs for this *Rashomon*-like theme, and the cumulative effect of presenting the repeated patterns breaks down the prosecution's case without ever needing to present an account called 'true'.

Specifically, the objects depicted in slow motion are foregrounded by their frame rate. They stand out as they occur in the film and in our memory of the film. It is impossible for Morris to show us what happened at the scene of the crime. We cannot see Officer Wood falling to the ground and dying. Instead of relying on the actor re-creating the event, Morris limits our view of the actor by filming him as close-ups of parts of his body (such as torso and feet), and uses a slow-motion shot of a flashlight falling and breaking as it hits the ground by the car as a metaphor for the dying policeman; in the sense outlined by Eisenstein's story of the pretzel-shaped shop sign, the depiction of the flashlight becomes an image of murder as it slowly bounces, the glass breaks, and the light goes out for ever. In real time, this transcendent meaning would not exist.

In the same way, the milkshake stands in for the incompetence of the partner. We can never see exactly how the policewoman reacted, or exactly where she was during the shooting, and so Morris uses the slow-motion image of the milkshake being thrown through the air and landing on the tarmac as a metaphor for this absence and the subsequent discrepancies in her testimony. The action is shown in three slow-motion shots following the sound of the first gunshot in the second re-creation, intercut with real-time close-ups of, first, the police radio which she didn't use, and, second, her car door opening. In the first slow-motion shot, her hand throws the milkshake across the frame and the milkshake leaves the right side of the frame; in the second, it flies through the air; and in the third it falls to the ground and the liquid flows out. The first shot is later repeated, immediately after Randall Adams describes the difference between her account of the crime at the time and her testimony at the trial. The slow-motion shot tells us we should throw out her testimony, which is as useful as a spilled milkshake on the side of the road: all the original properties of a milkshake are there, but they have been rendered worthless.

Slow motion is also used to delineate the re-enacted interrogation sequences. A slow-motion shot of a pen being tossed onto a prepared confession statement, and another of the statement being pushed away and out of the frame, places the sequence firmly in the re-created past, in the realm of memory. It also foregrounds our impression of Adams's defiance towards the police investigators, and thus his innocence.

The slow-motion shots of the swinging pocket watch, as a clichéd symbol for hypnosis, are very important. In addition to illustrating the investigators' interview, it also works as a metaphor. The film as a whole investigates the ways we can unlock inaccessible past events; the watch stands in for the ineffective means the Dallas police implemented to unlock past events, not just in hypnotising the policewoman, but by ignoring throughout the investigation all the evidence which pointed towards David Harris.

Each of these slow-motion objects occurs only once or twice in the film, but their visibility is extremely high. As a contrast, think of the image of the figure in the car adjusting the rear-view mirror. This occurs many times in the film in various re-enactments – sometimes close-up, other times in wider shots. This repeated element is another metaphor: it stands in for *the film*'s attempt to unlock the inaccessible past – to look more clearly in the rear-view mirror. The image is not as visible as the slow-motion objects, but rather provides an underlying, rhyming element, like the flashing red lights.

Both Randall Adams and David Harris express feelings of subjective temporality in their interviews. When Randall Adams was threatened at gunpoint to sign the confession, he says it 'felt like hours' before the policeman finally backed down. Similarly, David Harris, in describing the moments after the shooting, says that 'it seemed like time stopped'.

These are the subjective states in real life that film-makers aspire to create when telling stories of characters under extreme pressure. For Morris, the drama lay in another direction.

The final sequence of the film introduces a new formal element which combines object and interview in the form of a close-up shot of a tape recorder playing back a final conversation between Errol Morris and David Harris. The camera slowly revolves, but the shot is not in slow motion. We hear Harris tell Morris that Randall Adams didn't kill Officer Wood; he's sure because he's 'the one who knows'. This shot is not a re-creation; it did not happen in the past. Because the use of slow motion depicting the flashlight, the milkshake, the pocket watch and the pen makes the re-creation sequences processive, open, unresolved, conflicting, implicative elements, the lack of slow motion in connection with this new object, the tape recorder, suggests closure. It underscores, even creates, our reaction to the content of the conversation: we believe that Randall Adams is innocent and that David Harris killed the policeman. In Pudovkin's terms, Morris uses cinematics to 'consciously guide' our attention.[66]

The Thin Blue Line has been called a post-modern documentary,[67] which brings to mind the avant-garde film-makers and critics of the 1920s and 30s who saw the cinema in general, and expressionistic technique specifically, as modern. A parallel can be drawn which places slow motion in the context of post-modern experience. Its extensive use on television – as instant replay on sports programmes, in advertisement and music video, in news and documentary, in channel idents and programme introductions – attests not only to its power to heighten our awareness and hold our attention but also to its contribution to post-modern perception. Singer-songwriter Paul Simon's lyrics are reminiscent of the early French theorists:

> These are the days of miracle and wonder
> this is the long distance call
> the way the camera follows us in slo-mo
> the way we look to us all ...[68]

A dedicated examination of the ways slow motion works in this context provides ample room for future study.

Raging Bull

Raging Bull is an unequalled example of the ways in which slow motion can work on multiple hierarchic levels. At the shot level, it creates a defamiliarisation of images and marks them as processive and implicative. At the sequence level, it forms antecedent/consequent point-of-view structures, and also shapes the rhythm of the fight sequences. On a higher level, the slow-motion point-of-view sequences together form a compelling antecedent which resolves in a strong closure, and at the film level we can compare the differing applications of the device in the point-of-view sequences and the fight sequences, allowing us to see the film as a whole in the light of these comparisons.

As might be expected in a post-classical film concerned with the life of an athlete, *Raging Bull* uses slow motion to depict images of quick physical motion and the heightened emotions of sport, in this case boxing. It also acts to portray the inner state of the boxer Jake LaMotta, and, as a combination of these two elements, the title sequence establishes the dual role of the device. The titles appear over a single long shot of Jake alone in the ring, shadow boxing, filmed at 96 frames a second.[69] The rest of the film explores the nature of his violence toward himself and his family, as well as towards his opponents in the ring, and the image of Jake fighting with himself, head down, slowly bobbing and weaving against the laws of gravity, serves as a foundation for the narrative.

In a similar way, the opening lines of the film, spoken by Jake in 1964 while rehearsing in his dressing room before his night-club act, 'An Evening with Jake LaMotta', serve to internalise the film as a whole, to place it as a memory/flashback:

Those cheers remain in my ears,
and for years they remain in my thoughts.
'Cause one night I took off my robe and what I do,
I forgot to wear shorts.
I recall every fall, every hook, every jab . . .

The combination of memory and dream imagery fixes the film's introspective tone, which, following a cut back in time to 1941, is carried by its cinematic, rather than its narrative elements, and by the use of slow motion in particular.

There are five scenes which feature the use of slow motion in connection with Jake's point of view and inner perception. They are each structured differently, depending on the congruence of varying parameters such as camera motion, focal length, music, sound, the characters involved, and the point in the narrative. Indeed, as we will see, slow motion is used differently in each of the sequences: to generate implicative form, to create a strong rhythm, to link a system of details, and as combinations of these. The common parameter, however, is the point-of-view structure present in each sequence and the use of slow motion for the antecedent, objects shots. The distortion of time in relation to Jake's point of view provides the strongest cinematic evidence of Jake's obsessive, possessive attitude toward Vickie, and the fact that other men, including Salvy, Tommy and even his brother Joey, are threatening to Jake beyond a rational level. We can refer to these scenes as the gym, the pool, the dance, the Copa, and the hotel room.

In the gym, the sequence alternates between shots of Jake and Joey in the ring and shots of Salvy and the boys entering the room and sitting down to watch the workout. It consists of eight shots. First (the first shot of the sequence and the scene), Jake and Joey spar in close-up. None of the surrounding context of the gym is revealed, and Jake's face is not clearly visible due to his face mask and movements. Next, Salvy and the boys, in slow motion, walk through the room. The next six shots alternate between mid to wide views following Jake and Joey round the ring from outside the ropes, and progressively closer views, still in slow motion, of Salvy and the boys as the camera moves in towards them, from inside the ring. We never see Jake look at the action happening outside the ring. The camera position, movement and alternation suggest a possible point-of-view structure, but lack of a point-glance would make it questionable. Instead, Scorsese uses the slow motion to establish point-of-view firmly. Slow motion's inherently dynamic and processive elements make the sequence a system of antecedent/consequent phrases, but the resolving consequent is withheld until we actually see Jake look at Salvy. In the first six shots we gather not only narrative information but also Jake's attitude, without ever seeing Jake actually look outside the ring, or even seeing his facial expression at all. We get the impression that Jake senses their presence and is disturbed by it. It is not until the seventh shot that Scorsese, with a close-up of Jake clearly and aggressively looking beyond the frame to where we know Salvy sits, establishes in any conventional sense a point-of-view structure,[70] and the dialogue that follows as the scene continues proves our impressions to be correct. The tension of the slow motion reflects Jake's attitude, and its function to establish point-of-view forms a pattern which will recur in the film. It is important to see this sequence as linked to the other four, because it occurs before Jake ever sees Vickie, and yet his attitude toward Salvy is antagonistic, thus complicating the motivation for his desire for Vickie in the next sequence, and foregrounding the fact that his nature is obsessive in general, not just when it comes to Vickie.

The pool sequence occurs in the very next scene. Again, Jake encounters Salvy and has antagonistic feelings towards him, this time in connection with Vickie, who he sees for the first time as she sits with Salvy and the boys by the neighbourhood public pool. The scene alternates between Jake's point of view of the other group and his conversation with Joey. This time, Jake's point of view is firmly established by the presence of point-glance shots throughout the scene,

30

which includes point-of-view shots in real time of Vickie, Salvy and the group. The slow motion comes in a slightly slow shot of Salvy putting on sunglasses, and another of a close-up of Vickie, eyes closed against the sun and head leaning back, with the water of the pool gently rippling behind her head. The third and final slow-motion shot is much slower and also closes the scene; it is a big close-up of Vickie's legs, from the thigh down, splashing in the pool. In the sequence, the sound, focal length and camera movement, as well as the dialogue between Jake and Joey, add to the obsessive nature of Jake's gaze towards Vickie, but it is the slow motion which links it with the gym sequence and links Jake's desire for Vickie with his antagonism toward Salvy. The fact that the final shot of the scene is in slow motion leaves the tension unresolved and implies the continuation which occurs in the next slow-motion sequence, the dance.

The sound and music tracks work with the slow-motion shots in this sequence to underscore Jake's dedicated gaze. In a series of ten shots which alternate between Jake staring and slow-motion images of Vickie sitting at another table and Salvy approaching the table to take her away, all of the sound – voices, clatter, and the general atmosphere of a neighbourhood dance – drops out, leaving just the dance music. The juxtaposition of the speed of the music and the speed of the dancing couples who, in slow motion, cross Jake's view of Vickie lends a dreamy rhythm to the shots, and the lack of natural sound places us deep within Jake's personal interior territory, with all outside noise cut off. The outside world crashes back in the ensuing series of shots, as Jake follows Vickie, Salvy and their group downstairs and outside, but only over the shots of him; his slow-motion point-of-view of them on the stairs and outside in the car continues the unnatural lack of sound. After they drive away in slow motion to the accompaniment of an non-diegetic bongo and whistle tune, Jake is finally brought back to reality as the atmosphere track intrudes on his gaze and he looks left and right, as if to adjust himself to surroundings he wasn't aware he was in. The impact of the scene is especially strong because of the intensity of Jake's stare and the dreamy, vision-like quality of the slow-motion shots, established by the tension between the rhythm of the music and the rhythm of the dancers. Because Vickie shares a frame rate with the dancing couples, she and the others seem to move gracefully and rhythmically, within their shots and also when compared with the quick movement surrounding Jake in his real-time shots. The fact that the scene ends with Jake's consequent, real-time shot and that it consists completely of point-of-view structure makes the dance more formal than the pool sequence, although as a continuation of the implications of Jake's desire for Vickie the narrative is as yet unresolved. It is an example of parametric noncongruence, where some elements reach closure but one or more others imply continuance;[71] in this case we can interpret it as Jake's continued and growing determination to meet Vickie, which he contrives in the next scene.

The fourth slow-motion point-of-view sequence takes place quite a bit later in the film, after Jake and Vickie have been married a few years. At the Copacabana night-club, Jake, Vickie, Joey and his date sit at one table. We realise with Jake in a slow-motion point-of-view shot following Vickie across the room that Salvy, Tommy and the boys are at another table. In this shot Vickie and Salvy exchange kisses on the cheek, then they both turn simultaneously in opposite directions; Vickie leaves the frame on her way to the powder room, and Salvy heads straight to camera (Jake). The next shot, in real time, creates a marked jump in time as Salvy is at Jake's table immediately. In this way, this shot, while not from Jake's physical position, continues the point-of-view impulse. Salvy points out Tommy's table to Jake and we see them in Jake's slow-motion point-of-view. A few shots later, Vickie approaches Tommy's table.

A striking element of this shot of Vickie at Tommy's table is that it begins with a flash frame, an element used extensively in the fight sequences to denote photographers' flashes. On its own it creates a notion of stopped time, a photograph being taken. Physically it is a moment taken away, as it appears as a blank frame in the film. In slow motion, where it occurs in the film as two consecutive blank frames, the compounding of temporal distortion develops a rhythmic tension, in conjunction with the low, slowed-down sound of the shutters and flash explosions. In the Copa scene it serves not only as a warning flash to Jake but also as an echo of the fight scenes, and links Jake's vision of Vickie with his feelings in the ring.

The sequence continues using a mixture of real time and slow motion as Jake watches the other table: Tommy and Joey are linked in a slow-motion two-shot looking at Jake, and Tommy gestures Jake over; the scene ends in real time with the conversation round the table.

In the hotel room before Jake's championship fight, the slow-motion point-of-view shots zero in on close-up details as Vickie and Joey pay their respects to Tommy. In a four-shot sequence, we see close-ups in slow motion of Joey's torso with his hand on his hip, Tommy and Joey facing each other, Tommy kissing Vickie on the mouth while holding her face in both hands and then gesturing emphatically, and Vickie smiling at Tommy. The dialogue track and the picture are slightly out of synch. The individual shots do not alternate with shots of Jake looking; rather, the entire sequence is bracketed by him. The brevity of the jump-cut slow-motion shots combined with the intense nature of the close-ups and the separated sound imply that Jake's obsession with Vickie's betrayal has reached a kind of shorthand in his mind while at the same time it has deepened in magnitude. This is borne out in the rest of the scene, as Jake badgers Vickie about her behaviour with Tommy; he slaps her and continues to yell at her, and at Joey as well when he tries to stop Jake's violent outburst. In the final, prophetic line of the scene, Jake says he's 'disgusted with the two of you. I'll deal with you later.'

A consideration of Branigan's reflections on questions of subjectivity, point-of-view shots, and character reflection and projection[72] suggests that Scorsese has manipulated these slow-motion point-of-view sequences in very complex ways. Their legible narrative function within the scenes in which they occur attests to the classical arrangements of the shots into point/glance, point/object relationships; the deviant structure in the gym sequence outlined above is defined by Branigan as a discovered and delayed point-of-view, 'where a point/object shot is given but the point/glance shot is withheld'[73] – it functions in the ways we have discussed, but still falls within Branigan's formal delineations of point-of-view. The subjectivity of the sequences, then, falls clearly within classical point-of-view structure, unlike the 'modern texts' which Branigan points to as falling outside the forms he describes in these chapters.

Branigan defines subjective representation as occurring when all six units of narrative representation – origin, vision, time, frame, object and mind – refer to character.[74] The slow-motion point/object shots in all of Jake's 'visions' clearly conform to these rules. In further defining a 'perception shot' as a signifier of mental condition, Branigan sees the various expressionistic devices as metaphors for vision, as when a blurred image stands in for a drugged state or a zoom denotes increased or sudden attention. Slow motion, although not mentioned by Branigan specifically in this context, can be included in this definition to stand in for Jake's mental condition; his vision is heightened and intensified by combinations of desire, antagonism, jealousy and fear of betrayal, and the shots signify this mental condition.

But Jake's visions also conform to Branigan's definition of 'mental process narration', where the 'occurrence of undefined temporal markers and the existence of a character's mental condition [act as] the unity or coherence of the representation'.[75] He stresses that

what is important to the mental process sequence is that new, undefined temporal relations are introduced; time is no longer continuous or simultaneous. For instance, what is the temporal relation between that which slowly appears in superimposition and everything else in the image? When a temporal discontinuity is referred to – justified by – a mental condition of a character, then we label it, in the reading, as a 'subjective' sequence and when the temporal dis-

continuity is undefined, that is neither present, past, or future, then
we label it as a form of mental process narration.[76]

He goes on to include slow motion in a list of devices which mark
undefined time.

Branigan acknowledges that perception shots, mental-process
sequences and point-of-view can work together in a scene, as they do
in *Raging Bull*, but he stresses that perception and mental process
must be seen as distinct structures because of the differences in their
temporalities.[77] And yet the slow-motion point-of-view sequences of
Raging Bull do combine these structures. *By using slow motion as a
device in his perception shots, Scorsese has combined these two structures, and broadened Branigan's formal definitions.* The link between
the structures forms a tension of temporality; the visions take place in
the present of Jake's perception, and in the present of the point-of-
view structure, but they also exist in an undefined temporality linked
to Jake's mental state, and, on a larger scale, in Jake's memory (recall
the opening of the film). Thus we see that contrasting and comparable
senses of time work right through the film.

For Eisenstein, 'the progression goes from *metaphor* (i.e. the *pictorial function* of juxtaposition) to the *rhythm* of juxtaposition (i.e. to
generalisation). The rhythm of the juxtaposition of elements is the
fundamental means whereby the generalisation will express itself.'[78]
We see the slow-motion shots in *Raging Bull* working not only as
metaphors for Jake's distrust but also, on higher hierarchic levels, as a
generalisation of the obsessions which will result in Jake's pitiful
defeat in life.

Meyer explains how 'the more clearly and completely shaped a
[musical] pattern is – the more patent its order on a number of hierarchic levels – the more specific and compelling its implications will
be'.[79] In addition, he stresses that in most cases high-level patterns are
fully comprehensible only by retrospective analysis. When examined
in the context of Meyer, Eisenstein and Branigan, the slow-motion
point-of-view sequences in *Raging Bull* combine to form a profoundly
implicative antecedent to the scene following the championship fight
in which Jake's obsession explodes into domestic violence. At the end
of a long and drawn-out scene, Jake assaults Joey and Vickie in one
fell swoop of physical rage. The absence of slow motion places the
scene firmly in reality. It is the result of all of the inner turmoil
expressed by the previous slow motion. The impact of the scene over-
shadows Jake's victory in the championship fight, which immediately
precedes it. In fact, the slow-motion celebrations in the ring are cut
abruptly to introduce the more important fight.

The slow motion in the boxing sequences of *Raging Bull* works to depict rapid movement and create exciting rhythmic patterns. In addition, there are point-of-view sequences within the fights. These work in a more general way than the ones we have been looking at; some of the fight scenes include the point of view of various of Jake's opponents as he punches them, and the effect is one of heightened action and verisimilitude: we feel as if we are in the ring. As Eisenstein said, 'A fight filmed from a single viewpoint in long shot will always remain a depiction of a fight and will never be the perception of a fight.'[80] The slow motion picks out elements such as close-ups of sweat and blood flying after a punch, a close-up of Jake breaking an opponent's nose, blood gushing, and repeated punches to the head, as well as wider shots of Jake swaggering in the ring after knocking someone out. Technically the juxtaposition of fast and slow is brought to the fore when, for example, in the final section of the last fight, we see five successive shots of punches to Jake's head from different directions in the frame. Each shot is less than a second in duration – from 12 to 21 frames long – but the combination of slow motion, quick editing and the slowed-down low rumble on the soundtrack of the photographer's flash make the action legible as a barrage.

The photographers and their flashes are present throughout the fight scenes and spill over into the other sections of the film as well. In addition to the scene at the Copa mentioned earlier, the flash returns near the end of the film, when the LaMottas live in Florida. The poolside newspaper interview is punctuated by the flash, but this time it is slowed down to a rapid series of still images of extreme close-ups of the flash apparatus. The organic and fluid quality of the ringside flashes is stressed by this repetition. Overall, the repetition of the flashes – in slow motion, still images and real time – set against the pattern of the fights, within the context of the general repeated pattern of all the fights in the film, generates the rhythm to which the rest of the film proceeds.

Slow motion also supports the narrative events which the fights develop: Jake doesn't like Vickie calling his opponent Janero good-looking, and it is his nose we subsequently see demolished in slow-motion close-up, followed by a slow-motion point-of-view shot of Vickie in the crowd, Jake proud of himself and making sure Vickie has seen.

In a more complex fashion, the two most important fights in the narrative – first when Jake wins the title and then when he loses it – contain rhyming elements of slow motion. Most notably, close-ups of Jake's torso as he is sponged down by the trainer appear in both fights. The camera is at a 45-degree angle so the water falls against gravity both temporally and spatially. In the victorious fight the water is clear, and the camera pans down his body to the 'EVERLAST' logo on his waistband. In the losing fight, the rhyming shot repeats the image, only this time the water is bloody. The two shots stand out like the repeated objects in *The Thin Blue Line*; as in that film, these slow-motion shots act as metaphors. They become images of victory and defeat, but, more than that, they point outside the ring to the defeat Jake suffers in the time between the two fights, the extracurricular violence which cost him his only friend – Joey – and will eventually cost him Vickie as well.

The amount of slow motion, the dramatic montage, the expressive camera work, and the overall length and attention to the defeat of Jake LaMotta, as opposed to his championship victory, provide a parallel narrative to Jake's tormenting and tormented existence. In a similar way, a comparison of the use of slow motion in these parallel narratives is a comparison between Jake's physical and mental states. The two overlap in the realm of emotion, which Jake expresses in a violent and physical way.

Notes

1. Tom Gunning, 'The Cinema of Attractions', in Thomas Elsaesser (ed.), *Early Cinema: Space. Frame. Narrative* (London: BFI, 1990) p. 58. Gunning is borrowing the term 'attraction' from Sergei Eisenstein, who, when still in the theatre, defined it as a 'sensual or psychological impact' (Eisenstein, 'How I became a film director', in *Notes of a Film Director* (Moscow: Foreign Language Publishing House, n.d.), p. 16.)
2. Gunning, 'The Cinema of Attractions', in *Early Cinema*, pp. 56–7.
3. Austin C. Lescarboura, *Behind the Motion-Picture Screen* (New York: Scientific American Publishing Co., 1919), p. 326. He also notes: 'If the problems of making the exposures has been a difficult one, that of handling the insects has been at least equally difficult.'
4. Single-exposure photographs using this shadow, or silhouette, method were in use as early as 1881 by Austrian physicist Ernst Mach, according to Dr Harold Edgerton.
5. A forerunner of motion picture technology in general, this low-tech stroboscope was invented simultaneously in 1832 by Plateau in Ghent and Stampher in Vienna. Both were inspired by Michael Faraday, who in turn was inspired by Peter Mark Roget.
6. In a similar way, experiments with fast motion were stunning audiences with images of plants growing, flowers opening and buildings being constructed before their eyes. The use of both fast and slow motion in nature and natural history cinematography developed early and continues today. Slow motion serves to capture the intricate movements of birds and animals, and also smoothes out potentially jerky shots as a result of trying to film unpredictable and quickly moving subjects.
7. Ricciotto Canudo, 'The Birth of a Sixth Art' (1911), in Richard Abel (ed.), *French Film Theory and Criticism: A History/Anthology. Volume 1: 1907–1929* (Princeton, NJ: Princeton University Press, 1988), p. 60.
8. Ricciotto Canudo, 'Reflections on the Seventh Art' (1923), in Abel (ed.), *French Film Theory and Criticism*, p. 296.

9. Jean Cocteau, 'Carte Blanche' (1919), in Abel (ed.), *French Film Theory and Criticism*, p. 172.
10. Paul Ramain, 'The Influence of Dream on the Cinema' (1925), in Abel (ed.), *French Film Theory and Criticism*, p. 363.
11. Jean Epstein, 'On Certain Characteristics of *Photogénie*' (1924), in Abel (ed.), *French Film Theory and Criticism*, p. 316. Some seventy years later, perhaps the best dramatic purpose these images have been put to is in Saul Bass's opening titles for *Age of Innocence* (Scorsese, 1993).
12. Jean Epstein, 'Approaches to Truth' (1928), in Abel (ed.), *French Film Theory and Criticism*, p. 424.
13. Evgeny Mikhailov and Andrei Moskvin, 'The Cameraman's Part in Making a Film,' in Richard Taylor (ed.), *Russian Poetics in Translation. Vol. 9: The Poetics of Cinema* (Oxford: RPT Publications, 1982), p. 116.
14. F. H. Richardson, *Handbook of Projection for Theatre Managers and Motion Picture Projectionists* (New York: Chalmers Publishing Co., 1922), p. 78.
15. V. I. Pudovkin, *Film Technique and Film Acting (Memorial Edition)* (London: Vision Press, 1974), p. 180.
16. Ibid.
17. Ibid., p. 181.
18. Ibid., p. 181.
19. Ibid., p. 178.
20. Ibid., p. 178.
21. Both Eisenstein and Pudovkin hold up Epstein's adaptation of *The Fall of the House of Usher* (France, 1928) as an example. Eisenstein considers it 'the one case of the consistent application of this method' ('Beyond the Shot', in Richard Taylor (ed.), *Selected Works*, Vol. 1, *Writings 1922– 1934*, London, Bloomington and Indianapolis: BFI and Indiana University Press, 1988, p. 149), meaning the decomposition of movement described above, producing unusual emotional tension, while Pudovkin calls it 'not at all what I mean', since according to him the entire film is in slow motion, with no conjunction of fast and slow. Their disagreement is a bit pointless, however, as it seems that neither of them actually saw the film. Eisenstein is 'judging from press reports' and Pudovkin '[has] heard that Jean Epstein shot a whole film in slow motion (I think it was *The Fall of the House of Usher)*'. What *can* be learned from comparing the two is the difference between analysing slow motion in a shot, as Eisenstein does here, and as an edited sequence, which Pudovkin insists on.
22. Sergei Eisenstein, 'Beyond the Shot' and 'The Dramaturgy of Film Form', in Richard Taylor (ed.), *Selected Works*, Vol. 1, pp. 138–51 and 161–81.
23. Eisenstein, 'Beyond the Shot', p. 149.
24. Ibid.
25. Ibid.
26. Eisenstein's argument has, of course, its political implication, which equates the dynamism of montage with Marxist theory; and cinema-as-the-culmination-of-the-history-of-art with the-Soviet-state-as-the-culmi-nation-of-the-history-of-society.
27. These days the reverse is found as well, when, for example, a professor at the University of California at Berkeley explains passages in Homer's *Odyssey* in terms of cinematics, specifically slow motion. Homer period-

ically suspends the action of battle to describe in great detail warriors' armour and accoutrements, and their specific movements as they put them on.

28. Eisenstein, 'Laocoon', in Michael Glenny (ed.), *Selected Works*, Vol. 2, *Towards a Theory of Montage (1937–40)* (London, Bloomington and Indianapolis: BFI and Indiana University Press, 1991), p. 111. Italics mine.
29. Ibid., p. 155.
30. Ibid. This is an extrapolation of the text. Here Eisenstein is not referring to slow motion specifically, but 'composition itself, in its mature stages of development'.
31. Eisenstein, 'Montage 1937', in Michael Glenny (ed.), *Selected Works*, Vol. 2, pp. 25–6.
32. Ibid., p. 26.
33. Eisenstein, 'Laocoon', p. 124.
32. Ibid., pp. 130–1.
35. Ibid., p. 122.
36. Ibid.
37. Andrei Tarkovsky, *Sculpting in Time: Reflections on the Cinema* (London: Faber & Faber, 1989), p. 117.
38. Ibid., p. 118.
39. Ibid., pp. 66–7.
40. Ibid., p. 69.
41. Ibid., p. 120.
42. Ibid., p. 121.
43. Ibid., p. 69.
44. Ibid., p. 117.
45. Ibid., p. 66.
46. Jean Epstein, 'The Senses 1 (b)' (1921), in Abel (ed.), *French Film Theory and Criticism*, pp. 241–6.
47. Epstein attempted to put his theories to practice in *Coeur fidèle* (1924). In a review, René Clair discussed the film's use of rhythm and repetition: 'In *Coeur fidèle* it is created by means of the reappearance of earlier images; at first this is very effective but soon it becomes a burden to the overall movement. Periodic repetition of earlier images – like assonance or rhyme in prosody – seems to be the only effective rhythmic element the film now has at its disposal. But rhyme and assonance do not bring back the same word in a sentence, whereas the repetition of images summons up more or less the same vision. Something else must be found.' René Clair, 'Coeur fidèle (1924)', in Abel (ed.), *French Film Theory and Criticism*, p. 304.
48. Susan McClarey's, *Feminine Endings: Music, Gender, and Sexuality* (Minneapolis and Oxford: University of Minnesota Press, 1991), for example, explores the applicability of Vladimir Propp's morphological analysis of narrative relating to musical structure, where a piece starts in 'home' key, journeys to foreign, 'other', liminal zones, and returns.
49. Leonard B. Meyer, *Explaining Music* (Berkeley, Los Angeles, London: University of California Press, 1973).
50. Ibid., p. 91.
51. Ibid., p. 26.
52. Implication should not be confused with tendency, which refers to the

phenomenon in Western tonal music for certain tones in a scale (the second, fourth, sixth and seventh) to tend to move to more stable tones (the first, third and fifth). Implication involves making inferences and forming patterns *on the part of the listener,* not a tendency inherent in the music.

53. Similarly, Laura Mulvey, in a lecture to the BFI MA students on 28 May 1993, explored the inherent pleasure of puzzle solving and pattern building.

54. Meyer, *Explaining Music*, pp. 111–13.

55. Edward R. Branigan, *Point of View in the Cinema: A Theory of Narration and Subjectivity in Classical Film* (Berlin, New York, Amsterdam: Mouton Publishers, 1983) p. 79.

56. Meyer, *Explaining Music*, p. 53.

57. See, for example, Pam Cook (ed.), *The Cinema Book* (London: BFI, 1985), for codes of classical cinema conventions.

58. François Truffaut, *Hitchcock* (London: Secker & Warburg, 1986), p. 332.

59. Ibid., p. 429.

60. It is difficult to tell how the effect was produced; it does not have the slight jerkiness associated with step-frame printing.

61. See p. 11 above.

62. See p. 13 above.

63. Peckinpah himself was influenced by, especially, Kurosawa's investigations of time (*Rashomon*, 1950) and violence (*The Seven Samurai*, 1954; *Throne of Blood*, 1957, and others).

64. See Wayne Peters, 'A Cinema of Affects', BFI MA dissertation, 1993.

65. To summarise the film briefly, Randall Adams is serving a life sentence for the murder of a Dallas policeman, Officer Wood. The documentary presents evidence that the murder was actually committed by David Harris.

66. As a comparison, there are films which end in slow motion and consequently remain unresolved on one or more levels. *Yellow Earth* (Kaige, 1984) leaves us with the slow-motion image of a boy struggling to walk against the stream of hundreds going the other way. What will become of him? *Silkwood* (Nichols, 1983) ends with a slow-motion shot repeated from the film, the last moment Karen Silkwood, whose death remains a mystery, was seen alive. *Switched at Birth* (Hussein, 1991, TVM), about an adopted child reuniting with her natural family, ends with a slow-motion shot of the girl holding hands with both her natural mother and her adopted father. A resolution to the emotional court battle depicted in the film, but, on another level implied by the slow motion, the beginning of unforeseeable but inevitable events.

67. See, for example, Linda Williams, 'Mirrors Without Memories: Truth, History, and the New Documentary', *Film Quarterly*, vol. 46, no. 3, Spring 1993.

68. From 'The Boy in the Bubble', *Graceland*, 1986.

69. The frame rate is noted by Scorsese in a storyboard drawing reproduced in 'Drawings into Film: Directors Drawings', exhibition catalogue, Pace Gallery, New York 1993. It is nearly impossible to determine the exact frame rate of a shot by viewing a film.

70. Point-of-view structure depends on a point/glance point/object structure, or a permutation thereof. See Branigan, *Point of View in the Cinema*.
71. Meyer, *Explaining Music*, p. 85.
72. Branigan, *Point of View*, chapters 4, 5 and 6, pp. 73–141.
73. Ibid., p. 113.
74. Ibid., p. 75.
75. Ibid., p. 85.
76. Ibid., p. 86.
77. See Branigan, pp. 89–90.
78. Eisenstein, 'Laocoon', p. 131.
79. Meyer, *Explaining Music*, p. 27.
80. Eisenstein, 'Laocoon', p. 134.

STRATEGIES FOR SELF-SCRUTINY
Video Diaries 1990–1993

Sue Dinsmore

Introduction

This paper reflects upon the popular and critical acclaim of the BBC camcorder series *Video Diaries*,[1] and presents a textual exploration of the opportunities for self-reflection and self-presentation offered by the programmes. It seeks to extend the current restricted range of critical reference which has characterised other accounts of the series by examining the *Video Diaries* not just in relation to their television documentary heritage but also in connection with those strategies for self-scrutiny offered by the practices of diary-writing and home-movie-making.

The general assumption about *Video Diaries* which circulates among British TV critics, viewers, programme-makers, and TV satirists tends towards a definition of the series as essentially and exclusively *confessional* in tone and content. This assumption is neatly summarised by James Saynor's early observation of the first experimental series: 'There's something compellingly direct about the first-person visuals that helps to *take you inside* a subject – and a film-maker's consciousness – in a fresh and original way.'[2]

Like all assumptions, the equation that all *Video Diaries* are necessarily and exclusively intimate TV confessions possesses a certain degree of accuracy, for the series has indeed been 'a revelation in broadcasting personal testimony'.[3] But the experience of re-viewing all the programmes after a gap of up to four years since their initial transmission reveals not only the inadequacies of this assumption as an accurate description of the series as a whole, but also the extent to which those features of which one retains a vivid memory expand to fill the misremembered (or entirely forgotten) void into which the rest of the programmes may have fallen. The effect of this is that one's recollection of the programmes is in fact a simplified and condensed version of their 'highlights'; in the case of *Video Diaries*, the versions of the programmes which remain alive in the memory consist chiefly of their confessional moments. On closer inspection of individual pro-grammes it is evident that, while the confessional testimonies have an immediate and profound impact, these confessions are only part of a larger constellation of other features which simultaneously promote and undermine the notion of the subjective diarist as truth-speaker.

Partial Recall: Remembering the Diaries

The impact of the confessional pieces delivered direct to camera is such that, in recollection of the *Diaries*, it is those pieces which over-whelm the range of other relationships with the camera. In fact, in terms of screen time occupied, those pieces do not generally dominate the series to the extent that they seem to do in memory. The effect of the confessional piece to camera outweighs its limited duration: a little goes a long way.

The impact of such moments upon recollections of the programmes is clearly demonstrated by my own response to 'On the March with Bobby's Army', the first programme in the second series of *Diaries*. The programme made a profound impact upon me, and, having recounted the nature of my viewing pleasure to many people over the three years since I first watched it, I believed that I had retained a vivid and detailed memory of Kevin Allen's *Diary*. I possessed a particularly detailed recall of the piece-to-camera sequence which takes place at night in the cabin of a boat sailing from Sardinia to Rimini. Because the cabin is shared with a number of other sleeping travellers, Kevin Allen speaks in a whisper and describes, with many pauses to giggle or to contain incipient giggles, a conversation he has just had with a group of Italian policemen. His hilarity derives from the fact that his own contribution to the conversation was, as the policemen informed him, and as he delights in telling the camera, characterised by his confusion between two pieces of almost homonymic Italian vocabu-lary: the word for 'nappy' and a piece of slang which Kevin had recently acquired, and which he believed to mean 'blow-job'.

Such was the comic impact of this particular scene that I was sur-prised to discover on re-viewing that it actually included a distinctly worried reflection by Kevin Allen on the possibility of further trouble with violent fans. 'All the loonies have been arriving at Rimini,' he confides to the camera in a concerned tone, 'so I don't know whether to stay there or not. I've had a gutful of all that.' My surprise at the difference between my recollection of the nature of this scene and its actual tone was compounded by the discovery that, while I remem-bered it as a 'lengthy' excerpt lasting five or ten minutes, in fact it runs for barely three minutes. It was also a surprise to discover that, rather than the programme as a whole being characterised by the almost constant on-screen presence of diarist Kevin Allen, in fact, out of a running time of over two hours, Allen's on-screen presence accounts for only 18 minutes and 40 seconds. (I noted a similar discrepancy between the impact of a number of other diarists' on-screen presences and the amount of time during which they appeared in front of the camera.)

Diaries and Diaries

Bob Long (current executive producer of *Video Diaries*) and Giles Oakley (editor of the BBC CPU) have both testified[4] to their conviction that the naming of the programmes as 'Diaries' was a significant element of the success and acceptance gained by the series in the early days. The term 'Diary' gives the promise of an intimate personal encounter with the maker of the programme. But a number of critics have pointed out the paradox of a diary produced specifically for public consumption. These programmes, they argued, were not *really* diaries. 'Like any diary written for publication, these home movies are unreliable if not downright incredible,' censured John Naughton in *The Observer*. 'Seeing is not believing, even when the camera shakes.'[5] The *Independent*'s TV critic was a little more charitable: 'It was impossible not to ache for [Willa Carrol] and her sisters confronting memories of horrible child abuse at the hands of their stepmother,' he admitted, before explaining that 'the diary [*My Demons*] ... was just a bit too polished (even amateur television seems too slick these days) ... the juiciest, truest diaries are *those not meant for publication* [or for broadcast]'.[6]

These critics employ a rigid definition of the meaning of a diary against which to measure the *Video Diaries*, and their reluctance to recognise that the diary can be anything other than an exclusively private text is echoed by the tone of Alex Aronson's book, *Studies in Twentieth Century Diaries: The Concealed Self*, which contains a chapter entitled 'The Published Self' wherein Aronson claims that the published, public self is an 'exiled self'.[7] The publishing diarist, he argues, performs a species of self-betrayal: 'Having surrendered fragments of his identity to a nameless multitude, he has betrayed the gifts bestowed on him in his seclusion and has offered his most secret inner being to be investigated by whoever is sufficiently curious to do so.'[8]

The tone of Aronson's description is testimony to his belief in the essentially private and secret nature of diary keeping, a privacy which functions for the diarist both as a mirror, in which the writer's mind is reflected, and as a window through which 'he perceives and observes the world around him'.[9] However, the solitary and self-contained isolation of the diarist is questioned by Simon Brett's introduction to the Faber anthology of diaries in which he describes the wide variety of tones of voice which are used by diarists and the range of different images of themselves which they wish to project. 'Very few', he concludes, 'seem to be completely unselfconscious; all have the thought of a reader somewhere at the back of their minds.'[10] The diarist, in other words creates for herself a constant companion in the form of an imagined reader who may or may not be conceived as a facet of her own self.

Lynne Truss's pleasure in 'Desperately Seeking Nessie', the *Video Diary* recorded by Steve Feltham, derives precisely from the diarist's form of direct address to his imagined viewer, which means that although he appears to be 'a diarist apparently sitting casually indoors making his own entertainment, with just a camera for company', Steve Feltham can be 'at the same time refreshingly aware of an audience *beyond the camera*'.[11] Feltham's ease of movement between 'making his own entertainment' and demonstrating an awareness of his imagined viewer is characteristic of the flexibility and 'amazing versatility'[12] which Simon Brett identifies as the benefits of the diary form – a form which, he argues, can fulfil a wide variety of different roles:

> It can serve as confessional or as apologia. It can be used to colour reality or to vent spleen. It can be a bald record of facts or a Gothic monument of prose. It can chart the conquest of a libertine or the see-sawing emotions of a depressive, it can chronicle the aspirations of youth and the disillusionments of age.[13]

On Time: Commentary and Temporal Flexibility
The most direct link between the diarist and the viewer is forged by the complex connection between the voice-over and the video footage. This connection rests on a contradictory relationship between the notion of the diarist as an observer (behind the camera), as the object of observation (in front of the camera), and as the commentator who sutures these two selves together. The relationship in the *Diaries* between the spoken commentary (which takes the form of a voice-over, recorded during the editing process) and the footage taped by the diarist during the recording period of the *Diary* production is characterised by considerable grammatical complexity. This complexity allows the diarist great flexibility in the tonal range of distances from which to reflect upon herself, and positions the viewer together with the diarist on the boundary between the 'here and now' of the transmission time (voiced by the invisible commentator) and the 'past present' of the videotape footage (identified by the diarist who speaks directly to the camera).

Iain Sinclair, in his article about Patrick Keiller's film *London* (UK, 1993), characterises what he describes as the 'present debased form' of documentary as a 'script-approved argument' in which the commentary functions as a way of explaining (censoring) the world, a format in which: 'language [is] reduced to the function of cement – holding together disparate elements'.[14] In *Video Diaries* the commentary functions less as 'cement' than as a means to make tentative links between the 'past' (camcorder footage) and the present, providing the diarist with opportunities for viewing at a distance or with hindsight. This is, in effect, a particularly sophisticated form of televisual self-scrutiny which a number of diarists refer to as a privilege[15] and which clearly (through the tone, syntax and grammar of the commentary) places the viewer and the commentating diarist *together* at the same point in time, viewing the camcorder footage of the diarist's previous experiences together from the vantage-point of the present. The disjunction between the 'past time' re-presented in the video footage and the 'present time' occupied by the voice-over highlights what Geneviève van Cauwenberge has described as 'the problematic unity of the self in time'.[16]

The recording of videotape, in contrast with the writing of an entry in the diary, makes it possible to *be* in a situation, to be acting and reacting to what is happening *now* and, at the same time, to be recording it. In 'Sweet SA', when the military police are waiting in a car outside the door, Jenni's role as camera operator and commentator does not prevent her from sharing in Fritz's alarm, and rushing from window to window, trying to guess what is going to happen next. This simultaneity of action and record is an impossibility for the diary writer, who has to wait until after something has happened before she can sit down and record it in writing.

The necessary delay between action and record that is part of the process of keeping a written diary effectively creates an incomplete or a distorted image of the past. This distortion occurs chiefly in the act of remembering – an act which in many ways the recording eye of the camcorder accomplishes for the diarist, so that Alex Aronson's description of the use of the present tense in a written diary is not wholly applicable to the video diarist:

> Whenever a diarist uses the present tense he apprehends the moment of writing as existing outside and beyond time, for the act of writing in the diary produces an illusion of stability and permanence which is absent from life as experienced in the raw. Not being but becoming is the essence of a diary.[17]

Using Aronson's terms with reference to the *Video Diaries*, it appears that it is the commentary, the voice-over sections, which bear more resemblance to a written diary than the taped footage, which has a simultaneity with the present that makes it more like a replay rather then a recall of the past. The commentaries, on the other hand, are frequently reflective and have many of the characteristics of a delayed diary entry described by Aronson. Such commentaries can function as a re-reading of diaries, a process which can enable the diarist to stand outside herself, reviewing her own past actions from the perspective of the present. In *Video Diaries*, the diarists' comments in the voice-over not only provide the basis for the intimate relation to the viewer but also function as a reaction to re-reading/viewing the taped footage.

The piece to camera, even though it is part of the taped replay of the present, frequently has a reflective tone more reminiscent of a recollection than of a commentary on the past. In the context of a *Video Diary* these direct addresses to the camera are like pauses for breath, 'metaphors of the flux of time',[18] providing a space for self-reflection and reconsideration that performs a function very similar to the act of making an entry in a written diary.

In *Video Diaries* the combination of the taped, seen replay of the present and the spoken reflection on the present as the past creates a double-layering effect. A parallel effect is explored by André Bazin in his essay 'The Ontology of the Photographic Image'. At the heart of Bazin's analysis is his emphasis upon the filmed image as 'objectivity in time'.[19] Whereas the still photograph, he argues, halts the lives of those pictured, and 'embalms time', the projected film is at once 'the image of things' and 'the image of their duration, *change mummified* as it were'.[20] Watching the moving image, the 'mummified changes', the movements through time are replayed. It is this capacity of the moving image to re-present the past as if it were the present that makes possible the double-layering of the *Video Diaries* – their distinctive relationship between the self in the image and the self on the soundtrack. The actions of the visible self are present as evidence, as clues, which the words of the audible self piece together.

The relationship between the voice of the diarist as commentator and the on-screen self in *Video Diaries* is remarkably fluid. The commentaries frequently shift between the present, the past perfect and the past imperfect tenses, in order that the audible presence of the diarist (speaking now) may offer explanations for the behaviour of the 'past' version of his or her self visible on screen. This fluidity creates a paradoxical situation whereby the voice of the apparently more distanced 'present self', commenting with the benefit of hindsight, is actually in the position of revealing the 'truth' that might undermine the apparent situation depicted on screen.[21] For example, in 'Searching for a Killer', the diarist Geoffrey Smith, who has returned to Haiti in order to track down the assassin who shot him in the leg several years previously, is seen getting into a car with his friend Aboudja. The two men are, as the commentary informs us, about to set out on the

Video Diaries referred to	Diarist	Broadcast BBC2 Saturdays Transmission date	Times
SERIES ONE			
My Demons	Willa Carrol	12.5.90	21.50–23.00
SERIES TWO			
On the March with Bobby's Army	Kevin Allen	11.5.91	22.05–00.00
Spike and Clinton	Spike Ambrose and Clinton Smith	19.5.90	21.00–21.45
Surviving Memories	Jo Spence	1.6.91	23.00–00.00
The Man behind the Shotgun	Jack Murton	8.6.91	22.05–23.20
Sweet SA	Fritz and Jenni Joubert	13.7.91	21.25–22.25
Crossing the Frontier of Fire	Mirella Ricciardi	27.7.91	21.10–22.20
SERIES THREE			
Searching for a Killer	Geoffrey Smith	25.7.92	21.45–22.50
Desperately Seeking Nessie	Steve Feltham	1.8.92	22.05–23.05
Not a Transvestite	Mjka Scott	22.8.92	22.10–23.10
My Demons – The Legacy	Willa Woolston	5.9.92	22.00–23.15
Grope – The Movie	Jane Eller and Michele Howarth	18.9.93	21.30–22.30
SERIES FOUR			
Major, the Miners and Me	Brenda Nixon	4.9.93	22.15–00.15
Dying for Publicity	Chris Steele-Perkins	25.9.93	22.35–23.45
Love is the Drug	Jane Perryman	2.10.93	22.35–23.35
Rebel without a Pause	Bob Doyle	16.10.93	23.20–00.20

first stage of Geoffrey's 'search for a killer'. As he slips into the passenger seat and slams the door of Aboudja's car, Geoffrey answers his friend's enquiry about his state of mind with a breezy cliché: 'I'm ready as I'll ever be.' Almost before his on-screen self has finished speaking, the voice-over comments, 'I was putting on a brave face for Aboudja.' A similar reversal of the apparent truth of the screen image is achieved by Kevin Allen's spoken 'footnote' to the image of himself as an apparently assured interviewer, chatting informally with Bobby Robson on a hotel terrace. 'Although a certain amount of blag had got me this far,' comments the voice-over, 'I was unprepared ... I sat opposite Robson and froze in the midday heat. Groping for a question.'[22]

In his essay 'Cinema and Exploration', Bazin's account of the exhibition of anthropological or expeditionary films describes how the filmed images are themselves only one small part of a larger package which includes books, lectures, and TV and radio 'versions' of the trip on which the film was shot. Furthermore, he identifies that even during the screening of the film the moving images are set in a wider context by a spoken commentary on the images delivered by a member of the expedition team. 'This type of film is conceived as an illustrated lecture,' posits Bazin, 'where the presence and the words of the *speaker-witness* constantly *complement and authenticate* the image on the screen.'[23]

Aronson's description of the process of re-reading a written diary similarly identifies the extent to which the written text functions as only one part of the 'package' of the experience of being a diarist – an experience which affords the diarist the opportunity, in re-reading her written records, of acting as a 'witness' to her past self:

Diaries are rarely rewritten though they are frequently reread ... The effect on the writer is generally deeply disturbing, for things long forgotten are being recalled with a vividness that makes them part of a newly discovered reality at the moment of reading.[24]

As the 'speaker-witness' to images of themselves, re-viewing their filmed records, the video diarists' comments heard in the voice-over sections of *Video Diaries* not only 'complement and authenticate' the image on the screen; they also serve as a means to suture the present speaker to the image of themselves as they existed in the past time (delivered as present immediacy) on the taped footage.

Me – Myself – I: Strategies of Self-Reflection

Although video diarists never refer to themselves in the third person, there are frequent changes in the tone of the commentaries which accomplish a distancing effect very similar to that described by Alex Aronson in his account of written diaries. Commenting on the use of the third person in written accounts of one's own actions, Aronson posits that 'The metamorphosis from *I* to *you* occurs quite naturally as if it were a matter of looking into the metaphorical mirror in which [the diarist] finds himself reflected at the moment when the entry is made. The reflection acquires, as it were, a third dimension.'[25]

In *Video Diaries*, the effect of such self-reflexivity across time is less to establish the presence of a 'third dimension' than to create a species of polyphony, which enables a number of different tones of voice to alternate throughout the diary, providing a flexible commentary which can voice a variety of different attitudes to the visible self, offering responses that range from the ironic to the sympathetic, from the disapproving to the encouraging. Such voice-overs can also be expressions of tolerant forbearance, such as the scene in 'On the March with Bobby's Army' in which Kevin Allen tapes himself late one night, alone at a piano, accompanying himself in a wailing, drunken and tuneless paean. As the sounds of his singing on-screen self fade, the voice-over remarks dryly: 'I've no way of explaining this. I was tired and pissed ... after three pints of Malibu and blackcurrant, it somehow seemed essential that I compose a late night ode to Wolverhampton Wanderers' centre forward, Steve Bull.'

It is a fact almost universally overlooked by critics who characterise the *Diaries* as 'DIY psychoanalysis'[26] that the pieces to camera which have become recognised as the *Video Diary* trademark do not always take the form of a confession. In the same way that the commentary can adopt a wide spectrum of tones of voice, so too the piece to camera can perform a variety of different functions. The whispered comments to camera made by the diarist, alone in the middle of the night, can be expressive of angst, as when Bob Doyle in 'Rebel without a Pause' is seen tossing and turning in his bed in the small hours, agonising about his plan to erect a monument to his brothers-in-arms, the members of the International Brigade who were killed in Spain. 'Why do I bother at my age now', he complains to the camera, 'about this worry?' But the late-night piece to camera can also be a drunken song, such as that performed by Kevin Allen in 'Bobby's Army', or it can function as a brief news flash, providing the viewer with practical details about the diarist's current circumstances. For example, there is a single late-night piece to camera in 'Desperately Seeking Nessie' which occurs after Steve Feltham has been settled in his mobile library at the side of the loch for some months, and is beginning to discern what it may be like to live through a Scottish winter. The sounds of a raging gale can be heard outside the vehicle and the dark screen is illuminated by a single candle, as Steve reaches out from his bed, strikes a match and ignites the wick. 'It's about three o'clock in the morning,' he whispers as the candle flame sputters. He pauses to listen to the wind blowing, and then describes the force eight gale and the effects which it has been having on his wind generator. 'My fillings are being rattled,' he adds. There is another pause, and Steve signs off. 'I thought I'd share that with you,' he says, and then blows out the candle.

The practical circumstances of Brenda Nixon, as she keeps her 24-hour vigil on the picket outside the Hatfield Main pit, are also documented in two night-time pieces to camera in 'Major, the Miners and

Me'. In the second piece, her practical comments on the difficulties of sleeping on wooden slats in a draughty caravan develop into a moving and reflective testimony on her reasons for fighting against the pit closures. The apparent frankness that characterises Brenda's testimony, and many of the pieces to camera in *Video Diaries*, creates a situation in which the authentic voice of the author, making a direct address to the camera/viewer, establishes an immediately and particularly intimate relationship between the diarist and the viewer.

Christine Geraghty describes the highly personal but more flexible viewer–text relationship that characterises soap opera viewing as a 'position of simultaneous engagement and distance'.[27] This dual positioning is not on offer to the *Diary* viewer in terms of the shift between personal engagement with the characters and distance from them through the formal conventions of the construction of a fictional worlds, but is made possible through the syntactical and tonal shifts between the direct address of the camcorder footage recorded as 'evidence' and the diarist's own commentary, which, like a written diary entry, provides some space for emotional distancing through hindsight. In *Video Diaries*, the differing degrees of self-reflection which such hindsight permits, and the tone of voice in which they are expressed, can be understood to correspond to the distinction between the voice of the diarist as it is heard in the taped video footage ('the *I* that makes the entry in the diary'[28]) and the voice of the diarist in its role as commentator (the *I* re-reading the diary).

These 'aspects of consciousness' correspond also to the distinction which Roland Barthes draws between speech and writing in his essay 'Writers, Intellectuals, Teachers'. In a section of the essay subtitled 'The odour of speech', Barthes characterises speech as 'remanent', as retaining the 'odour' of its context, in contrast to writing, which, he argues, has no such contact with the moment of its creation, 'has no past'. In the context of *Video Diaries*, Barthes's distinction between speech and writing provides a precise analogy for the difference between the 'evidential' nature of the videotaped material – which, like speech, is 'subject to remanence', and derives its immediacy from its firm grounding in the context of the time and circumstances in which it was recorded (and which, by reviewing, it is possible to *replay*) – and the reflective tone of the commentary, which refers to the past-present moment visible on screen, but which, by its very nature (like writing), is necessarily distant from that experience: 'In order to write *of* speech (about speech), I am compelled to *refer* to illusions of experiences had by the subject I am when I speak, that I was when speaking ...'[29]

The fluidity and flexibility of the relationship between commentary and footage in *Video Diaries* is extended by editing strategies, particularly those which split the original relationship between sound and image, effectively using the direct comments of a piece to camera as a commentary. Jane Perryman's *Diary* ('Love Is the Drug') begins with a montage of her life, showing her at work, at play, at home. The images are accompanied by the sound of her voice making a direct address to the viewer. 'It's important,' she explains in the voice-over, 'no matter what happens at the end of the day, by the time I finish making this – doing my diary – no matter what happens, you don't judge me.' At this point, the edited montage sequence ends with a cut to a mid-shot of Jane sitting on her bed, speaking to the camera/imaginary viewer. It then becomes apparent that the words which were juxtaposed as a commentary to the montage sequence are in fact part of a lengthy piece to camera which continues:

> Because if you think you're judging me, have a good look at yourself – see if there's anything, if you had a camera on you at every high and low for a year or so, just think what would happen, and what would be shown in your life. It's not as easy as you think it is, you know.

Home Movies: The Absence of the Everyday

Although there are many striking similarities in the tone and textual characteristics of home movies/videos and the *Video Diaries*, a major distinction separates the two forms. In footage shot at home for private viewing, 'impromptu realities', as Richard Chalfen explains, are 'greatly outnumbered by scenes of self-conscious hamming or "acting-up" for the camera. Capturing an impromptu reality [is] ... by far the exception rather than the rule.'[30] On the contrary, in *Video Diaries*, there are relatively few scenes of self-conscious hamming,[31] and the majority of footage falls into the category which Chalfen identifies as 'impromptu reality'. What Chalfen means by this term is most clearly presented in his consideration of precisely which domestic activities are recorded by the home-movie-maker.[32] He prefaces this consideration with the comment:

> What is supposed to be a documentation of daily family life [home movies], isn't at all. Rather than finding that anything can be filmed, we find a very selective choice of topics ... the list of excluded topics is much longer than that of included ones ... only a narrow spectrum of everyday life is selected for recording on film.[33]

Chalfen then provides a comprehensive checklist of the range of 'prohibited' activities. In order to demonstrate that it is precisely those activities which he identifies as absent from home movies that are so

51

characteristically, and frequently, present in *Video Diaries*, I offer an 'amended version' of his list: the following 'reworked' extract from Chalfen's text includes a set of strategically inserted parentheses, containing indications of the *Video Diaries'* response to these 'excluded' activities.

In home movies, begins Chalfen, 'one seldom, if ever, finds family members preparing, eating or clearing up from breakfast, lunch or dinner' (diarists in all series are frequently seen engaged in routine culinary activity in their kitchens). 'We don't expect', he continues, 'to see people getting dressed in the morning (nine diarists from the first three series film themselves getting dressed or applying make-up) 'or going to bed at night' (a large number of diarists are all seen either in, or on their way to or from, bed). 'We don't see family members going to the bathroom to either wash or use the toilet' (it is common practice for diarists to film themselves washing, and although nobody films themselves using the toilet in a *Video Diary*, Sophia Brignone is seen explaining to a Brazilian chemist in 'Crossing the Frontier of Fire' that she is constipated, and then canvassing opinion on the efficacy of the laxatives on offer; and Bob Doyle, in 'Rebel without a Pause', does fart in front of the camera after eating beans for lunch, and responds to his companion's giggles with a chuckle: 'What did you expect – chimes?') 'We don't see children going to school' (Brenda Nixon's son is filmed in the classroom in 'Major, the Miners and Me', and both he and his sister are seen going to and coming home from school; Clinton Smith is seen in 'Spike and Clinton', accompanied by his adviser, talking to his teachers at a parents' evening). 'Nor do we see scenes of washing dishes, cleaning house, or doing home repairs' (many diarists make a special point of showing themselves working at a wide variety of daily domestic tasks). 'We don't see family members reading books or magazines, [or] watching television' (fourteen diarists across the first four series are all seen performing at least one (and, in most cases, all) of these activities) or 'using the telephone' (extensive footage of diarists talking on the telephone appears in practically every single *Diary* in all four series). '[In home movies] we do not see scenes of children being scolded,' concludes Chalfen, completing his list with the two greatest home movie taboos, 'family quarrels [and] scenes of intimate lovemaking' (there are no sex scenes in *Video Diaries*, but there are innumerable examples of people arguing in front of the camera. Such instances are especially frequent in programmes which feature a married or cohabiting couple.)[34]

The 'exclusive' range of topics which are filmed in home movies is, argues Chalfen, matched by the selective character of its audience.[35] His identification of the 'home mode' of communication as that intended for essentially private viewing is corroborated by Chuck

Kleinhans in his account of 'My Aunt Alice's Home Movies', in which he characterises the home-movie viewing situation as primarily a family event, in which the pleasures of spectatorship are dependent upon the existence of a social or familial relation to those people who appear on the screen: '[Home movies] fascinate those who can share in the immediate sensation of recognition . . .'[36]

Made for broadcast on national network television, *Video Diaries* are clearly a more 'public' form of communication than home movies. But, paradoxically, this more 'public' form of film-making includes a far greater range and proportion of 'private' activities than does the essentially domestic home-movie format. Whereas the publicly broadcast *Video Diary* tends to present (as my 'amended version' of Chalfen's list clearly demonstrates) intensely private activities and feelings, the privately screened home movie tends rather to depict the 'public face' of family life: 'the symbolically created world of home movies is a very happy place, full of smiling people engaged in enjoyable and important activities'.[37]

This distinction is eloquently demonstrated by Willa Woolston's use of home-movie footage in 'My Demons – The Legacy'. Intercut with scenes from interviews which she conducted with her sisters – in which both Willa (off camera) and her relatives (on camera) break down and weep at their childhood memories of the extreme physical and emotional cruelty inflicted upon them by their stepmother – are excerpts from the family's home movies. Without exception, these excerpts are filled with the smiling faces of an apparently happy, 'normal' family enjoying lakeside vacations: the stepmother, elegantly poised in boats and gardens, smiles broadly, while the tanned little girls grin, giggle, and cavort in their swimming costumes. The home movies give no indication whatsoever of the private torments endured by the sisters. Precisely the same discrepancy between memories and home-movie footage is noted by film-maker Michelle Citron, who comments in a brief account of her film *Daughter Rite*, which used a step-printed excerpt from one of her family's home movies, that

> I somehow expected the movies to confirm my family's convoluted dynamics. But when I finally viewed them after a ten year hiatus, I was surprised and disturbed that the smiling family portrayed on the screen had no correspondence to the family represented in my childhood memories.[38]

Concluding Remarks
The most prized function of written diaries, as Brett observes, may be that they make it possible for the diarist to impose some sense of order upon their personal experience,[39] providing a valuable guide in the

'desperate search for meaning' which Aronson[40] also identifies as a chief characteristic of diary entries. In the case of *Video Diaries*, as in written diaries, or indeed in home movies, the only criterion for the inclusion of material is that it should have some direct bearing upon the diarist (or amateur film-maker) herself. Quotidian triviality, be it routine or unforeseen, is frequently recorded with the same degree of attention to detail as social or political upheaval, national catastrophe and family trauma. Whatsoever the nature of such material, it is always mediated through the diarist's individual perceptions of the world and her position within it.

The textual sophistication of the *Video Diaries* is such that, although these subjective perceptions are united by the fact of their shared original source (the diarist), they rarely serve to present an unproblematically coherent or 'monolithic' sense of self that might define the diarist as a fixed entity occupying a stable position. On the contrary, the image of the self which is presented to the *Video Diaries* viewer is fragmentary, shifting, and fluid. Its fluidity derives from the *Diaries'* distinctive combination of the diarist's footage of events from her life (including scenes of both action and reflection) with her own commentary upon that record. The complex layering of shifting temporal and syntactical positions in both the audiovisual (taped) and oral (commentary) texts creates the possibility for subtly self-reflective programmes in which the personal, subjective discourse of emotion and self-reflection, which is frequently denigrated by other factual televisual forms, is privileged as an intensely sophisticated strategy for self-scrutiny.

The private, individual concerns of the self-scrutinising diarist are broadcast, via a public national TV network, into the private, domestic sphere of the viewer's home. The camcorder records *private* life, which is brought into the *public* domain, for consumption in the *private* world of the living room – creating a closed circuit which begins and ends in domesticity, and depends upon the intimacy of the relationship established between diarist and viewer.

The intimate relationship between those people on and in front of the television screen is not just based on a body of experience of daily life, aspects of which may or may not be shared, but is articulated in the public sphere in a language of self-reflection and self-scrutiny which is recognisably private. The tone of voice and the intimate nature of the viewer–diarist relationship established in the programmes ensures that the level of recognition necessary for the spectating pleasures of home-movie watching is replaced with intimacy: the language spoken by the diarists is recognised as the language of personal communication.

The viewer recognises that the diarists are communicating in a publicly agreed language of privacy. As the most domestic of all media, television's position as 'the box in the corner' makes it appear less paradoxical that a public national network should be the means for communication in private and domestic tones of voice. In the context of other factual television programmes in the schedules, the *Video Diaries*' use of a private language which is recognised as domestic and familiar claims a space in the public airwaves not simply for voices that would otherwise be unheard, but also for a tone of voice that is rarely privileged as part of the public discourse of television.

Although the precedents for many of the textual approaches to the recording of everyday life, which is the main focus of the *Diaries*, do derive from the heritage of television documentary forms and techniques, to trace precedents for the *Video Diaries*' strategies of self-reflection and self-presentation requires recourse to other inheritances, to the essentially private cultural practices of diary writing and home-movie-making. The resulting shared intimacy between viewer and diarist and the domestic nature of much of the diaries' footage serve effectively to 'seal off' the effects of public transmission – bypassing the public domain, and forging a direct connection between the domestic conditions in which the *Diaries* are produced, and the domestic conditions in which they are consumed.

Notes

1. *Video Diaries* is a series of programmes produced by the BBC Community Programme Unit (CPU) and broadcast on BBC2. All footage in each *Diary* is shot on a small camcorder over a relatively long period (sometimes up to twelve months) by a non-professional 'diarist'. Diarists are unpaid members of the public who make films about aspects of their own lives. They shoot an average of 150 hours of videotape and have the right of editorial control over their material, which is cut to make a programme between 50 and 90 minutes long. The first series of five *Video Diaries* was broadcast between 21 April and 26 May 1990. A further four series (thirty-one programmes in total) have been broadcast, as well as two series of *Teenage Diaries*. The success of these series has also led to the current CPU project *Video Nation,* in which fifty people have been simultaneously equipped with camcorders in order to record their everyday lives. At the time of writing a fifth series of *Video Diaries* was in production and intended for broadcast in Autumn 1994.
2. James Saynor, 'Authorised Versions', *The Listener,* 3 May 1990, p. 46 (my italics). Saynor's relatively positive formulation of the 'essence' of *Video Diaries* is inverted by the growing number of critics who have elected to identify 'first-person visuals' as a species of self-indulgent, spectator-sport navel-gazing.
3. Bob Long, 'Video Diaries: Our History', National Film Theatre programme notes to 'Broadcast Lives: Oral History on Film', 1993.
4. In an interview with the author.

5. John Naughton, review of 'Off the Rails', *The Observer*, 26 May 1991, p. 76.
6. Review of 'Crossing the Frontier of Fire' (no byline) in the *Independent*, 29 July 1991, p. 12.
7. Alex Aronson, *Studies in Twentieth-Century Diaries: The Concealed Self* (Lampeter: Edwin Mellen, 1991), p. 105.
8. Ibid.
9. Ibid., p. 1.
10. Simon Brett (ed.), *The Faber Book of Diaries* (London: Faber & Faber, 1987), p. x.
11. Lynne Truss, 'Cult of the Camcorder Celebrity', *The Times*, 29 August 1992, p. 3.
12. Brett (ed.), *The Faber Book of Diaries*, p. x.
13. Ibid.
14. Iain Sinclair: '*London*: Necropolis of Fretful Ghosts', *Sight and Sound*, June 1994, pp. 12–15.
15. 'This Video diary gave me a chance to tell my own story' (Chris Steele-Perkins, 'Dying for Publicity'); 'I am quite glad that I have the opportunity to evaluate my life, and I think for the first time since I married Steve I am actually able to stop and think: am I doing the right thing? (Jane Perryman, 'Love is the Drug').
16. Geneviève van Cauwenberge, 'Self Reflexivity in Contemporary Documentary Film: Chris Marker's *Sans Soleil*', in Willem De Greef and Willem Hesling (eds), *Image–Reality–Spectator: Essays on Documentary Film and Television* (Amersort: Acco, 1989), p. 159.
17. Alex Aronson: *Studies in Twentieth-Century Diaries*, p. vii.
18. Ibid. p. ix.
19. André Bazin, 'The Ontology of the Photographic Image', in *What Is Cinema?* (ed. and translated by Hugh Gray) (Berkeley: University of California Press, 1967), Vol. 1, p. 14.
20. Ibid., p. 15.
21. The commentary is never used to undermine the veracity or authenticity of the unsmiling straight-to-camera piece.
22. Every *Diary* provides numerous examples of this type of 'hindsight' commentary. The instances are especially frequent in those programmes where diarists' voice-overs have a particularly reflective or self-reflexive tone, for example 'My Demons' (and 'My Demons – The Legacy'), 'Surviving Memories', 'The Man behind the Shotgun', 'Not a Transvestite' and 'Love Is the Drug'.
23. André Bazin: 'Cinema and Exploration', in *What Is Cinema?* Vol. 1, p. 156. My italics.
24. Aronson, *Studies in Twentieth-Century Diaries*, p. xv.
25. Ibid., p. 31.
26. Paul Barker: 'The Spread of the Cult of the Camcorder', *The Times*, 27 July 1992, p. 1.
27. Christine Geraghty, *Women and Soap Opera: a Study of Prime Time Soaps* (Cambridge: Polity, 1991), p. 6.
28. Aronson, *Studies in Twentieth-Century Diaries*, p. 63.
29. Roland Barthes, 'Writers, Intellectuals, Teachers', in *Image–Music–Text* (London: Fontana, 1977), p. 205.

30. Richard Chalfen, *Snapshot Versions of Life* (Bowling Green, Ohio: Bowling Green State University Press, 1987), p. 54.
31. With the notable and sole exception of 'Grope – The Movie', which features many scenes of the diarists, Jane Eller and Michele Howarth, larking about (singing, dancing, dressing up and dangling their legs over the edge of the bath) specifically for the camera.
32. His research is based specifically on collections of amateur films on 8mm and 16mm, but the range of topics which he identifies is recognised by other writers as an accurate description of the favoured topics of amateur video-makers.
33. Chalfen, *Snapshot Versions*, pp. 61–3.
34. After Chalfen, *Snapshot Versions*, p. 62.
35. Chalfen, *Snapshot Versions*, p. 8.
36. Chuck Kleinhans, 'My Aunt's Home Movies', *Journal of Film and Video*, Summer/Fall 1986, p. 26.
37. Chalfen, quoted in Patricia Erens, 'The Galler Home Movies', *Journal of Film and Video*, Summer/Fall, 1986, p. 18.
38. Michelle Citron, 'Concerning Daughter Rite', *Journal of Film and Video*, Summer/Fall, 1986, p. 93.
39. Brett, *The Faber Book of Diaries*, p. xi.
40. Aronson, *Studies in Twentieth-Century Diaries*, p. viii.

For further reading on *Video Diaries* the following texts are particularly valuable: Jon Dovey, 'Old Dogs and New Tricks: Access Television in the UK', in Tony Dowmunt (ed.), *Channels of Resistance* (London: BFI, 1993); Peter Keighron, 'Private Eyes', *New Statesman*, 17 May 1991; Peter Keighron, 'Video Diaries: What's Up Doc?', *Sight and Sound*, October 1993.

ABSENCE AND REVELATION
Photography as the Art of Nostalgia

Patrizia Lombardo

The Pleasure that Kills

Any research into photography, cinema, video and television necessarily entails a reflection on questions of technique. This reflection is not merely technical in nature; it is also cultural since it explores the impact of such media on the ways in which we live, think and act. In making such an assertion it is impossible to avoid citing Raymond Williams, one of the most important critics of our time, who, from the 1950s to his death in 1988, worked to redefine the meaning of culture in the post-war world. Against the conception of culture as a given and eternal set of universal references – epitomised by the canon of 'great works of art', the idea of high culture that informed British national education for almost two centuries – Williams put forward a notion of culture which corresponded to the realities and tensions of Western liberal democracy. In *Culture and Society* (1958), he wrote: 'The history of the idea of culture is a record of our reactions, in thought and feeling, to the changed conditions of our common life.'[1]

These changed conditions of life are connected to technical advances and therefore include material shifts as well as shifts in feeling and thought. Any mutation is measured by our reactions to it, to its effects on our minds and gestures. Williams believed that 'particular changes will modify an habitual discipline, shift an habitual action'.[2] The term 'discipline' here can also be pushed to its academic sense, embracing the disciplinary struggle that Williams found himself caught up in during the 1950s and '60s.[3]

What I want to argue is that one cannot trace a general history of the study of media without taking into account photography, the technique underpinning both film and television. There can be no cinema without photography, since, as Christian Metz notes,[4] film is comprised of immobile images which are projected on a screen at a regular pace and separated by black pauses resulting from the occultation of the camera by a rotating curtain. A discontinuous movement, passing from one photogram to another, creating the impression of continuity. Moreover, as Walter Benjamin suggested in a famous essay, photography is *the* technique that precipitated a radical change not only in the production of the art object but also in our perception of the world. For Benjamin the invention of photography marked a new configuration in the consumption and meaning of the work of art, since technical reproducibility ensured that art would lose its 'aura' of uniqueness. The birth of photography in first half of the 19th century accompanies the beginning of industrial mass production, but it also marks the starting point of art itself as mass phenomenon, bringing together both the artistic object and its reception – the response of men and women confronted by that object. Therefore the spark of cultural analysis, as opposed to a supposedly pure art history or a total critique of ideology, relies on the attention given to the interaction between individuals and the artistic product.

Benjamin proceeds to suggest certain shifts in the nature of that interaction. One has to reconstruct the initial surprise – or rejection – provoked by the technical miracle of fixing transient images. Benjamin cites an article from the *Leipzig City Advertiser,* which regarded photography as scandalous on the grounds that only the artist who is 'divinely inspired' was allowed to produce such images. The *Advertiser*'s journalist wrote: 'To try to catch transient reflected images is not merely something that is impossible, but, as a thorough German investigation has shown, the very desire to do so is blasphemy ...'[5] However, Benjamin continues, after they had recovered from this initial surprise or shock, people developed an indifference to the multiplication of images in much the same way as they did towards the proliferation of information through print – that other technique which did so much to change human perceptions of the world.

Benjamin and Williams share both a Marxist concern for the history of technique, and that other Marxian touchstone, a vision of the 19th century as the inauguration of our modernity, of our culture, which occurs at that point in history precisely because of the explosion of technique and, in particular, the beginning of the mass production of words and images. Such new techniques break with past habits and disciplines, forging new modes of perceiving and feeling.

However, there are slight differences in emphasis between the two commentators. Benjamin regarded journalism *and* photography to be at the root of the 'absent-minded attention' of modern men and women, and, in his *Short History of Photography* (1931), he sketches a brief comparison between the two. Williams, on the other hand, identified printing as a 'major technical advance'[6] – one of the greatest technical developments in human history that created new means of communication – but photography, which was so crucial for

Benjamin, is not central for him. Indeed, in Williams's list of the important technical advances, photography is not even mentioned:

> The major advances in transport, by road, rail, sea, and air, themselves greatly affected printing: at once in the collection of news and in the wide and quick distribution of the printed product. The development of the cable, telegraph, and telephone services even more remarkably facilitated the collection of news. Then, as new media, came sound broadcasting, the cinema and television.[7]

However, Williams does suggest that, similar to the recorded voice, photography implies the *absence* of people, which in turn suggests a possible major effect of these new means of communication: that of absence as an indispensable component of the audiovisual dimension of contemporary life. In the attempt to show how culture today indicates a process rather than a conclusion, he considers the 'neutral' or impersonal aspect of techniques:

> The only substantial objection that is made to them is that they are relatively impersonal, by comparison with older techniques serving the same ends. Where the theatre presented actors, the cinema presents the *photographs* of actors. Where the meeting presented men speaking, the wireless presents a voice, or television a voice and a *photograph*. The point about impersonality often carries a ludicrous rider. It is supposed, for instance, that it is an objection to listening to wireless talks or discussions that the listener cannot answer the speakers back. But the situation is that of almost any reader; printing, after all, was the first great impersonal medium. Much of what we call communication is, necessarily, no more in itself than transmission: that is to say, a one-way sending. Reception and response, which complete communication, depend on other factors than the techniques.[8]

Photography here appears as a substitute for human presence, as the reflected image that stands at the basis of contemporary communication. The impersonality of media, of one-way sending, voices without bodies, photographs of actors and people rather than their physical presence – all these are the elements which constitute our everyday life where we constantly face absence as the existential foundation of our experience, from politics to domesticity.

Indeed, today (much more than at the time Williams wrote *Culture and Society*), in what we call our post-modern world, we find ourselves constantly dealing with hundreds of absent bodies. We are bombarded by images, voices, computerised instructions, by technical

60

glow and murmuring, and have become indifferent to the lack of human presence that the impersonal media carry within themselves. The reception of media is therefore founded on this almost automatic pact with absence: in the world of mass communication, in the glimmering metropolis of computers, TV screens, electronic devices, we act without surprise, without regret for a type of exchange that implies the presence of interlocutors. Meanwhile the young generation has become as acquainted with the remote control as the inhabitant of the big city is used to traffic, automatic movements and anonymous passers-by.

This contemporary familiarity with absence is a fundamental product of the process of alienation that nineteenth-century writers such as Poe and Baudelaire and, of course, Benjamin (in the tracks of major German sociologists such as Max Weber and Georg Simmel writing at the turn of the century) identified as typical of the modern condition. Indeed, alienation was *the* founding experience of metropolitan life. Simmel called it the nervous life of the modern metropolis; Benjamin, the interiorisation of shocks – with shock and anguish becoming such a mental habit that they preordain human perception. In his essay 'On Some Motifs in Baudelaire', Benjamin regards a poem from Baudelaire's *Les Fleurs du mal*, 'A une passante', as exemplary of metropolitan alienation. In the big city even eroticism is a solitary experience: the lyrical voice tells of a sudden street scene, where a man glimpses a beautiful woman quickly disappearing in the crowd and traffic. There is no conversation, no human contact, only one-way communication conveyed in broken sentences that cannot even hold together in the continuity of syntax as the poet mentally addresses a few words to the woman, an anonymous 'you' who will never give an answer:

> Fugitive beauty
> Whose glance suddenly made me reborn,
> Will I ever see you again if not in eternity?
>
> Somewhere else, far from here! too late! probably *never*!
> Because I ignore where you flee, you do not know where I go
> You! whom I would have loved, oh, you who knew it![9]

This short and convulsive meditation on the ephemeral and the impossible derives from the power of a glimpsing vision, of two gazes that seem to cross briefly but fail to meet in any real encounter. The Baudelairian gaze to the passer-by, her sudden and inaccessible glance, epitomise a situation which is the opposite of any phenomenological continuity, of any intersubjective exchange. The broken desire reproduced in the fragmented rhythm of Baudelaire's poem, in the spasm of

61

its lines, suggests the reaction to the purely visual as the act of gripping a person through the eyes, of reaching the most unconscious desire, the barest and bluntest demand of love, for an other who is constitutively absent. As vanishing image, unattainable body (as inconsistent as the photographs of actors which, in Williams's words, mark the shift from theatre to cinema and television), the Baudelairean passer-by is symptomatic of the metropolitan reality that brutally changed the culture of the nineteenth century, and softly continues to change thoughts, feelings, desires and relationships in our late twentieth century audiovisual world.

While technological advance has enhanced the effects of the nineteenth-century metropolitan phenomenon, the alienation inherent in the *reception* of mass-media stands as a reversal of the conditions of representation prevalent during the 19th century and the first half of the 20th century. Prior to the ascendancy of the techniques of mass communication the world was comprehended through direct experience more than through images whereas today one can argue, rather paradoxically, that there is more representation than material world. Nineteenth-century artists who have been labelled as 'realist' had to respond to the richness of reality and cope with the poverty of representational means caused by limitations in particular techniques, certainly when compared with our own technological power. Particular forms such as the novel or painting were slow, even if an individual artist, such as Balzac, tried to produce at a frantic pace – almost as if the human being could follow the machine rhythm of printing. And, even if printing in the 19th century did undergo major technical advances, those transformations seem almost irrelevant compared with the quickness of the media world.

The development of photography served to clarify the connections between the histories of techniques and of ideas – particularly anthropological and sociological perspectives. However, the study of the new medium could not be comfortably integrated into the nineteenth-century disciplinary structures of universities. Photography may relate to the concerns of fine art, history, communication studies, or sociology, but yet cannot be subsumed under any of these categories. How can one really separate the concern for chemical elements reacting to the sun or the lights in the photographic studio from the surprise caused by the rapidity of technical reproduction, and the blasé attitude towards the very quickness with which representations and images can circulate? This quickness of reproduction increasingly occultates photography's initial scene when the camera caught what was present in front of it – be it a person, an object, or an urban or natural landscape. Nevertheless, as always when our historical memory is blackened by some technical ease, collective reminiscence is powerfully and unconsciously at work. Consequently, I would suggest, the indifference of our electronic age is actually built upon on that inaugural surprise of the first mythical photographs, the astonishment which, in the 19th century, produced something akin to a collective mirror stage, when humankind perceived its own image in the silverish mirror of the camera and the black-and-white shades of the photograph.

The human subject, acquainted with the world, has forgotten the inaugural scene of the discovery of his/her own image. Yet that scene is formative and dictates the function of the self. In his famous 1949 paper, 'The Mirror Stage',[10] Jacques Lacan drew attention to the euphoric, foundational moment in which the child – when it is approximately six months old and is as yet unable to walk or talk – recognises with exultation its own *imago* in the mirror, as well as the image of its reflected environment, and enjoys the repetition of this scene. It is a crucial episode which frames, before the effective acquisition of language, the human subject as belonging to the inextricable network of the real, the imaginary and the symbolic. In fact, that identification of his/her own image – of his/her own self or body as image – takes place within the symbolic order, the order of language, since the subject's enjoyment lies exactly in the *fictional* construction of the specular reproduction of himself or herself, and the 'reality' of his/her environment. Alienation – in the literal sense of *alius*, other – stands at the basis of identification: the subject needs that alienating process in the presence itself of a 'technical' object – the mirror – in order to recognise his/her self, his/her existence. Lacan stressed the transformation produced in the subject after he/she has hold of the image.

I would suggest that photography constitutes the mirror stage where the enlarged self of humanity recognises its own image in a 'fiction' where the imaginary, the real and the symbolic are tightly connected. Consequently, one of the primary objectives of media studies should be to stress the transformation that took place in human life with the global holding of the image. Such is the advent of photography, and its continuation in the filmic image.

It is important to note that in the Lacanian narration of the mirror stage the subject's taking on of the image, and the whole fiction, is related to the concept of the real. It is as if the *infans* (speechless) child could say in front of the object that is the mirror: 'That image is really me, my body, myself, here and now.' The imprint of what Benjamin called photography's 'here and now' (*hic* and *nunc*) is always there in the photographic print itself, which therefore accomplishes the miracle of a mirror marked for ever by the outlines of the reflected image, fixing for all time the transient reflected image. The *real* presence of the photographed person, place, object – vanishing in an inexhaustible absence, always lacking – lingers forever in the halo of photography as the unconscious memory of its historical dimension, even in the most sophisticated contemporary montage and *truquage*, which do not need the presence of anything in the flesh. If it were not so why would we insist on photography's documentary value? Isn't the whole CNN operation, in the United States and in the rest of the world, based on this photographic-documentary conviction stamped into our cultural unconscious? We see, therefore how could we not believe what we witness as recorded in the very place (*hic*), at the very moment (*nunc*) it happened or is happening? Don't those images tell the truth of what really happened, or even what is taking place just now, in front of our (I would argue, televised) eyes – such as the images of the Gulf war, or the insurrections in Moscow? The realist value of photography is exactly what embodies the possibility of information-disinformation, the more or less nuanced manipulation of the interplay between fiction and reality.

Michelangelo Antonioni's film *Blow-Up* (1966) probably offers the most acute reflection on the intertwining of truth and *truquage* in photography. How could photographs be falsified if they did not carry within themselves the trace of photography's power, linked to its inaugural scene – that is, its possibility of grasping the ephemeral moment as it happens? Doesn't language carry a similar double bind, since we lie with language exactly because it holds within itself the reference to truth? If the reproduced image is hellish and dangerous for the correspondent of the *Leipzig City Advertiser*, that is because photography is a sort of *ménage à trois*. It is where the object (what is photographed) and the subject (the viewer) face themselves with a precise mental perception: the idea of a presence turned into absence. In other words, the object appears to the subject as the *manque d'objet*, the lacking of the object.[11] The three terms, then, are: subject, object, and lack (or absence). Simultaneously true and untrue, real and evasive, photography, like Baudelaire's passer-by, exists in the gap between what it is and its reception, in that discrepancy between the object and the subject, where the subject, far from mastering the situation (the object), is subject to, or subjugated by, an endless questioning of the object which continuously eludes the subject through its ineluctable absence.

The interplay between reality and absence (and the subsequent interplay between truth and falsehood) constitutes the status of photography. Williams understands this when he speaks of the photograph of absent actors in cinema and television, and Benjamin analysed that absence as a new phenomenon – one which is, I insist, a variant of the situation of the Baudelairian passer-by. In his essay on the history of photography, Benjamin did not simply reflect on the

64

technical aspect of photography – what can be called the photographic object – he also speculated on the reception of photography, on the way in which the subject feels and thinks in front of the photographic object, which in this way marks its difference from art:

> In photography, one encounters a new and strange phenomenon: in that fishwife from New Haven [1843, by David Octavius Hill], who casts her eyes down with such casual, seductive shame, there remains something that does not merely testify to the art of Hill the photographer, but something that cannot be silenced, that impudently demands the name of the person who lived at the time and who remaining real even now, will never yield herself up entirely into art.[12]

Although written in an impersonal mode or in the passive form – 'something that cannot be silenced, something that impudently demands' – what is active in Benjamin's passage is the spectator, who, in the moment in which he or she receives the image, cannot but question its state of reality, and in doing so almost misses that piece of reality when the person in the portrait was there, present in the flesh. The spectator of photography holds the same position as Baudelaire looking at the passer-by in the street, being in that same situation of alienation and thirst for reality, imprisoned in that 'impudent demand' for the other, that eventually splits up in the many questions of the Baudelairian character. Benjamin continues:

> However skillful the photographer, however carefully he poses the model, the spectator feels an irresistible compulsion to look for the tiny spark of chance, of the here and now, with which reality has, as it were, seared the character in the picture.[13]

That irresistible compulsion, that 'tiny spark' of time and reality, which the spectator is seeking is rather different from the famous situation of the *regard de l'autre* (the gaze of the other) in Sartre's *L'Être et le néant*, when one person reaches consciousness of himself or herself trough the gaze of another human being. In a public park, two people look at each other, they realise that they themselves are looking because of the other, and they realise that they exist in a perfect two-way balance. In what can be called the phenomenological stream, one person has the sense of his or her own identity thanks to the recognition implied by the other, mirroring with his or her own eyes the received gaze. The Sartrian scene implies the impact of physical presence, the consciousness (not the unconscious) of the self in an, adult rather than infantile, intersubjective exchange where the subject has obviously full control of his/her own motion and language, as if the human subject could annihilate or quietly forget the unbalanced situation of his/her need demand-dependence as a child. The Sartrian action is a dual fulfilment of the Cartesian *cogito*:[14] I look at you looking at me; we both know that we are looking at each other. The action is slow. Time has, so to speak, a chronological dimension between the extremes of the ephemeral and the eternal which we are able to master.

But the passer-by episode, on the other hand, is constructed on the overlapping of the ephemeral and the eternal and takes place in a 'tiny spark of chance, of the here and now'. The two gazes are irredeemably discrepant; they never meet, their temporal dimension is, literally, that of the twinkling of an eye, and then the solitude of the meditation on eternity. One person watches the other; he looks with desire – an already violent nostalgia for what is taking place negatively as something which will never happen. The other is simply on the other side of the street – she is beautiful, desirable, impossible, real and unreal at the same time, as if her action were frozen in the intransitive verb to look, and not to look at, a verb suspended with no preposition and no object, or the object being so removed that it will never be reached. The woman is an image, an optical object, and the subject is left without one-to-one recognition, burning in the tension of a desire that, far from being fulfilled, stands as alienation, as an anguishing desire for the other. Desire flickers in a continuous questioning, to which absence inevitably gives rise, reiterating the quest with a powerful phantasmic activity. Perversion, in its most literal sense, is implied in the whole operation, where the visual *per se* has an almost total power, and rejects the merely physical for an endless mental visualisation or representation.[15]

Benjamin had a clear insight of this when he briefly suggested that photography 'makes aware for the first time the optical unconscious'. One can connect with the theme of the cultural effects of technological changes indicated by Williams, and suggest that it is this very 'optical unconscious' which is at stake for spectators of film and, especially, television – the fragmented, sparkling, interrupted production of images rhythmed by the remote control, or glimmering in the clips. What you have in the act of spectatorship are subjects situated beyond the possibility of being recognised by the gaze of the other, anonymous viewers whose desire is enticed. We look, for example, at Madonna's body moving with music and song, ungraspable in the vertiginous spasms, the jumps and cuts of the convulsive editing of the images. In this act we undoubtedly resemble the inhabitant of the metropolis perceiving the passer-by in the middle of traffic and noise, strained in erotic contraction: 'And I, tense like an eccentric / Drank in her eyes, sombre stormy sky, / The sweetness that enthrals, the pleasure that kills.'[16]

But images have an inevitable pornographic character. Fredric Jameson begins his book *Signatures of the Visible* (1992) by stressing the irony of our civilisation which has transformed human nature into just one sense, that of sight:

> The visual is essentially pornographic, which is to say that it has its end in rapt, mindless fascination; thinking about its attributes becomes an adjunct to that, if it is unwilling to betray its object; while the most austere films necessarily draw their energy from the attempt to repress their own excess (rather than from the more thankless effort to discipline the viewer). Pornographic films are thus only the potentiation of films in general, which asks us to stare at the world as though it were a naked body.[17]

The production of images is founded on both the provocation and the boredom of pornography – the indifference we can have towards it, even if we look for excitement. Our perception, our mind and our senses are so used to the excess of images and their enticement, to the naked body of the world, that there is no surprise, no possible shock, because, as Benjamin understood, the shock is already interiorised, is already part of our internal world, of our psychic predispositions. Our reactions to the overwhelming world of the audiovisual oscillate between indifference and appeal. We know that Madonna is absent, yet we are compelled to question her reality, to desire the fragments of her body so carefully constructed as sexual machine, as fetish. She, the image *par excellence*, wants to be wanted, she is the object of scopophilic pleasure (pleasure in looking) *par excellence*, shining on that spark of unfulfilled desire posed as the condition of desire itself. The scenario is inevitably, and abstractedly, sadomasochistic: we will never touch her, she can go on torturing her spectators, giving glimpses of the pleasure that kills.

It is possible to develop these ideas into a feminist analysis of what is at stake in vision. In her famous article, 'Visual Pleasure and Narrative Cinema', Laura Mulvey argues that 'it is woman as representation that crystalizes'[18] the paradox or the tension between sexual instinct and narcissistic identification with the image seen. She also identified that these two crucial terms as used by Freud were 'formative structures, mechanisms without intrinsic meaning'.[19] They could only become meaningful thanks to a work of idealisation, but their major feature is non-realistic: 'Both pursue aims in *indifference to perceptual reality*, and motivate *eroticised phantasmagoria* that affect the subject's perception of the world to make a mockery of empirical objectivity.'[20]

67

While a thorough theory of the image would necessarily have to take into account the question of gender (and is a type of analysis perfectly coherent with my reading of Baudelaire's female passer-by), this is not my objective here. Rather, in the remainder of this paper I will consider some theoretical and historical issues in relation to photography, and, more specifically, attempt to construct a network of concerns around photography and the image in general through the interplay of key texts by Williams, Benjamin, Bazin, Barthes and Jameson. My aim is not a critique of their various positions, either explicit or implicit, which in several cases obviously lack an investigation of gender. Rather, I would like to highlight, within the puzzle offered by some texts by those writers, a double bind essential to the understanding of photography, and therefore cinema: that is, the rapport between absence and reality. If photographs are different from filmic images and even more so, as Jameson suggests, from 'from the glossy images of postmodern film', nevertheless one cannot forget that 'they are technically and historically related'.[21]

Black-and-White Is Blue

We might think that photography and cinema are a part (alongside painting) of the history or the anthropology of the idea of the real. Eric Auerbach, rejecting any narrow academic conception of realism as a school founded in the 19th century, identified realism as *the* major concern of Western art from Homer to modernity. The point, of course, is not that of identifying an eternal cultural value that would project a Western mould over any human experience, in a sort of teleological comparative history, but rather to examine the insistence on the notion of the real, and to ask certain questions of it. For example, what are the different values given to the real in various historical periods and in various geographical areas? When and how was it charged with a particular meaning, so that it became central to the way in which knowledge has been organised or epistemological problems posed? How have various techniques and optical means – perspective, photography, cinema – intersected to produce antagonistic significations? How mutually dependent are a positive (and positivistic) and a negative sense of the real?

I would like to argue that, from Balzac to Brecht and Lacan, the notion of the real has primary importance. Writing in the 19th century, Balzac drowned in the excess of the real world – where objects, matter, things, books, people, ideas, words piled up in an uncontrollable quantity. But the master of the French realist novel was already perceived by Baudelaire as a visionary. Forcing the limits of the realist experience culminating in Balzac's descriptions of the big monster, Paris, Baudelaire carved out another notion of reality: an allegorical one, where Paris became indescribable, but haunting as a spectral presence – which is absence. Consequently Paris can be totally identified with the mysterious woman, the ephemeral passer-by tinged with the colour of eternity. On the other hand, it is precisely because of the shifting meanings of the term 'realism' that Brecht could later talk of another realism which does not correspond to the great organic genealogies of the realist novel, but rather to the technical power of montage, as in Dos Passos's novels, or to the allegories of Shelley.[22] Neither did the thirst for the real escape the surrealistically conceived investigations of Lacanian psychoanalysis. The hard core, the impossible kernel of the real holds up, ineluctably tied to the order of the symbolic and the imaginary. To speak of the real is already to be part of the symbolic order because, as Lacan insists, 'the real, whatever disruption we might operate, is always and in any event at its own place'.[23] The real will still be there even in the aftermath of the most devastating nuclear destruction.

Visible or invisible, easy or impossible to grasp, full or empty, concrete or abstract, opaque or virtual – reality has been a cultural obsession. In the modernist era a whole host of concepts move around the real, allowing all the paradigms from reification to dereification, passing through the exaltation of the concrete, the nostalgia for the physical thing, the search for the truth, the belief in the document, the allegorical value of the fictional, the imprint of the symbolic. Behind all of this an old dream is lurking – the desire to be reality, to be the thing itself beyond the representational power of words and images. It is a dream of blind materialism to immediately turn into the idealism of the full thing, dispensing with the need for representation in the fullness of the presence of the present. God stands at the horizon, in the divine mystery of creation. Yet how is it possible even to conceive of such a desire for reality without that gap that is our thinking and speaking about it? In the moment I see reality, I am marking the distance that makes reality problematic, tingeing with absence/presence itself. Such is the drama of representation. Any artistic theory – either holding onto representation or denying it – is part and parcel of the same drama. Hence the misery and splendour of the term 'realism.'

In 1945 André Bazin wrote one of the most important essays on photography, at a moment when the medium was already one century old, and cinema half a century. In this essay, 'The Ontology of the Photographic Image', Bazin established a link between cinema and photography within the perspective of the psychological history of the plastic arts. Moreover, in his subsequent writings, including the seminal work on Italian neo-realist cinema, Bazin established himself as one of the great interpreters of realism. His modernist fight to endow cinema with artistic dignity is paradoxically constructed upon what I would call a non-modernist vision of the world. This is probably due to his Catholicism, inevitably infused with a conception of some essential human unity and the belief in some inner signification of things. If modernism is born with Baudelaire and his poetics of the 'modern' – of the modern metropolis as the only (completely alienating) reality – then any belief which is founded on unity, continuity, and the fullness of some spiritual experience through matter, is inevitably idealist and non modernist.

As already suggested, *Les Fleurs du mal* continually hints at the presence of Paris, not by describing it but by showing its effects on human perception. Baudelaire's poems subvert the poetic idealism of a world where nature, God and human life respond to each other in a perennial harmony. Disharmonious, satanic, cruel, but nevertheless innovative both at the stylistic level of a versification, which did not respect traditional metrics, and at the content level, which was striking in the scandalous choice of themes, the lyric poems of Baudelaire mark, as Benjamin has shown, the essential cultural switch in the 19th century which corresponded to the new forms of production, and to the market economy typical of the metropolitan reality. 'Modern' here means fragmentation, expressed in the very form of the other crucial work by Baudelaire, *Paris Spleen*, in which the intuition of montage is already present. The poet announces to his friend Arsène Houssaye that these poems were conceived as segments, as pieces whose order was irrelevant but whose rhythm corresponded to the 'abstract modern life', to the broken rhythm of the modern metropolis where the human subject is constantly divided, constantly exposed to the nervous life of his or her inner perception moulded on the nervous reality surrounding all his or her gestures:

Which one of us, in his moments of ambition, has not dreamed of the miracle of a poetic prose, musical, without rhythm and without rhyme, supple and rugged enough to adapt itself to the lyrical impulses of the soul, the undulation of reverie, the jibes of conscience?

It was above all, out of my exploration of huge cities, out of the medley of their innumerable interrelations, that this haunting ideal was born.[24]

The reality of modernism is abstract where the Catholic vision of the world is spiritual – pointing to a mysterious correspondence between things and their significations. However, I would argue that realism cannot exist without some degree of allegory, because even the most flat conception of it – namely, that realism is a copy of things – must refer to some organising notion, such as the positivistic idea of the evidence of facts. Catholic realism is allegorical in the sense of it being a transfiguration of something concrete into its hidden meaning, while the modernist realism – that of Baudelaire – on the other hand, derives from an intellectual, almost mathematical, operation. It refuses both description and transfiguration but it believes in a process of idealisation that turns reality into mockery; it has the power of abstraction and deformation. A famous poem, 'Les Sept viellards' (The Seven Old Men) recounts the hallucination of the poet-inhabitant of the metropolis, who is convinced he sees an old man multiplying in front of him. The poem begins with a powerful vision bordering on absurdity:

Swarming city, filled with dreams,
Where ghosts grab passers-by at full day!
Mysteries rise all over like sap
In the narrow channels of the mighty giant.

One morning, when, in the sad street,
Buildings, whose height was increased by the mist,
Were similar to the two embankments of a grown river
When, like a stage setting resembling the actor's mind

A filthy and yellow fog flooded all the space around,
My nerves stiffened like a hero's, I followed ...[25]

As in many of Baudelaire's poems, if we examine this work, if we catch its reel-movement when, in the following lines, the old man multiplies to the number of seven, we see hallucination implanted in the real, or one inextricably connected to the other. The modern resides in this realistic hallucination. In painting and cinema modernism moves towards expressionism – exactly that allegorical, disturbed and distorted technique which perverts 'realist' (in the simplistic sense) reproduction into symbolic colours and shapes, such as those deformed buildings and that yellow fog hitting the eyes and the ears of the reader in Baudelaire's poem, not unlike the violent images of Fritz Lang's *Metropolis* assaulting the viewer's perception.

Not surprisingly, expressionism was exactly the type of cinema that Bazin could not stand, and against German expressionism he fought for the virtues of Italian neo-realism. His enthusiasm for Rossellini and neo-realist cinema in general was founded on the awareness that the illusion of reality given to the spectator 'can only be achieved in one way – through artifice'.[26] But Bazin did not see a violent tension between the epistemological and the aesthetic senses of the phrase 'reproduction of reality'. On the contrary, for him:

> The 'art' of cinema lives off this contradiction. It gets the most out of the potential for abstraction and symbolism provided by the present limits of the screen, but this utilisation of the residue conventions abandoned by technique can work either to the advantage or to the detriment of realism. It can magnify or neutralise the effectiveness of the elements of reality that the camera captures.[27]

Technique, so important for Bazin, is at the service of reality, of the world that cinema is supposed to represent according to the movement of our desires. Nothing in Bazin's writing, not even his most acute concerns for technical devices, such as in his famous analysis of *Citizen Kane*, leads to an identification of technique as that primary force within which human beings live and change, as that breaking-point from which a cultural jump is activated in spite of some delays in mentality and habits. Rather, for Bazin technique is always an instrument; it is never above human spiritual life.

But, on the contrary, technique is often the tangible shape taken by human spirituality. The difference between Bazin's progressive Catholic approach[28] and the modernist-Marxian relies exactly in this value of technique. (We know, of course, that there is a militaristic and Fascist conception of technique which certainly does not underscore its primary importance, since it becomes the necessary means of power: technique is the instrument a few people use to dominate and crush other people.) Jameson, who pinpointed, in 'The Existence of Italy', the ontological-metaphysical Bazinian project, puts it clearly:

> I am tempted to say that all technological explanation has, as its strong function or 'proper use', demystification, generally in the service of a materialist philosophical position: de-idealization, then, de-spiritualization in whatever sense or context, provided it is understood that is is not a position but rather an operation, and *intervention*, whose aims and effects depend on what is being demystified, generally the innate tendency of literary or cultural critics to an idealism of meaning or interpretation.[29]

But arguably the main source of Bazin's enthusiasm for neo-realism is what might be called his passion for the peculiar melancholy of the black-and-white – the historical nostalgic essence of photography, that inescapable longing for reality imprinted in any photograph before the advent of colour. Jameson is again full of insight on this point. Quoting Kracauer on Benjamin, he stresses the 'global relationship between melancholy and the visual'.[30] In the essay 'In Defence of

72

Rossellini', Bazin developed what Jameson saw as his 'ontological' nostalgia:

Neo-realism ... is always reality as it is visible through an artist, as refracted by his consciousness – but his consciousness as a whole and not by his reason alone or his emotions or his beliefs – and reassembled from its distinguishable elements. I would put it this way: the traditional realist artist – Zola, for example – analyses reality into parts which he then reassembles in a synthesis the final determinant of which is his moral conception of the world, whereas the consciousness of the neo-realist director *filters* reality. Undoubtedly, his consciousness, like that of everyone else, does not admit reality as a whole, but the selection that does occur is neither logical nor it is psychological; it is ontological, in the sense that the image of reality it restores to us is still a whole – just as a black-and-white photograph is not an image of reality broken down and put back together again 'without the colour' but rather a true *imprint of reality* [my italics], a kind of luminous mould in which colour simply does not figure. There is ontological identity between the object and its photographic image.[31]

Bazin, within the context of neo-realist cinema, once again stressed his thesis on photography, establishing a necessary link between neo-realism and black-and-white, which is the kind of *rapprochement* we cannot avoid now, in the era of the glamorous colours of the postmodern. What Bazin called the ontological identity between the object and its photographic image rises up in the consciousness of the spectator like a revelation.

The idea of revelation is actually crucial in 'The Ontology of the Photographic Image', which begins with the precise intention of finding a continuity in a human endeavour. Photography is part of the history of the plastic arts, whose primordial human intention was the sacred battle against death. Embalming the dead as in Egyptian religion and the painting of the portrait of Louis XIV both demonstrate the same human impulse: the attempt to preserve life by a representation of life, the need to remember, to win time through the immortal character of form. Bazin described the tension implied in the history of the plastic arts by way of the concept that would become his favourite theme in film criticism: realism. The history of the plastic arts is the history itself of resemblance or realism. A double realism glimmers through Bazin's argument, articulating the aesthetic and the psychological as the two halves of the same question. Human beings are thirsty for reality and they move between the aspiration to spiritual reality and the replacement of the external world thanks to its duplication, what Bazin calls *eidolon*, or image of the external world.

Bazin reveals his idealistic-spiritual vision as fundamental for human experience. It is not that he doesn't see that human beings live in alienation, but rather that they are perceived as going beyond their alienation, exactly in those miraculous moments in which an ontological identity – a coincidence – is found between the thing and its image. The spiritual tension is a promise, a fulfilling *Aufhebung,* or a reassuring return to some previous golden age, before the split. The history of the visual arts, culminating in photography and cinema, leads humanity towards that aim.

Unlike the Marxist-modernist oriented idea of periodisation which emphasised the new conditions of life in the 19th century, Bazin's periodisation endowed photography and cinema with the power of the happy rediscovery of a more spiritual age. For him they echo back to some miraculous balance that existed before the invention of perspective, what Bazin calls 'the original sin of Western painting'. Medieval painting was, in his opinion, beyond the conflict of the spiritual and the psychological, while the invention of perspective on the other hand was the result of that conflict. This rather obscure idea hints, I think, at the illusory and especially abstract character of the *representation* of reality in the technique of perspective. The essential task for Bazin is not to represent but to re-create or create anew. Such is the incantatory power of revelation. Niepce and Lumière can therefore be seen as redeeming the plastic arts, freeing them from what Bazin calls 'their obsession with likeness'. Photography jumps away from the original sin of Western painting, from the prejudices with which it affected our perception of the object, and, it can be added, from the subsequent sin of expressionism – for isn't expressionism in fact connected to the *a priori* of perspective, because it needs to transgress and deform it, and, by doing this, it reconfirms perspective's hegemony? Silent and sober, renouncing perspective's dream of likeness, focusing on what can be called the existential solitude of things and beings, their phenomenological density, their mysterious life – photography is, for Bazin, the revelation of the real:

> The aesthetic qualities of photography are to be sought in its power to lay bare realities [but the French text is condensed on the term *revelation*: 'Les virtualités esthétiques de la photographie résident dans la *révélation* du réel.']. It is not for me to separate off, in the complex fabric of the objective world, here a reflection on a damp sidewalk, there the gesture of a child. Only the impassive lens, stripping its object of all those ways of seeing it, those piled-up preconceptions, that spiritual dust and grime with which my eyes have covered it, is able to present it in all its virginal purity to my

attention and consequently to my love. By the power of photography, the natural image of a world that we neither know nor can see, nature at last does more than imitate art: she imitates the artist.[32]

Bazin's argument builds up dramatically, surveying human history, casting light on unconscious attempts and desires, sketching a compelling anthropology capable of finding the dazzling emotion that *reveals* the real. In that luminous moment of revelation photography moves away from the path of the visual arts and fulfils the quest for the object, giving the certainty that what has been photographed really existed in space and time. Bazin's intuition on this point is similar to that of Benjamin, despite their ideological differences, in that photography's revelation is close to Benjamin's tiny spark of chance which I commented on above.

But who, when looking at a photograph, can escape that shade of the nostalgia for the real? In his 1980 book *La Chambre claire*, Roland Barthes, from a structuralist-phenomenological perspective, reached an understanding of photography similar to Bazin's revelation. Barthes is convinced that photography's essence relies in the *ça a été* (it has been). Following Sartre's work on the imaginary and Lacan's conception of an impossible real, Barthes insisted on the absence of the photographed object, finally realising an experience of 'hallucination' that is not too far removed from the revelation Bazin talked about:

The image, says phenomenology, is an object-as-nothing. Now, in the Photograph, what I posit is not only the absence of the object; it is also, by one and the same movement, on equal terms, the fact that this object has indeed existed and that is has been there where I see it. Here is where the madness is, for until this day no representation could assure me of the past of a thing except by intermediaries; but with the Photograph, my certainty is immediate: no one in the world can undeceive me. The Photograph then becomes a bizarre *medium*, a new form of hallucination: false on the level of perception, true on the level of time: a temporal hallucination, so to speak, a modest, *shared* hallucination (on the one hand 'it is not there,' on the other 'but it has indeed been'): a mad image, chafed by reality.[33]

The startling personal experience of Barthes researching the essence and meaning of photography culminates in the astonishment of a resurrection, when, while contemplating (not unlike Proust's narrator looking at his grandmother's picture) the photograph of a six-year-old girl, he *recognised* his dead mother as he had never seen her. Photography is a snapshot, in the technical and existential senses; it catches the instant, fixing it for all time. In front of that picture, Barthes is taken by cathartic revelation that blends the sorrow for an absence with the melancholy beauty of time, of the time we have never lived but we can long for in the faded light of the black-and-white image.

Discussing film history and its periodisation in his essay 'The Existence of Italy', Fredric Jameson rejects a simply linear or evolutionary chronology progressing from 'realism' to 'modernism' to 'post-modernism'. He nevertheless considers that this 'three terms' trajectory is valuable 'at a more compressed tempo',[34] and, beyond the analogies between what has been called the realist moment of film and the nineteenth-century realist novel, he faces 'realism' as a 'peculiarly unstable concept owing to its simultaneous, yet incompatible, aesthetic and epistemological claims, as the two terms of the slogan, "representation of reality," suggests'.[35] Jameson follows the conceptual tensions implicit and explicit in that slogan, since the strength of representational techniques undermines the truth content, stressing the illusory character of realistic effects, while the simple claim of a correct representation of the world – of reality – annihilates the very existence of an aesthetic mode of representation, exalting a documentary value beyond the realistic artifice, or art. But, in a very anti-Bazinian way, Jameson insists that we cannot avoid taking into account the conceptual instability posited by the simultaneity of the epistemological and the aesthetic claims, 'prolonging and preserving – rather than "resolving" – this constitutive tension and incommensurability'.[36]

Photography is condemned to be inextricably linked with the real and its fluctuations as it necessarily embodies the paradox of the phrase 'representation of reality'. But Jameson perceives photography as crucial to the understanding of something else, which is, I would argue, at the basis of any historical research – namely the paradox of history itself. Both share a concern with the relationship of an event to the present, or with the presence of an event beyond its primary phenomenological appearance in that disquieting reinvention or re-enactment or rediscovery of it – a process that combines immediacy with representational distance:

Still photography remains, however, the archetypal embodiment of this process and of its paradoxes: in it even 'fiction photography' (19th century *mise en scène* and costumed poses) ultimately becomes 'realistic,' insofar as it remains a historical fact that 19th century bourgeois people did put on costumes to pose for such tableaux. On the other hand, one is also tempted to say that in another sense there is no photographic *realism* as such – all photography is already 'modernist' insofar as it necessarily draws attention (by way of framing and composition) to the act by which its contents are 'endowed with form', as we used to say in the modernist period. 'Realism,' in this view, would simply consist in the space of the family photograph and the 'likeness' of some sheerly personal association and recognition ...[37]

Jameson's major point of interest is in film history, but he must investigate it through a reflection on photographic image and on what I would call the 'trembling', or the flickering, of the term 'realism', which is always logically (rather than chronologically) first, even in the compressed sequence of realism-modernism–post-modernism. Through photography and its use in certain kinds of cinema Jameson perceives the nostalgic character inevitably attached to the medium. The embodied possibility of nostalgia provokes a startling reversal: Jameson reads Benjamin as being on the side of nostalgia, in spite of what can sound as a non-nostalgic slogan – Benjamin's idea that photography marked the end of art's aura. In the age of video and television, according to Jameson, we can identify in cinema a sort of return to the splendour and uniqueness of the work of art, the famous aura Benjamin saw as characterising the artistic object before the advent of mass production. Because of this return, the 'good print' of a film acquires the value of a renewed authenticity.

Nostalgia also lingers in the immobility of photography, in the fading away of its nuances. What separates our perception of photography from Benjamin's is obviously a technical aspect: the glossy colour picture of our age that changes the meaning and perception of the black-and-white photograph. This glossiness is the presence itself of the post-modern, which can cast a nostalgic light on the melancholy technicality of black-and-white, somewhat blurring the distinction between realism and modernism, while marking the post-modern. Jameson tracks down the tie with the past:

In photography, however, as Susan Sontag has pointed out, things are somewhat different, the marks of aging – fading, yellowing, and the like – increase the value of a black-and-white print and heighten its interest as an object for us. Colour prints, however, merely deteriorate with age. The distinction is strikingly dramatised in the Cuban film, *The Opportunist!* (*Un Hombre de éxito*, Humberto Solas, 1986), which begins with streaked and faded black-and-white (fictional) newsreel footage of the return of the police chief figure to La Havana in 1932, wondrously transmuted into colour while the camera pauses on the monumental interior of the palace ...[38]

I would insist on the value of Jameson's perspective and reinforce his non-linear understanding of the sequence realism–modernism–post-modernism, while maintaining that realism holds a primary position and can be mapped with different degrees of intensity and carry various values. Within his thesis on the nostalgic character of photography, which he argues from the standpoint of a materialist cultural history of cinema, I will draw attention to what I call his snapshot, or photographic, method in writing, in the sense that his argument is constructed not according to a linear narrative development, but is, rather, a mode of writing and thinking which escapes both the old-fashioned Hegelian analytical-synthetical endeavour, and the post-modernist taste for a sort of random jamming together of quotations. Rejecting any master narrative, Jameson presents neither a linear account of the history of film, nor a theoretical system, nor a one-sided ideological demystification. He himself probably gives a perfect definition of his non-historicist mode of writing through the term 'alternate accounts'.[39] He precipitates – in the chemical sense, as in photography – theoretical questions and cases: an interrogation on the status of the visual, or the problem of realism, blending with the interpretation of certain films or literary or critical texts. Moreover, the cases modify their exemplary value, because they are positioned according to different angles of vision, triggering off in multiple clicks.

In the sequence realism–modernism–post-modernism there is no eternal value judgment, since the logical and the chronological level are interchangeable, and because Jameson's aim is not to stand for one type, or school, against the other – that, for example, modernism is better than realism, post-modernism is better than modernism; and so on. We cannot, like Bazin, argue that Italian neo-realism is better than expressionism, because, in the age of post-capitalism, our memory is filled with films' reminiscences, we see films that mix all categories or use them laterally. While there are undoubtedly moments in which it is clear that Jameson's battle is against what he calls 'high modernism', which is so ineluctably tinged with nostalgia, nevertheless a very cogent example of his discourse is the reading of Antonioni's *Blow-Up*, a classic in film modernism, effectively a double-bind modernism in the sense that its subject is the modernist art technique *par excellence* – photography.

Jameson wrote that photography is 'already a philosophically existentialist medium, in which history is subject to confusion with finitude and with individual biological time; and whose costume dramas and historical records are therefore always close to the borderline between historicity and nostalgia'.[40] But he can never be said to advocate the cause of a triumphant and perfectly liberatory post-modernism, one which would finally get rid of history and its melancholia in the triumphant glossiness of coloured images. For he understands too well the hammering question:

> Is this then to say that even within the extraordinary eclipse of historicity in the postmodern period some deeper memory of history still faintly stirs? Or does this persistence – nostalgia for that ultimate moment of historical time in which difference was still present – rather betoken the incompleteness of the postmodern process, the survival within it of remnants from the past, which have not yet, as in some unimaginable fully realised postmodernism, been dissolved without a trace?[41]

Jameson is always aware that any 'strange form of vision has formal and historical preconditions'.[42] Take for example his suggestion of the post-modern insight at the end of *Blow-Up*: whether 'by fulfilling the realist ontology – that is, by revealing Bazinian realism openly as ontology (and as metaphysics) – it can be seen as the inauguration of all those non-ontological impulses which will take its place and which we loosely term postmodern?'[43]

I would suggest that the borderline 'between historicity and nostalgia' which Jameson talks about is inevitably there in the term 'inauguration' (which recurs frequently in his essay to indicate the input of certain works). To invoke this idea of 'inauguration' places one in the stormy position of Benjamin's angel of history. Looking at Klee's 'Angelus Novus', Benjamin pictured it as the emblem of history: the angel seems to be about to move away from something he contemplates – his eyes are staring, his wings wide open, caught in the wind. He suggested that the angel's face is turned towards the past, and that he cannot close his wings because he is violently pushed forward by a storm. 'This storm irresistibly propels him into the future to which his back is turned, while the pile of debris before him grows skyward. This storm is what we call progress.'[44]

The term 'inauguration' is also charged with the momentum of a surprise, and points to the paradoxical position of all who cannot believe in the high modernist phenomenon of the avant-garde, who reject any idealism, of history conceived as progress, but nevertheless understand that techniques are framed by history and that our collective unconscious struggles with the debris, the remnants of the past. We critics remain at the borderline, like spectators of photography who inevitably look for that 'here and there' of the thing, the event, the theory, knowing that what we have is an image, a piece of an alternative account. The borderline between historicity and nostalgia is imprinted as in a black-and-white photograph in the very form of writing – black on white. Consequently, perhaps the only coherent post-modern position would be to give up writing altogether, to dissolve our bodies in gleaming letters breaking the flux of images. By writing we cannot avoid some lingering between historicity and nostalgia.

Nostalgia here is not exactly for the past. Nostalgia is not only conservative (I would venture that the conservative type is not nostalgic at all, just moralising about contemporary evil and wanting to capitalise the *status quo*): there is also the ontological nostalgia of Bazin; the phenomenological variety of Barthes; and something I would call radical nostalgia, which is an impossible nostalgia for the future coloured by the past, as well as for the past readable only through the wind of its future. Radical nostalgia refers to the longing for the *ça a été* in the moment when we face images, being inhabited by endless questioning. Barthes felt this while looking at an old photograph of 1854, Charles Clifford's 'Alahambra' – an old house, a porch, a deserted street:

> This longing to inhabit, if I observe it clearly in myself, is neither oneiric (I do not dream of some extravagant site) nor empirical (I do not intend to buy a house . . .); it is fantasmatic, deriving from a kind of second sight which seems to bear me forward to a utopian time, or to carry me back to somewhere in myself: a double movement which Baudelaire celebrated in 'Invitation au voyage' and 'La Vie antérieure'.[45]

But the alternative account is also at work. Barthes's perception is also openly inscribed in Baudelaire's modernism, in his interrogative and phantasmic meditation about time in 'A une passante'. Nevertheless, this double movement of being carried back and forward in time is symptomatic of a decentring, which is our historical condition, our situation when we try to have a view on historical events – exactly what Jameson has perceived as the paradox embodied in photography, the tension between immediacy and the representational distance which prescribes some re-enactment of what happened. It was this double movement of history's tension which Benjamin seized through the expressionist violence of Klee's painting.

But the point I want to make is that the condition of our thinking and being in the world is decentred *par excellence*, or – using the concept Jameson suggests in his brilliant interpretation of Antonioni's *Blow-Up* – 'lateral':

> There is a crucial structure of laterality at work here (demonstrable elsewhere in contemporary literature), by which perception or ex-

perience requires a kind of partial distraction, a lateral engagement or secondary, peripheral focus, in order to come into being at the first place. The empty common is therefore not an image in any of the full or even post modern senses of the word ... Indeed, in these supreme moments the screen defeats the Gestalt structure of normal perception, since it offers a ground with a figure, forcing the eye to scan this grassy surface aimlessly yet purposefully in a spatial exploration that is transformed into time itself: there is nothing to be seen, and yet we are, for one long lost instant, looking at it, or at least trying to.[46]

Thanks to Jameson, via the ideas of Bazin, Barthes and Benjamin, I believe that the technical strength of photography can be perceived today in something other than the medium itself, but something which carries the effects of that theory/history of photography I have attempted to sketch in this paper. Writing takes place today in world of cinematography – something Jameson understands. To write in a certain way is not simply a question of style: I would argue that it is not simply a question of writing but also of seeing. Photography, cinema and television are in our blood. The point is not just to write about contemporary media, giving dignity to them, in the way Bazin fought a battle against a stifling high culture, pushing for the dignity of cinema. It is to write today within the world of media, and to write theory or criticism with the rhythm of media. Perhaps the crossed roads of photography, cinema and writing will launch us back to the crucial debate on photography which neither Barthes nor Bazin could fully articulate, since they were too busy searching for the real. Photography and cinema, like language, and writing itself, anchored in the figurative element, are driven into the real of the symbolic; they display the immense hieroglyph of a collective mirror stage, of the identification of a plural alienating *imago*, of a fiction line that ties up the image at the crossing of the real and the symbolic. But did not Bazin get close to this insight by ending his essay on photography with the bare sentence: 'On the other hand, of course, cinema is also a language'?[47]

Only the idea of the snapshot can help. There is no theory today that flows in a linear narration. Intermittencies and intervals cannot be ignored; they offer new beginnings, another montage, another use of elements where reminiscence is displaced into another meaning and continuously decentred and decentring. Jameson offers a perfect example of his critical writing and successful post-modern use of quotations in his essay 'On Magic Realism in Film'. Interrupting his concern with history via the consideration of some Latin American

81

films and literary works, he suggests the importance of colour in post-modernism and focuses on a long quotation by Lacan concerning the distinction between the eye and the gaze. Lacan's point in the original passage (on Zeus's grapes) had the purpose of illustrating the Freudian concept of instinctual drive. But here Jameson displaces its theoretical input into his own argument – which is akin to the rotating curtain in the succession of the photograms, moving on to another element: a wonderful quotation from Pablo Armando Fernandez's novel, *Los Niños se despiden*, about colour, where the whole spectrum of multiple colours is nuanced 'in a wide and varied register from a almost pure white to jet black'.[48]

Photograms are at the basis of the filmic image. We must work like the protagonist of *Blow-Up*, with a host of shots, made and unmade by history, following the snapshots of language, of writing. We must be able to write – and to read – with the remote control, following pieces of different stories and histories at the same time, 'laterally', knowing where we are, in a sort of dense, nervous journalism – aimlessly yet purposefully. Distracted and concentrated at the same time, we must see, in writing, through writing, the 'signatures of the visible' that shape our everyday experience, and condition the making of our experience and existence in the mass-media metropolis of this end of the century.

Notes

1. Raymond Williams, *Culture and Society* (London: Penguin, 1963 edn), p. 285.
2. Ibid.
3. The Birmingham Centre institutionalised the existence of a new discipline, communication or cultural studies, with its emphasis on cinema and television. The master's degree programme at the British Film Institute follows, in the 1990s, the project of giving scholarly dignity to media studies within an institution which is not a university with a media department but a whole centre active in film production, research, press, library and museum collections.
4. See Christian Metz, 'A propos de l'impression de réalité au cinéma', *Cahiers du Cinema*, nos 166–7, 1965, pp. 75–82.
5. Walter Benjamin, 'A Short History of Photography', *Screen*, Spring 1972, vol. 13, no. 1, pp. 5–6.
6. Williams, *Culture and Society*, p. 290.
7. Ibid.
8. Ibid., pp. 290–1. My italics.
9. Charles Baudelaire, *Les Fleurs du mal, Oeuvres complètes* 1 (Paris: Gallimard, Bibliothèque de la Pléiade,1975), p. 93. My translation. Benjamin commented on this poem in 'On Some Motifs in Baudelaire', *Illumination* (New York: Schocken Books, 1985), p. 167.
10. Jacques Lacan, 'Le Stade du miroir comme formateur de la fonction du Je', *Écrits* (Paris: Seuil, 1966), pp. 93–100.

11. See on the question of the *manque d'objet*, Jacques Lacan, 'Les trois formes du manque d'objet', *Le Seminaire* (Paris: Seuil, 1994), book 4, especially pp. 36–9.
12. Benjamin, 'A Short History of Photography', *Screen*, p. 6.
13. Ibid. My italics.
14. One should also investigate the distinction between the eye and the gaze. Lacan sketched this distinction, as noticed in a remarkable analysis of colour and glossiness by Fredric Jameson, 'On Magic Realism in Film', *Signatures of the Visible* (New York, London: Routledge, 1992), pp. 139–40.
15. Some psychoanalysts maintain that the era of neurosis is over and psychosis is much more representative of our age. Wouldn't this be confirmed by the psychic effects of the contemporary plethora of images? See Contardo Calligaris, *Introduction à une clinique différentielle des psychoses* (Paris: Points-Hors-Ligne, 1992).
16. Baudelaire, 'A une passante', *Les Fleurs du mal*, p. 92.
17. Fredric Jameson, Introduction, *Signatures of the Visible* (New York and London: Routledge, 1992), p. 1.
18. Laura Mulvey, 'Visual Pleasure and Narrative Cinema', in *Visual and Other Pleasures* (London: Macmillan, 1989). This article, written in 1973, was first published in *Screen*, 1975.
19. Ibid., p. 18.
20. Ibid.
21. Jameson, 'The Existence of Italy', *The Signatures of the Visible*, p. 186.
22. See Berthold Brecht, 'Uber den Realismus 1937 bis 1941', *Schriften zur Literatur und Kunst 2, Gesammelte Werke*, Vol. 19 (Frankfurt on Main: Suhrkamp Verlag, 1967). Jameson made a Brechtian point when he wrote:

> Returning now to the historical issue of realism itself, the most obvious initial way of estranging and renewing this concept would seem to consist in reversing our conventional stereotype of its relationship to modernism. The latter, indeed, we celebrate as an active aesthetic praxis and invention, whose excitement is demiurgic, along with its liberation from content; while realism is conventionally evoked in terms of passive reflection and copying, subordinate to some external reality ... Something will certainly be gained, therefore, if we can manage to think of realism as a form of demiurgic praxis; if we can restore some active and even playful experimental impulses to the inertia of this appearance as a copy or representation of things. ('The Existence of Italy', *Signatures of the Visible*, p. 162)

23. Jacques Lacan, 'Le Séminaire sur "La Lettre volée" ', *Écrits*, p. 25. My translation.

It would be reductive of the Lacanian implications to reduce the mirror stage to the epiphany of the image, to the triumph of the imaginary. The human being does not believe – as the animal would – in the reality of the image. The human being understands that the image is fictional. He or she – at such an early stage of development before the usage of language – enters the symbolic structure of language itself; therefore understanding the function of the image:

This jubilant assumption of his specular image by the child at the *infans* stage, still sunk in his motor incapacity and nursling dependence, would seem to exhibit in an exemplary situation, the symbolic matrix in which the *I* is precipitated in a primordial form, before it is objectified in the dialectic of identification with the other, and before language restores to it, in the universal, its function as subject.

I am led, therefore, to regard the function of the mirror-stage as a particular case of the function of the *imago*, which is to establish a relation between the organism and its reality – or, as they say, between *Innenwelt* and *Umwelt* ('The Mirror Stage', *Écrits*, English translation, London: Tavistock, 1977, pp. 2 and 4).

24. Charles Baudelaire, *Paris Spleen* (New York: New Directions Books, paperback, 1970) pp. ix–x.
25. Fourmillante cité, cité pleine de rêves,
    Où le spectre en plein jour raccroche le passant!
    Les mystères partout coulent comme des sèves
    Dans les canaux étroits du colosse puissant.

    Un matin, cependant que dans la triste rue
    Les maisons, dont la brume allongeait la hauteur,
    Simulaient les deux quais d'une rivière accrue,
    Et que, décor semblable a l'âme de l'acteur,

    Un brouillard sale et jaune inondait tout l'espace,
    Je suivais, roidissant mes nerfs comme un héros

    (Charles Baudelaire, *Les Fleurs du mal*, p. 87.)
26. André Bazin, 'An Aesthetic of Reality,' *What Is Cinema?* (Berkeley, Los Angeles, London: University of California Press, 1972), vol. 2, p. 26.
27. Ibid., pp. 26–7.
28. Dudley Andrew stressed in his study on Bazin (*André Bazin*, Oxford: Oxford University Press, 1978; Paris: Éditions de l'Étoile, 1983, pp. 35–49) the importance of the intellectual atmosphere around the Catholic and Bergsonian journal *Esprit*, and the influence of the Catholic critic Albert Béguin. Béguin believed in a double reality, where things have a natural relationship to mystery and spirituality, not unlike the medieval religious tradition, where reality is the revelation of a spiritual sense.
29. Jameson, 'The Existence of Italy', *Signatures of the Visible*, p. 178.
30. Ibid., p. 209.
31. Bazin, 'In Defence of Rossellini', *What is Cinema?*, Vol. 2, p. 98.
32. Bazin, 'The Ontology of Photographic Image', *What Is Cinema?*, Vol. 1, p. 15.
33. Roland Barthes, *Camera Lucida* (London: Vintage, 1993), p. 115.
34. Jameson, 'The Existence of Italy,' *Signatures of the Visible*, p. 156.
35. Ibid., p. 158.
36. Ibid.
37. Ibid., p. 191.
38. Jameson, 'The Existence of Italy', *The Signatures of the Visible*, p. 217.
39. 'What has been absent from these *alternate accounts* of realism – the experimental-oppositional, Hollywood, documentary, and photographic-ontological – is any trace of the older valorisation of a realistic "work"

within a dominant stylistic or narrative paradigm ...' (ibid., p. 197). My italics.

40. Ibid., p. 191.
41. Ibid., p. 229.
42. Ibid., p. 196. Jameson wrote this sentence while analysing Antonioni's *Blow-Up*.
43. Ibid., p. 194.
44. Walter Benjamin, 'Thesis on the Philosophy of History', *Illuminations* (London: Fontana, 1992), p. 249.
45. Barthes, *Camera Lucida*, p. 40.
46. Ibid., pp. 195–6.
47. Bazin, 'The Ontology of the Photographic Image', *What Is Cinema?*, Vol. 1, p. 16.
48. See Jameson, 'On Magic Realism in Film', *Signatures of the Visible*, pp. 139–41. This quotation from Fernandez is on p. 140.

FILMOSOPHY
Colour

Daniel Frampton

1

In the history of film studies philosophy has not played much of a part. Disciplines such as literature, sociology and psychoanalysis have sped away with 'cinema', and a significant philosophical reassessment of the ground of moving images has been continuously passed over (usually in fear), and placed in the margins of film studies. The sense in which I am sliding in 'philosophy' here is for a more ruminative thinking about film, with a healthy distrust of inherited terms and concepts, and the setting about, where necessary, of forming new words and concepts to open up and reveal the workings of film.

The reason for introducing a new term, 'filmosophy', is that, while the ideas of this paper skirt around some recognisable theoretical areas, the whole, loose and contingent as it is, cannot be constrained by any single one of them. Furthermore, the neologism signals an important concern of the project as a whole: that is, film study must progress conceptually to survive (how else does film art move on but with new sounds and images?) The work in progress that is filmosophy encompasses a variety of components: the understanding of film composition as steered by a film-mind – how film decides and considers its own objects; a type of meditative, open thinking by the experiencer onto the film (partially gained by understanding, and thus unconsciously utilising, filmosophical terms and indicators); the coining of those filmosophical terms using words, regular or invented, that fulfil filmosophy's aim to get as near as possible to revealing linguistically the experience of film; the performative, poetical writing of analyses that attempt to feel the (sometimes philosophical) power of moving images; the use by the films themselves (as intentional, willing film-minds) of all types of thinking in their composition (a standard conventionally constructed film can be studied for its thinkings, while the films of, say, Antonioni and Kieslowski might be written about as *being* 'filmosophical'). Filmosophy also covers the philosophical importance of moving-image thinking, and the possibilities of utilising this non-conceptual thinking for philosophy and the teaching of both visual literacy and the new home cinema of the camcorder.

First, *our* thinking. We mix life to our own production quality, taking in certain things in favour of others available, continually interpreting. Simple experience is always a thinking action – conscious or unconscious. Thinking is the fact that we do anything at all. As Martin Heidegger noted, 'the field of vision is something open, but its openness is not due to our looking'[1] – our eyes don't work on their own, our thinking is what reveals things to us. (We might say that an awareness of these 'interpretations' is a philosophical extension of those experiences.) From my sound world I can similarly focus on particular sources, can think in or out certain noises. I can think out the traffic noise down in the street below, usually unconsciously, but always significantly. I can steer my hearing to a sound that I want to identify – like a squeak in a car.

Then, we *do* thinking; we engage and practise thinking at certain times when we feel the need. I sit at my desk and I go over certain key words around 'thinking' such that I may elucidate on the subject in my writing. I work things out. Abstractly, in this case, but at other times I may call up images to help my train of thought, but images that are in every way 'referenced' – that is, linguistically understood. These images can themselves move into a sort of day-dreaming, a non-localised mode of thinking, free-ish, and creative. Imagination can be part of this thinking, trying out situations or images that have not come to me before, testing how they would fit in my current thought. Remembering, attentiveness, concentration, belief (what do you think about it?), reasoning, reflection, pondering – all these are types of thinking, thinkings which we do daily.

Gilles Deleuze, in his two-volume *Cinema*, argued that a certain type of contemporary cinema gives birth to 'mental-images'. Deleuze sees in the mental-image an attempt to make the mental

> the proper object of the image, a specific, explicit image, with its own figures ... which takes as objects of thought, objects which have their existence outside thought, just as the objects of perception have their own existence outside perception. *It is an image which takes as its object, relations, symbolic acts, intellectual feelings.*[2]

This is not to say that this image represents some person's thoughts, but that the image links directly *with* thought. For Deleuze, an image is defined as being a mental-image if it makes *relation* its object – that is, if it requires of us the act of *interpretation*, to work out what the image relates *to*. Deleuze means his mental-image to embody the two 'faces' of the image, 'one turned towards the characters, the objects and the actions in movement, the other turned towards a whole which changes progressively as the film goes on'[3] – a thinking steering our knowledge of what is happening, while also being in full control of the film's overall concerns. According to Deleuze, this new image, this new mutation of cinema, strove to become 'truly thought and thinking, even if it had to become "difficult" in order to do this'.[4] But the real importance of Deleuze's new situations (images or sequences) is their power, the power of pure image and sound, to 'replace, obliterate and re-create the object itself ... to give rise to a seeing function'.[5] Here Deleuze is at his most incisive in realising that the image can direct our attitude towards the object, in the image, in effect subordinating any independent reference to the object. In this new thought-cinema Deleuze finds

> a camera-consciousness which would no longer be defined by the movements it is able to make, but by the mental connections it is able to enter into. And it becomes questioning, responding, objecting, provoking, theoramatizing, experimenting, in accordance with the open list of logical conjunctions ('or', 'therefore', 'if', 'because', 'actually', 'although ...').[6]

Filmosophy, rather, reveals the *whole* of film as (exhibitionist) thinking, which also, unlike Deleuze's thesis, does not include any semiotic linkage to the spectator's thought. This is thinking constantly out loud, never covert or secret. When we are watching and listening to a film what exactly is it doing? Is it not making its *own* decisions? Switching to a different scene here, focusing away from a character there, moving up the side of a building, framing a room from a low angle – thoughts of a film-mind (but not one phenomenologically analagous to our minds). *Once you see a film as thinking, nothing is wasted; everything achieves the same, significant level of importance.*

This is not to belittle the role of the creators of cinema – the director, writer, cameraman – but to allow for a more fluid and poetical understanding of film. The words and opinions of the creators are of importance, in that they may be *translated* into our more poetical talk about film, and thus onto the experience of film. If in talk we say the film 'does' this, or 'does' that, then the talk will elicit less obstructive language than if we were talking of the director, or the 'camera', where you end up just seeing what the director was supposed to have 'done', or how the 'camera' moved, and the film will be lost to either authorship or technology. Also, filmosophy is not a value claim.

All films think, whether quietly, boringly, excitingly or confusingly. A film that thinks out loud – a 'flashy' De Palma film, say – is not inherently better than one that thinks in a less 'up front' way – *A Winter's Tale* (Eric Rohmer, 1991), for example. A film can think suitably and intelligently – that is, with its subject and interestingly. Or it can stop trying and just be (that is, be boring). A staid film is just one which has almost given up the capacity to think, and merely thinks on convention-autodrive. Heidegger's handling of 'thinking' is pertinent here, as he gave it as large a role as I do. 'Man is a *thinking*, that is, a *meditating* being,' he wrote.[7] Thinking is not the summation of film, but its constituting means. An actor can act without being in a film, but a film can't *be* without thinking. *Film* is a thinking. *Thinking is the ground of the world of film, and the ground of the life of filmosophy.*

2

Fernand Léger once wrote that 'color is a vital necessity. It is raw material indispensable to life, like water and fire. Man's existence is inconceivable without an ambience of color.'[8] There are three main aspects to descriptions of colour: 'hue' is the variety or shade of a colour; 'tone' is how light or dark the hue is; and 'saturation' is how close the particular colour comes to its deepest and most vivid type. Seeing is part of thinking; they are never divorced, and thus, in a very simple sense, colour is thought by us. A red book, let's say, is *interpreted* by us – not that it is worthwhile saying the book has a true 'ontological' colour that we only produce a response to. The book is the colour we feel it to be. And it is not worth saying much more than this – the 'epistemological' questions get boring and die before us.

There are different primary colours for light, paint and vision, but all revolve around red, blue and green. Primary ones are dominant in impression – beating the rest to our senses. Thus red is 'advancing', while blue is 'receding' – the trouble is that you may like blue more than red, or it may simply be brighter, and thus you spot it first in a crowd of colours. (I am led to think of the blue of the documentary *Atlantis* (Luc Besson, 1991), a blue that strikes deep, in a film which is like cinematic oxygen, and eventually provides every natural shade of watery blue.) Under differing conditions the same object will still be thought of as having the same colour, even though it is perceived as slightly off the 'original' colour. It is only in controlled tests that red is found to be focused in front of the retina, blue behind, and green right on the retina (whence its 'calming' quality). And, as Deleuze notes, 'according to Goethe, blazing red is not merely the frightful colour in which we burn, but the noblest colour, which contains all the others, and engenders a superior harmony as the whole chromatic circle'.[9]

How does colour in life affect us? How different is the 'effect' under the conditions of experiencing a film – that is to say, aesthetically? Colours are seen as stimulants by psychologists, and are so used in packaging and fashion, in offices and playgrounds. Culture, situation, expectation, prior knowledge – all play their part. Associations must play an important part so any colour could mean anything to anybody – depending on their previous experience. But in analysing film this cannot be accounted for and should not be given voice: what we can't tell, we shouldn't attempt to say. Red, blue, green – hot, cool, calm? But in the cinema we must ask: what type of red, what depth of blue, what are they 'on' – clothes, walls – when do we see them and in what order? It is not so much what colour but 'what and when and where and how colour'. Seeing a colour where it's not really supposed to be can elicit a completely different response from the usual one to the object. In *Willie Wonka's Chocolate Factory* (Mel Stuart, 1971) virtually all the colours in the factory are disjointed in their object relations – such as the blue chewing-gum that one of the children takes, and which tastes of a whole meal, including dessert.

All the main colours, abstracted, eternal – the colours of the rainbow – have historical and social associations. Some examples. Red, along with black and white, has the longest history, stretching from its Roman indication of class to today's sexy abundance of meanings: lust, heat, sin, sacrifice, blood (consider the reds of *Bram Stoker's Dracula* (Francis Ford Coppola, 1992)). Blue is the best-liked colour in Europe, being a modest medium between dark and colourful. Its historical links began with moral and religious codes, moving through hierarchical and royal denotation, to a simple, functional, stable meaning epitomised in work clothes. Yellow has the most powerful history, solidly indicating madness and illness, folly and stupidity, fear and envy, defamation and cowardice. White was seen by Isaac Newton as the true base element of the universe, and as such should be the guiding colour of life – civilised, natural and pure. Black remains linked with negativity and death. But, as Sergei Eisenstein notes, 'to this day attempts continue to be made to arrange the subjective and largely personal sensations into meaningful relationships, that are, frankly, just as vague and remote'.[10] And here, in his essay 'Colour and Meaning', Eisenstein goes on to provide an encyclopedia of colour meanings in poetry and art, finding consonance as well as opposites in associations. It becomes a beautifully indirect exercise in passion about *film* colour. Colour meanings are evolved in cultures, but never remain set for very long, if we can say they do at all. The problem here is one that John Gage has noted, that is, 'the definition of culture itself. Which sector of a given society is in question, which profession, which

90

class, which gender, which age group?'[11] The only way to interpret colour seems to be in actual situations – taking account of where and on what they occur: namely, as Eisenstein realises, *'the sole source for the attendant complex of concepts and associations, with meanings dependent only upon the general system of imagery that has been decided upon for the particular film'.*[12]

Before colour celluloid was perfected films were sometimes hand-painted (in some early films as many as six colours were added to each frame), or tinting and toning was used to get that added overall effect.[13] William Johnson notes the 'impressive red-tinted night scene of Babylon under attack by fire in Griffith's *Intolerance* (D. W. Griffith, 1916)'.[14] *The Lodger* (Alfred Hitchcock, 1926) decides on a creamy indoors and cool blue for night, while a club is thought yellow, and the lodger leaves the house in a pinky light. But all ends in red and love. In the history of colour film technology 'accuracy' has been the guiding aim. Technicolor was 'truer' than Eastmancolor, and better for studio shooting than Agfacolor. With Technicolor the balance of colour could be fine-tuned in the processing stage. Colours were thick and bright; dark scenes were weighty, like black on black. Like a landscape produced in felt-tip, Technicolor really was a new window on the world. (But, within filmosophy, it becomes a certain historico-thought, a place in movie history, instantly recognisable and thus 'reusable'.) The first colour films tended to connote magic, luxury, fantasy, because people, after the first shocks of cinema, still saw filmic reality in black and white – that was their convention. For some, colour diverted attention away from the story, and thus had to be subdued for serious pictures. (Nowadays we might see something as being more 'real' if it is presented on suitably amateur shaky video rather than black-and-white or colour celluloid.)

For filmosophers, what matters is what we see, not what we are told is the name behind the technique. The amount of technological innovation in the history of the development of colour film is astounding. It almost seems that weekly there was some advance or addition to film stock's capacities and dispositions. Thus we come to the question of how much this possible knowledge, these available facts, could affect our sense of how (especially early) films are thinking. A film of burnt-out whites was a common problem at that time; a film in degraded colour, a problem with stock longevity (do we restore a painting to *truly* understand it?). *In filmosophy the technology is only interesting in so far as it tells all that is aesthetically possible* – knowledge of just what can be done with cranes and steadicam to move the camera *can* help us formulate poetical translations (of image flight and fluidity), but the sole discussion of technology can kill a film stone dead. I'd much rather see what the film is doing than how the 'camera' created what we see. Knowing how celluloid works and acts is helpful, but the decision to discuss those facts in film talk is a question of audience and style. Often talk of a film's degradation or technical mistakes leaves it closed off to the sort of analysis you may have been *enticed* to submit after a first naive viewing. *Those naive thoughts, and attendant film talk, must not be lost to the rules and foibles of technology.*

Film thinking can *be* more than our thinking, and the decisions a film makes about colour are a prime example of its difference. We cannot suddenly become colour-blind, nor flip in completely monochrome vision, and only tone a scene by perhaps whipping out some tinted spectacles. *Film has the thoughtful freedom to enter into any colour.* Film has its own *will* as regards colour use - and can give a scene a hue at the drop of a stetson. If the most distinctive aspect of film among the arts is time/duration, then possibly a temporal thinking/evolving of colour(s) in a single film can be seen as the most cinematic. It's fine having striking scenes, designs, and lighting – but if they remain static and individual then a certain flow is lost. A film can so easily be picturesque or 'photographic' (think of the quirky framings of *Sweetie* (Jane Campion, 1989)) instead of *cinematic*. Filmosophy is less concerned to research the effect of colours than with the way film *has* colour, *uses* colour, and how we should *approach* that use in talk about film.

Sergei Eisenstein stands out in his writings on colour:

> Before we can learn to distinguish three oranges on a patch of lawn both as three objects in the grass *and* as three orange patches against a green background, we dare not think of colour composition ... the first condition for the use of colour in a film is that it must be, first and foremost, a dramatic factor.[15]

He argues that it is best used when it, and only it

> can most fully express or explain what must be conveyed, said, or elucidated at the given moment of the development of the action. .... In its own place, at a given moment, each is the protagonist for the moment, occupying the leading place in the general chorus of expressive elements which yield it this place – for the moment.[16]

Eisenstein recognises that colour can be an independent role player – that it can move the action on as well as, or even better than, an actor's words.

Victor Perkins makes the distinction between lighting and colour that is *naturally* within the diegesis, and that which is more intellectual in its obviousness. In the 'chicken run' scene from *Rebel Without a Cause* (Nicholas Ray, 1955) lighting forces the stage-managed sense of the contest, but in a completely natural sense: 'The illumination is traced to a quite credible source: the head lamps of the cars which other gang members, spectators, have drawn up along the sides of the course.'[17] For Perkins, cutting from one natural colour to another and giving a scene a meaning is better than 'those which, by rejecting credibility, encourage a purely cerebral recognition ... We are so busy *noticing* that we respond rather to our awareness of the device than to the state of mind it sets out to evoke', citing *Red Desert* (Michelangelo Antonioni, 1964).[18] Rather, 'it is just because we are not given reason to question the credibility of the colour [in *Bigger Than Life* (Nicholas Ray, 1956)] that we can give the full emotional response that the arrangement of colour requires'.[19] Perkins is not completely right in linking cerebral and emotional effects with, respectively, 'obvious' and natural lighting. There can, of course, be 'cerebral' natural colour (as in Godard), as well as emotional 'obvious' colour use (as in *The Sheltering Sky* (Bernardo Bertolucci, 1991), red filtered early on, and blue washed from when the female protagonist takes over the story). Perkins at one point makes a reference to 'the most literal-minded spectator'[20] and thus gives away part of the reason he raises natural devices: they can be understood by plebeians, by the man in the street. 'Credibly motivated ... credible purpose' chime in his prose,[21] as if all we ever wanted from the cinema was subtlety. Here I might even let Eisenstein reply, from a letter to Lev Kuleshov:

> This viewpoint holds that in a good colour film you are not conscious of colour. To my mind, this viewpoint, raised to the level of a principle, is the reflection of a creative impotence, of inability to master the complex of cinematic expressive means needed to make an organic film.[22]

On the thoughtfulness of colour use we may come back to Heidegger. He made the distinction between 'meditative' and 'calculative' thinking – and we might do the same for colour thinking. Meditative is 'thinking which contemplates the meaning which reigns in everything that is',[23] a thinking that is a continuous interplay of thought and argument, a slow, and deep mode of attention. Calculative thinking is a mode that merely *computes* possibilities economically; a *thoughtlessness* that 'never stops, never collects itself',[24] that takes in and then forgets. The analogy with colour thinking is not so simple, though. I would distinguish between the kind of colour thinking in *Dick Tracy* (Warren Beatty, 1991) and that in *A Short Film About Killing* (Krzysztof Kieslowski, 1990). The latter pulls us in with its thinking, meditatively colouring the film with the mind of its protagonist, sick with his world, and looking for a victim. The former can be seen to employ calculative thinking – where the film brings in primary colours as signals of a very simplistic presence, of evil or love or danger. (Of course that is how the film intends its thinking – calculating emotions like a comic book.) We might distance this with films that have almost given up the capacity to think with colour, that shy from intervening in any way in the sacred narrative to bring forward a colour, or alter a light, or, God forbid, use a filter. Heidegger noted that 'man today is in *flight from thinking*',[25] and we could say that the majority of popular film today has taken a similar flight, with a similar denial of its thoughtlessness, opining that their inquiry is full with possibilities. It is but a planning, researching and organising towards those oh-so-important *results* (emotions, thrills), but, without much thinking.

Edward Branigan finds that most colour theorists 'maintain that color has neither an absolute perceptual base, nor an absolute meaning (emotional or intellectual): color depends on relationships and comparisons'.[26] The only trouble is that Branigan never really moves on from this assertion. Like most theorists he comes to a theoretical dead end – he wants to say more, but finds he can't. Again like most, he ends up just listing certain uses of colour. Some seem to think it's like adding them up to work out their 'meaning'. Filmosophy asks that we move on from inventorying the occurrence of colours in a film towards finding words that might even partially translate their presence. The experience of them is important, and we do not experience a listing, a roll call of colours – the effects are much less calculable. The possibilities of talk about colour lie not so much in 'what colour where' but in realising what we are doing when we approach colour, and more importantly *how* film works in colour(s).

Filmosophy brings us to the use of *any* colour rather than the use of *a* colour in a situation. If we can offer possibilities of colour use then the weight will be taken off the pinning down of colour meaning. Blue is more *easily* used in a cold or melancholy way, red more easily in a hot and dangerous way, and so on – because of convention *and* of physiological reasons? But blue has not always been associated with coldness. Think of a room painted floor to ceiling in red – what would we feel? In blue – what? Branigan rightly asserts that 'we see only after we have acquired the cultural categories for seeing';[27] we see only *with* language. Does our physiological experience of blue hold the same throughout different cultural meanings, or does a deeply embedded meaning alter our physical reactions? What matters for filmosophers is the power and forcefulness of colour use in particular films. Eisenstein again: 'In general the "psychological" interpretation of color is a very slippery business. ... In art it is not the absolute relationships [associations] that are decisive, but those *arbitrary* relationships within a system of images dictated by the particular work of art.'[28]

The cinematographer Vittorio Storaro suggests that colours have identifiable meanings: 'Cinema is a language of images, formed by light and darkness, and by the internal elements of colours, through which stories must be interpreted.'[29] Black is the unconscious, red the greatest symbol of vital energy, orange the family and warmth, yellow the arrival of consciousness, green is knowledge, blue our intelligence as a human being, indigo our power, violet the last stage of human life, and white is the sum of all these: balance, equilibrium. This simplistic colour coding when applied to film lessens the impact. On stage at the National Film Theatre Storaro asserted that he doesn't 'paint' with light, but sees himself as 'writing' with colours and light. Here he elevates definite, controlled, precise *meaning* over beauty. His cinematography *is* amazing, but his desire for reason closes down the possibilities of aesthetic pleasure, and we find him working in a similar vein to the project of Newton himself – that is, to classify, close, and reduce the experience of colour to a set of numbers – such that the metaphoric might become retrievable, reusable (dead). Film is under the context of an aesthetic experience, not a laboratory one, and, even if 'tests showed' occurrences in the laboratory, in the cinema, in the film itself, the thinking attention is a wholly different one. Black is aligned with negation and evil. Whether it 'means' those things is no matter, whether it is *used* those ways *is* important. In *Blue Velvet* (David Lynch, 1986), Dorothy's apartment, its colour, doesn't just make us *feel* something, but also gives birth to a thought: a relation of colour to character to story to film *to thinking*.

3

So let us look at examples, from black-and-white to contemporary colour films. (What is important for the moment is explaining through film examples just how films think with colour, including all shades and image grains, and in the film discussions that follow I shall be primarily concerned with pulling from the films their colour use, simply feeling *how* they think their colours, while only attempting some of the poetical, ruminative talk that I call for in the latter part of this paper – where 'thinking', as a term, would be much less used – in some of the longer examples. The films discussed are also fairly randomly chosen and certainly not a listing of great colour films, such that the idea of 'colour thinking' should be shown to be applicable to any and all.)

We never saw in black-and-white before celluloid came along, and even then it seems we 'add' colour to our experience of it, filling in the colours we think are 'actually' there. Black-and-white film gets its degrees of light and dark from colour just like colour film. We can thus see that shading of black-and-white can behave like colours, where shade is actively used to give an immediacy of meaning in and around characters, or indeed without them. Early grainy, contrasty emulsions (orthochromatic) recognised blue, green and ultraviolet – red would just come out black. Panchromatic stocks rectified that, recognising red and having a finer grain. Now it is almost possible to follow snooker on a caravan 10-inch portable black-and-white (as I remember from some of my family holidays). But also 'black-and-white' is just what the tiny amount of writings about that form call into dramatic usage: the bad guy and the good guy – that is, conflict, dramatic contrast, counterpoint. And it is never less than well intended, but usually less than engaging. Yet Deleuze has called expressionism 'the precursor of real colourism in the cinema',[30] and Eisenstein talks of utilising 'the outlines and tonal "sounds" of grey photography'.[31]

The Lodger simply, effectively, casts aspersions and shadows on the mystery tenant, while *Knife in the Water* (Roman Polanski, 1962) has the monochrome cling like fog to the edges of the characters, smudging and claustrophobic (the film *understanding* the drama). *Sunrise* (F. W. Murnau, 1927) knows that the man's wife is his real true love from the beginning, bathing her in fresh cool light, while leaving him and his mistress in half shadow, before ending with them back together and brilliant light. *Nosferatu* (Murnau, 1922) thinks a grey twilight world (somewhere between the natural and the unnatural, pushing a certain 'undecidability' or 'uncannyness') with heavy shadows, such as the one that crosses the face of the innocent Nina at the beginning. With Jonathan over the bridge on the way to the count's castle, the 'other side' is thought as just that, in negative, and the flipping of light to dark rebounds in the opposition that the film thinks of Nina's light to the count's dark. In the end its is 'shadow' that becomes evil, creeping up on Jonathan, and gripping Nina's heart. The film has made it literally into a contest of dark against light, with light filling the climax, but fought in a moral and spiritual twilight of indistinguishability and drowned (thought *out*) contours. *Wild Strawberries* (Ingmar Bergman, 1957) thinks (reveals) Isak's innermost thoughts, feeling the thick black-and-white dream that replaces detail (in the image) with emotional force (whiteness to the left, receding black to the right – the future?), and recognising his previous life in blemish-free white, while putting him against black, watching, inventing, imagining. A film that also decides its ending with whiteness.

Both *Virgin Machine* (Monika Treut, 1992) and *Triple Bogey on a Par Five Hole* (Amos Poe, 1991) announce their *decision* to use monochrome by having colour titles over their opening shots. The latter then amplifies the memories of the home movies the main character shows by leaving them in colour, while even the monochrome is thought bluey for exteriors, and greeny for inside scenes. Most colour films use black-and-white to refer back in time – for example, to the blissful marriage of the hero of *Passenger 57* (Kevin Hooks, 1993), or the previous murderous events of *Dead Again* (Kenneth Branagh, 1991), while in *Leon the Pig Farmer* (Vadim Jean, 1992) it is used to denote a camcorder in action. *Being at Home with Claude* (Jean Baudin, 1992) decides on monochrome for its opening sex and death scene between the two guys, letting the blood, when it comes, splash colourfully, significantly, across the kitchen. *Spellbound* (Hitchcock, 1945) blasts us with fleeting red as the doctor shoots himself at the end (a few frames were hand-tinted red in each print of the time). The film-maker Norman McLaren finds that it is possible 'to sort out an image more quickly, grasp it sooner in color than black-and-white, especially if the image is at all complex and moving fast'.[32] McLaren seems to find that, in being nearer to ordinary experience, colour film has no delay in its effect, and that black-and-white is seen more as a 'fiction', in another world. It is this level of seriousness that colour films can engage with when they call in the thinking that black-and-white brings.

Filmosophy gives film an autonomy that we feel but previous film talk has failed to reveal. The film chooses to be somewhere – in a room of the protagonist say. It can decide the time of year, the hour of the day, the weather. The film then can choose to show us certain colours – pointing, colliding – lessening one, arcing to another, using movement to force colour, to bring it to our attention. In films such as *Delicatessen* (Jean-Pierre Jeunet and Marc Caro, 1991), *Léolo* (Jean-Claude Lauzon, 1992), *Les Parapluies de Cherbourg* (Jacques Demy, 1964), and *Jamón, Jamón* (Bigas Luna, 1992) colours provide a visual holiday from our humdrum days – kaleidoscopic films, pushing variety and versatility,[33] profuse and scattered colours, messy and cluttered sets. In a similar sense, Léger talked of the explosion of colour after the First World War, and asked: 'Where are we going? Quite simply we are going toward a rapid evolution in external plastic life, which will develop logically until its means are exhausted, until something else is discovered.'[34] And this, in a way, is how these films are thinking – they are filling up with colour to think their moral and socio-political gaudiness. They are at the end of something (modernism is the usual candidate) and are pushing such that something else must come along to replace it.

Branigan refers to Godard's 'colour strategies', and to Eisenstein's 'textual system of color', as though they were precise army moves.[35]

To talk of 'horizontal and vertical lines ... blocks and regular shapes'[36] that colours mark out is to sound as though you're advancing knowledge, but really you're just collating forms. One can notate colours and characters, but the point is whether that thinking provokes anything in us – is it intellectual and after the fact, or emotional and simultaneous with the experience? Theorists often say that the director probably used this colour here, on these people, to say this, or to mean that, and it's possible they are right to an extent. What these analyses lack is fluency of expression, and thus a certain sprouting of interest and importance: the use of colour in the films Branigan refers to – *Alexander Nevsky* (Eisenstein, 1938), *Deux ou trois choses que je sais d'elle* (Godard, 1967) – is much more powerful than these types of talking can *cope* with. Branigan is *almost* barking up the right tree when he notes that 'a textual system of colour – as a "discourse" involving repetition, variation, permutation – may actually propose new ways of reading color and color organisations, and so may recast cultural formulations',[37] – that is to say, films can create their own colour meanings and references. But mainly his analysis of *Deux ou trois choses que je sais d'elle* hides behind monotonous descriptions of the film's 'blocks' and 'stripes' of colour.

Film can bring our *attention* to clothes or decor; it can think them important by montage or movement. *Wittgenstein* (Derek Jarman, 1993) thinks its colours against pure blackness, thus realising and heightening their force and depth. This is not so much colour coding as use of 'colour'. If we cannot ever completely define colours, as Wittgenstein himself found, then the thought of *Wittgenstein* is one that plays with their apparentness and yet elusiveness – something that is obvious to us, but requires of us the attempt to leap over language to really get to them. Again, we find colour's resistance to meaning as its beingness. It is as Wittgenstein's work becomes more rounded that the film will move from that blackness on to the setting of where he is thinking, a move such as Wittgenstein himself made from ideas to physical language. *Vertigo* (Hitchcock, 1958) thinks the powerful self-deception of Scottie with a sickly green light that covers the body of Judy after he has completed her transformation, a light that is brought in by the film from the neon sign outside, and thought over the whole image, such that Scottie's obsession brings the image to his control. Think of *Raising Cain* (Brian DePalma, 1992) bringing in the simple thought of a distorting orange light on the evil father of the twins; *Bad Lieutenant* (Abel Ferrara, 1992) reddening its central rape scene, colouring (feeling) the horror; or the lime green thought of the hospital in *Blind Chance* (Kieslowski, 1990), feeling the painful memory of the young man. *Yellow Earth* (Chen Kaige, 1984) is a paean to earth, water and sky, thinking long on their colours of dusk red, brown-blue, and white. It thinks a sense of respect for these tones that mark daily life for the characters.

Passion (Godard, 1981) begins by studying a blue sky and a plane's white trail across it (a light that will put Isabelle's face in darkness later on), and rocks back and forth from this natural light to the 'artistic' lighting of the studio set-up: 'something separated from the real world by calculated approximations of probabilities', we hear. What is studied within the aura of the set – a lit subject in between darkness – is simply given to us in the outside scenario. Room lamps are moved about as much as the studio blondes. Darkness often comes with thought – ideas discussed, as with Jerzy typing in his hotel room, or talking on the pitch-black set. Lightness – as in the factory – arrives with the ordinary beauty of living. 'What bursts into light is the echo of what the night submerges. What night submerges prolongs in the invisible what bursts into light', we hear. What the artist attempts is what happens anyway; you just have to see it around you. *Prénom Carmen* (Godard, 1982) also gives us unlit interiors looking out to the brightness, faces and bodies masked by natural backlight, human umbras, straining our eyes for the information we thought we were to get, while the film is thinking somewhat differently. *Je vous salue Marie* (Godard, 1983) decides on similarly precise natural images, adding more spiritual montage, with a blue/white moon brought alongside a warm yellow sun, brought alongside a Mary searching for understanding. In a suitably coloured café in *Prénom Carmen* Godard himself says: 'Van Gogh looked for yellow at sunset. You have to keep looking'. We still have to find out how to see and understand colour.

The Long Day Closes (Terence Davies, 1992) realises its protagonist's journey, and gives us a sense of its place and force. The boy is in need of light, whether from a fire, a torch, the circus, or the cinema, and thinks his future as one of creeping darkness as he moves schools. The film decides this against its own background of subdued colours, a memory of England, a memory by the boy of his own life, calmingly brown, like the bricks that make his home. The film will travel to the right, moving from the boy's house into a lump of dark night, unlit by street lamps.[38] With his solitude the film brings him down to his cellar, and next to blackness, again to the right, dropping in from the street, and the final thought of his childhood is that of the last wisps of cloud edged with the soft light of a setting sun – a setting of his future, set, prescribed, in the memory of the thought of the boy of the film.

Darkness can also be thought to blot out others, to match the concentration or exclusion in the mind of a character – the darkness in *The Long Day Closes* which closes in around the boy when he imagines the force of the old ship while sitting in class, or in *Wild Strawberries*, when Isak is in the car surrounded by his fellow travellers and again returns in mind to his earlier life and loves. In another way both *Bad Lieutenant* and *The Double Life of Véronique* (Kieslowski, 1991) bring a dark border to their look, a soft blurring of the frame thought when the lieutenant and Véronique are reeling from their experiences (a thinking of their perception), one from drugs, the other from an inner pain.

But inside the film-mind *any* colour can be thought. In *L.627* (Bertrand Tavernier, 1992) it is a thinking of tone; the harshness of the image is *with* the work of the Parisian cops, just as *The Story of Qui Ju* (Zhang Yimou, 1992) is *with* the journey of the woman seeking her justice. *Apocalypse Now* (Francis Ford Coppola, 1979) marks a journey of another kind by thinking a difference in light, a movement from the artifice of war's brightness to the serene natural light of the inner jungle – the film *is* Kurtz. In another way, focusing can give us colour: *Vacas* (Julio Medem, 1992) brings us the wood where most of the magical events takes place by thinking its *whole* colour – that is, by pulling back such that the many greens and browns merge as a single freckled hue, the wood itself from a magical thought. Some films think in calm, bleak colour such that a significant colour may stand out – the red of Marnie's dreams in *Marnie* (Alfred Hitchcock, 1964), or the revolutionary red flags of both *The Fall of Berlin* (Mikhail Chiaureli, 1949) and *The Hunters* (Theo Angelopoulos, 1977), floating in against dull grey mountains.

The Double Life of Véronique thinks like no other film I know. It is a film that spreads it beauty across all the elements of cinematic form. While experiencing it everything works with and for the feeling you come out with, but even remotely describing it afterwards remains problematic. Its world denies words, even as they struggle to the surface of your mind as you leave the cinema. Colour and light are essential parts of its mood and perception, and enhance for us the lives of the unknowing twins. Central to this colour thinking is a sharp lime that floods in through windows when we are inside, and an ochre light that, as in the fateful concert, cuts its hue across faces and figures. It is the light that wakes the French Véronique from her slumber, and also from her malaise over feeling her other self. In *Three Colours: Blue* (Kieslowski, 1993) it is the power of Julie's memories that the film feels through colour, blushing blue with her as the past surges up to the present.

Intensely thoughtful are both *GoodFellas* (Martin Scorsese, 1991) and *Malcolm X* (Spike Lee, 1992), thinking their histories as they proceed. Both are a thinking through history with colour image, *a thinking that takes its concepts from cinema's history*. Both begin with hazy morals and images – the films flushing and softening all colours into oranges and browns. Filmosophically they are feeling

100

how the past is forever a diffused memory, a happening that is thought uncertainly as any act of remembering is – but distinctly a film-memory, taking its thought-processes from how cinema has itself decided to view history, a plastic past remembered through cine-images. (*Orlando* (Sally Potter, 1992) is a much more direct account of the grain and colour of the image being a history of the cinema – here virtually a history of film melodrama.) While *Good-Fellas* moves into sharpness with the rush of cocaine, *Malcolm X* feels the harshness of the prison into which Malcolm goes, blackening his surroundings, bringing the light into a cutting forcefulness. A cool blueness is this film's measure of his entry into knowledge via a dictionary, and on his release a preciseness of light fills the frame. Only when the film fills with the yellow-green of a stage curtain does his life end.

Zabriskie Point (Michelangelo Antonioni, 1969) taints its opening heated discussion by students with a yellow that moves into red, the film quickening and closing in on gestures and faces. The film is then washed of this colour until one of the students kills a cop and it brings in a green with his bus journey. Only after his girlfriend has mentally exploded 'civilisation' does the film move up to the sun and bring back its opening colour. *The Ox* (Sven Nykvist, 1992) emotively moves its desperate husband through a colour thought world. In a cold, blunt light, dying of hunger, he kills the ox of his master. The film feels their temporary warmth, but as quickly reveals the colour-sucked prison that he ends up in. There no brightness or colour is let through the film's blue-grey thought, the cold further thought through the brittle surface. When he is released into the same world as before his deed, the film pushes his new eyes, and sky and grass are made to bloom in his mind, and for us.

A distinctive, if calculative filmosophy is that of *Tetsuo II: Body Hammer* (Shinya Tsukamoto, 1992) and *Basic Instinct* (Paul Verhoeven, 1992). Both films feel their subjects with a steely grey, a colour in between life and death. *Tetsuo II* thinks it in concert with the mechanisation of its future-industrial characters (who in the end turn into full-blown Lister engines), while showing their earlier life in warm orange to make things bluntly clear. *Basic Instinct* provides no comparison, perhaps believing there to *be* no rosy way of existing. Added to the fact that it is set in present-day America, the chrome thinking of even the most simple of scenes seems to breed a disgust in its attendant amorality. Paul Virilio has called this sort of colour 'our post-historic, or post-modern colour, the colour of transparency, of the gleam or brilliance of metal ... and in the future it may be the colour of the stealth bomber, that is, an absorbent colour that has no reflection ... a colour in reverse'.[39]

4

What is important for filmosophy is how we are thinking while experiencing film, how the thoughts of film are 'translated' into words, and how those words are arranged in filmosophical talk. Film viewing is always a little different from our daily sensations, with different expectations, and needs. We are attentive in the cinema, we are thinking with and against it, but we are thinking towards it, not passively positioned (in life we usually think *from* our experiences). Meaning does not come via interpretation, but directly from experience. Meaning is what we *feel* when watching the thing, and that immediate feeling is our useful (and hopefully interesting) truth of the film. The film has no defence; it cannot shout, 'Hey, you, you got me all wrong, I never said anything like that.'

For filmosophers the most fruitful attitude to film comes from meditative thinking in the experience, onto the film (out to talk). Feeling along with *its* (thoughtful) feeling.[40] Attending to a film with our whole self we might think with it, instead of via stuttering terminology and against it. To achieve an (un)thought, intuitive, flexible, original experience, some new tools are needed. In our thinking upon the film's thinking, we select a mix of *its* thoughts as the film proceeds. We mix (selectively attend to) the colours thought by film, and *how* we mix them depends on the language we have (the experience is a thinking), and thus the language we employ when writing or chatting about the experience of the film. For filmosophers this language is best derived from realising film as an autonomous film-mind.

Where interesting talk about film lies is in the *unachievable* attempt to equal the film in power and precision and feeling (a call for experience to come forward and take a bow).[41] It is the *journey* towards that goal that is important, not any idea of getting there; listening to the film's thinking, and *pointing* to the power that a film has. There is no implicit/explicit distinction – everything is see/hearable and thus there. In effect this works as a *continuance* of the film in words, a *prolonging* via a *resonating* excursion of talk about film. Here the performance of a certain filmic rhetoric is constitutive; it needs to be just like colour, in fact, living on past its immediate experience, growing and thickening as it comes back into contact with the film it talks of. What reads better than fluid flowers of printed marks hanging on to the cliff-edge of sense, of knowledge, of that oh-so-boring city of logocentrism, with its narrow push to find the ends of theoretical roads?

Take *Blue Velvet*. There are plenty of analyses that talk of its colour, perhaps saying something like: 'Lynch contrasts the bland colours in Jeffrey's home life with the thick colours in the world of Dorothy and Frank.' But who is this analysis for? Where is it coming from? What it points out is fairly true – there *is* a sort of contrast of

102

colour. However, the language of the writing leaves something to be lusted after. It seems to die on being uttered. The origin the reading gives for the colour use is in the director – he did this – so we go back to the film and its form becomes synonymous with author direction. You might say, 'What's wrong with that?' Well, why put the director between us and the film? So you're watching a film and you notice an interesting use of colour, you get home to write, and just plop down what the colour did for you, and you rest easy that you've provoked new knowledge about that film, and about film in general. Well, no, I don't think you have.

Contemporary film writing is lumpish, bulky, as well as grabbing wildly at the so-called deeper meaning of a film (cancelling out our learning curve of intellectual adoption in the process). It employs descriptions straight from the film-making manual such as 'tracking shot', 'close-up', two-shot', and 'deep focus'. There are also reams of film analysis that take great pride in noticing *so* much in the image, and force everything to have a meaning, locatable, understandable. These 'close' (read: definitive) readings move into the film like train-spotters, noticing, and then giving raw to us: blotches of red, shafts of light, diagonal framings, which move left or up or off frame. Yet classical aesthetic terms are hardly any better: second-hand and faintly obnoxious in their 'high-art' aspirations, they must go the way of old art historians, and float silently up to heaven.

What is needed is a sort of training in film talk, and, as regards colour, it should be talk that very much *leaves* the colour for the audience to experience, directing their attention *to* the colours, situating them, revealing them. Terms such as 'contrast', 'counterpoint' – what do these really do for our experience? Even saying that something is 'lit' in such a way brings us back to forces outside the film. Why bother? Because that is how our 'film studies' language has so far been constructed. To bother is *not* to use those words: to find a better way, to find a filmosophy. *The Long Day Closes*, we are told, was put through 'the bleach by-pass process, in which colour is desaturated in the final wash of the printing ... [this] in combination with coral filters, Eastmancolor, and "old Cooke lenses"'.[42] *Where* does one want to say this, and to what possible audience – to film buffs, to film-makers, to media students? Where does the experience of film go when its technical make-up is explored as though by a cine-scientist? All we would ever see is technique, technology, authorship, a plethora of 'in-betweens'. That is, *experience is stunted, like a child's mind given the secrets it was intellectually, imaginatively feasting on.* It is this language which builds a structure that in the end denies thinking, repressing our experience by steering our language into a brick wall. Instead of uncovering it in fact covers up.

The drive in filmosophy is to renew the language of film talk, to provide words that *feel* the workings of film, and prolong the experience, both aesthetic and intellectual. Filmosophy recognises that how we watch a film is creatively tempered by the thinking framework of previous knowledge. Seeing a film as the immediate work of creators and their technology ('cameras', 'split screens', 'shots', 'edits') is to produce a certain mode of attention. A mode that is continually *delayed* at every point by the translation of film into an immediately created work of people and technology. This continual delayedness to our attention works against the possible poetic nature of film. People and technology *are* important outside the viewing experience as knowledge. But direct film analysis can do the translating before we watch the film. *Filmosophy is a translation of technology and people towards the thoughtful poetics of film.*

The Element of Crime (Lars von Trier, 1984) thinks not only its protagonist's memory, but also a beyond point of interpretation of that memory – knowing more than he, Fisher, can yet think himself: his guilt. For him the film provides a reliving that is suitably hazy – not all is recognisable at once, but dark, itself receding into the background. The skin of the image is jaune(diced), thought by the film in concert with Fisher's obstructed and disordered vision/version of criminal events, a colour to the events that Fisher can't keep from rising to the surface. Is it any wonder that the film only shows us Fisher viewing himself in dirty puddles, or tarnished mirrors? Puncturing this pallidness are lights from elsewhere – thought in from holes of understanding: television, surgery lamps, flashing police lights, fresh blue 'bulbs' sprouting from a piece of rare dry earth; and hot Cairo, the place from which he remembers the story, is now felt cool blue-grey (as is a church halfway through).

The depth of *Europa* (Lars von Trier, 1991), its complete world-life-mind, is most beautifully realised when the concentration and attention of the characters is thought by the film. Early on, when Leo is listening to his uncle, the setting of the train yard is seen subtly divorced, faded and distant – the instructions of his masters taking up the whole of his concentration, and the film matching his mind. The first thought of colour occurs when the film feels Leo's idealistic reaction to the sight of Zentropa's cars (and this layered thinking by the film unsettles our brain, as though we were seeing through two sets of eyes at once – and this is what the film does, and should be doing: *letting us view what ordinarily we just physically couldn't*, the narrow *with* the expanse, catching detail *along* with a wider scene). Colour is then introduced in what will become a gorgeous rhythm of images throughout the film between Leo and Katrinna. When Leo sees her on the train the film thinks his feeling of her with soft, dark colours. With her then taking him in, the film reverses the effect (the thought) and he almost appears as one big blush, being both infused with the colour he 'caught' from her, and in being coloured by the film thinking her attention this time. The film then brings them both into colour against a faded grey compartment (the film *knows* their perceptions – just of each other), before Leo again takes up his role of gazer in the background. Later, when he sees her from a car, he again 'catches' or receives her colour as the film cuts between them. The film thinks for all, though. It can *colour* that which is important: the bullet that drops to the floor, *for* the werewolf kid; the kid in turn, *for* the old man (the kid who safely divorces the old man into a large greying head – such that it becomes only a 'target' that he has been ordered to shoot); the old man's blood for us; and the younger boy for the soldiers. Leo, too, is realising things, about innocence and involvement, and the film reddens him thus. The death of Lawrence, the bomb package, the lovers' parting hands – all are decided by the film to be relieved of their grey origins and brought closer to our minds. For Max the questionnaire is not simply black and white, and the Jew's list no small matter. In his bath, about to shave, the razor takes precedence, and, from below, blood could never have been brighter. And then, when the rest find him dead in the bathroom, like the moment when Leo discovers Katrinna to be a werewolf, *Europa* gives us full colour, thinking for us the full impression made on all.

Part of filmosophy's idea of *embracing* the film is the resultant action on readers. If they feel the film has changed the writer, then they too will be sincere to the writing's subject. In seeing a film with its attendant writing, that writing, that talk, must rejuvenate the film for the person. This force again comes from the initial experience – when we step from the cinema are our eyes oiled or glassed over, do we act or feel differently?

Richard Rorty's paper, 'The Pragmatist's Progress', is a minor *tour de force* within his relatively recent engagement with critical ideas.[43] Here Rorty explains his post-Nietzschean no plans, no code of codes, no keys to codes, no great dualisms, anti-logocentric, YES to sensation and the use-fulness of texts, where descriptions 'are evaluated according to their efficacy as instruments for purposes'.[44] He sees no distinction between interpreting and using texts, as 'all anybody ever does with anything is use it [by] putting it to work'.[45] For Rorty, reading texts 'is a matter of reading them in the light of other texts, people, obsessions, bits of information, or what have you, and then seeing what happens'.[46] My experience of a film can be picked up by another writer if it provides interest, maybe if I've led the reader to feel that the film has changed me, has made me see something I didn't know I could.

Filmosophy attempts to elucidate both our thinking and the film's thinking. The resultant talk is one that would be a poetic translation of those joined 'thinkings'. No sign of technological terms but chat that leaves the film purer, not hidden behind a mass of industrial workings, but out in the open as a world-mind-life-thought. *Filmosophies should point back to the film to let its whole voice be heard.* The study of film needs these new concepts, and in one sense to do that it needs to become philosophical – that is (within my sense of philosophy) to consider (to mistrust) inherited concepts and terms, to analyse their referential 'basis', and to experiment with compounds and neologisms that might better redraw the lines of our inquiry. (Philosophy can also reorganise interpretative arguments concerning truth and interpretation, and the possibilities or horizons of meaning in film, forcing a sceptical eye on hard teleological theoretics.) This move itself requires the sort of mood of thought that Heidegger was trying to elucidate – a thinking that flows into the task, and towards a more *human* understanding. *An understanding that relates to us, rather than to any logistics or mechanics.*

These new concepts, these new filmosophies – even if youthfully shaky in their applicability and persuasiveness – are needed to provide voices that speak to be heard, and thus challenged, in halls of learning, in journals of research, and in homes of media bombardment. As Deleuze and Félix Guattari write,

> The concept is not given, it is created; it is to be created. It is not formed but posits itself in itself – it is a self-positing. Creation and self-positing mutually imply each other because what is truly created, from the living being to the work of art, thereby enjoys a self-positing of itself, or *an autopoetic characteristic by which it is recognised.*[47]

A new, or newly applied, word in filmosophy is an act of creation, and as such *decides a way of being/attending that only came about when it did* – a miraculous birth that immediately sets itself apart from others, leading all spotlights on to it, from no matter how far away. For example, colours have simple names, but they are deep in reference with earth or cloth or chemicals or fluids, and the original naming of some colours gives an idea of the creative possibilities of our talk about them in film – that browns came from earth and bark, and how a certain grey-brown got the name London Smoke. Also, with celluloid colour the image may actually be grainy fast stock, but is it really not 'brittle', 'harsh', or perhaps 'alive with its surface'? Which *reveals* the film? Which *revels* in the film?

We have seen that film, as a 'Mind', as a *World*, as a *Life*, handles its own images and sounds. It can consider possibilities (film with a pipe in an easy chair, thinking). But, uniquely, film can think without recourse to language to immediately interpret what it thinks (while we, of course, largely translate the experience back into language-ideas). It is a pre-reflective action (*film-intentionality*), with no 'brain' actually behind it, even though film, like ourselves, can engage in independent reflective action (*film-will*). A film may collide images, or situate a character such that an understanding is subtly arrived at, while never needing linguistic tools. It is, in a sense, freed of concepts, to meet the world head on. Its ideas, thoughts and concepts are not distinct and exact, but indicative, aesthetic, and emotional. Of course *we* automatically interpret its thoughts – we reduce its thinking to our thinking. This philosophical way of approaching film may give us clues to the possibilities of our own thinking, beyond language (film as another kind of artificial intelligence?). How were people 'thinking' before language was formed? Philosophers have searched for 'the mind' via 'mental states', have attempted intellectual, theoretical constructs in relation to the physical brain. But the idea that somehow 'beneath' language our minds work in images seems redundant, and the 'mind' remains as hypothetical and fictional as the brain is soft tissue. In a sense the brain is the 'word', while the 'mind' has remained the picture, unlocatable in set meaning. Film is the mind, is the metaphysical thinking that can, philosophically, *helpfully*, mirror our own ways of thinking. Film can stand in for the world in a metaphysical game, can be the new metaphysics, with its own abstract universal truths, a mind freed to conceive anything, whether pure colour as in *Blue* (Derek Jarman, 1993) or living dinosaurs as in *Jurassic Park* (Steven Spielberg, 1993), thus helping us understand the limits of *our* thinking. In being thinking, film can thus also become interpreting, and we can see some film as being as intellectually creative as anything philosophically can be, only not having to build strict concepts as philosophy does (while I also admit the possibility of a philosophical disenfranchisement of film).

In filmosophy our thinking upon film thinking is an action that also parallels our coping with existence. That is, it requires of us an act of reduction (although not from an understandable, ontological 'whole'), of subsuming the experience to copeable language. Filmosophy can here link with the struggle to find adequate ways of teaching visual literacy, by providing education with proper words to help children and adults breathe a critical mode of attention into their viewing habits. It may also provide words for thought for the creators of the burgeoning home cinema of the camcorder, providing them with similar tools that enable them to use film to help them understand, interpret and possibly transfigure their surroundings, their lives and their actions. And it is *how* we formulate the language of filmosophy that decides our involvement with the world (of film), that marks our *capacities* of knowledge, understanding, and communication. Filmosophy is not just the contemplation of film, but the correspondence with film via talk, and against a background, in a circular sense, of meditative thinking upon the film. It is a stylistic, performative cognitising of our experiences of film. Colourful film thinking (a place of meaning creation) demands colourful filmosophies. These writings can only come from an attempt to say the ineffable (the effort to attend poetically). If images and colours are a surpassing of our thinking (a picture paints a zillion words), then how we 'translate' is a measure of our philosophical maturity within the cinema house. Film works as though our present thought had never come. In filmosophy, film is the *beginning* of our thought, and colour is its most persuasive mood.

Notes

1. Martin Heidegger, *Discourse on Thinking*, trans. John M. Anderson and E. Hans Freund (New York: Harper & Row, 1966), p. 64.
2. Gilles Deleuze, *Cinema 1: The Movement-Image*, trans. Hugh Tomlinson and Barbara Habberjam (London: The Athlone Press, 1986), p. 198.
3. Ibid., p. 203.
4. Ibid., p. 215.
5. Gilles Deleuze, *Cinema 2: The Time-Image*, trans. Hugh Tomlinson and Robert Galeta (London: The Athlone Press, 1989), pp. 12 and 19.
6. Ibid., p. 23.
7. Heidegger, *Discourse on Thinking*, p. 47.
8. Fernand Léger, *Functions of Painting* (London: Thames & Hudson, 1973), p. 119.
9. Deleuze, *Cinema 1*, pp. 53–4.
10. Sergei Eisenstein, *The Film Sense*, trans. Jay Leyda (London: Faber & Faber, 1970), p. 90.
11. John Gage, 'The Spectrum's Shades of Meaning', *The Times Higher Education Supplement*, no. 1083, 6 August 1993, p. 15.
12. Eisenstein, *The Film Sense*, pp. 104 and 112.
13. Toning is the printing of black-and-white film on to colour stock through a filter, with the grey gradations taking on the varying degrees of the filter colour, but with white areas remaining white, and was usually done with yellow for sunlight, and blue for night. Tinting involved dyeing black-and-white film, with all gradations taking in the dye to different strengths, and white areas taking on the dye colour itself. In the twenties 80–90 per cent of films were tinted, but the chemical baths reduced sound quality, and so were phased out with the talkies – see Edward Branigan, 'Color and Cinema: Problems in the Writing of History', *Film Reader* 4, 1979, p. 20.
14. William Johnson, 'Coming to Terms with Color', *Film Quarterly*, vol. 20, no. 1, Fall 1966, p. 3.

15. Sergei Eisenstein, *Notes of a Film Director*, (New York: Dover, 1970), pp. 127 and 121.
16. Ibid., pp. 121 and 122.
17. V. F. Perkins, *Film as Film* (Harmondsworth, Middx: Penguin, 1972), p. 84.
18. Ibid., p. 85.
19. Ibid.
20. Ibid., p. 86.
21. Ibid.
22. Eisenstein, *Notes of a Film Director*, p. 119.
23. Heidegger, *Discourse on Thinking*, p. 46.
24. Ibid.
25. Ibid., p. 45.
26. Edward Branigan, 'The Articulation of Color in a Filmic System: *Deux ou trois choses que je sais d'elle*', *Wide Angle*, vol. 1 no. 3, 1976, p. 21.
27. Ibid.
28. Eisenstein, *The Film Sense*, pp. 106 and 112.
29. Vittorio Storaro, in *Writing with Light*, directed by David Thompson (Happy Valley Films, 1992).
30. Deleuze, *Cinema 1*, p. 52.
31. Eisenstein, *Notes of a Film Director*, p. 128.
32. Norman McLaren, quoted in Johnson, 'Coming to Terms with Color', p. 8.
33. *Pace* Johnson, 'Coming to Terms with Color', p. 18.
34. Léger, *Functions of Painting*, p. 120.
35. Branigan, 'The Articulation of Color in a Filmic System', pp. 20 and 21.
36. Ibid.
37. Ibid.
38. This left-to-right movement perhaps gets its association with moving forwards to the future from our Western style of writing. How are right-to-left movements understood in Arabic-writing countries? How are top-down movements regarded in Eastern societies, which write from top to bottom?
39. From an interview in *A Question of Colour*, director-writer Henry Colomer (Europimages/ Les films d'ici le sept, 1992).
40. 'The feeling is the immediate *welcoming* of what is given' – Jean-Francois Lyotard, *The Inhuman* (Oxford: Polity Press, 1991), p. 111.
41. Stanley Cavell ponders this: 'It is as if we and the world had a joint stake in keeping ourselves stupid, that is dumb, inarticulate' (*Pursuits of Happiness*, Cambridge, Mass.: Harvard University Press, p. 42).
42. Pat Kirkham and Mike O'Shaughnessy, 'Designing Desire', *Sight and Sound*, vol. 2, no. 1 (N.S.), May 1992, p. 14.
43. Richard Rorty, 'The Pragmatist's Progress', in *Interpretation and Overinterpretation*, edited by Stefan Collini (Cambridge University Press, 1992), p. 92. It's so lovely the way that the older a philosopher gets, the shorter his writings become, and thus the clearer the ideas. Quine now only ever seems to publish a few pages at a time, and this essay of Rorty's is so relaxed in tone that I'm sure he's writing it while reclining on a chaise-longue listening to Mahler's Fourth on a hot drunk summer's day in Virginia.

44. Richard Rorty, 'The Pragmatist's Progress', p. 92.
45. Ibid., p. 93.
46. Ibid., p. 105.
47. Gilles Deleuze and Félix Guattari, *What Is Philosophy?*, trans. Hugh Tomlinson and Graham Burchill (London: Verso, 1994), p. 11. My italics.

VERSIONS OF UNCLE TOM
Race and Gender in American Melodrama

Linda Williams

The following work-in-progress is part of a book tentatively titled *Moving Pictures: Melodramas of Black and White*.

In July 1914 carpenters working on a large vacant, weed-covered lot between Sunset and Hollywood Boulevards began to construct the primary set of D. W. Griffith's new film *The Clansman*. According to Karl Brown, assistant to Griffith's cameraman Billy Bitzer, force of habit instilled by years of backstage training resulted in these carpenters including hinges on scenery so it could be easily 'folded up and shipped to any op'ry house in the country'.[1] These stage scenery hinges on film sets for a scene in an ante-bellum Southern town were the tangible vestiges of a melodramatic stage tradition feeding into Griffith's film. The most important single element of that tradition, as Brown explains, was *Uncle Tom's Cabin*:

> I doubt if there was a man on that work crew who hadn't been out with a 'Tom' show, as the *Uncle Tom's Cabin* shows were called. There were Tom shows scattered all over the country by tens and dozens. It was not so much a show as an institution, a part of the American stage scene for the past sixty-odd years.... Stage crews had been constructing Tom shows for so long that there wasn't a detail of the Civil War period, inside or out, that they hadn't built, up to and including wobbly ice for Eliza to flee across, one jump ahead of the bloodhounds, which were usually Great Danes.[2]

Brown's anecdote begins to suggest some of the confluence between what was the most popular and influential play of the nineteenth-century American theatre and, correspondingly, *the most popular and influential film* of the first half of the 20th century. For 'Tom' plays – theatrical versions of *Uncle Tom's Cabin* – seem to have occupied a similar position of importance in the history of the melodramatic theatre that *The Birth of a Nation* certainly does in the history of cinema. Each brought an unprecedented length and legitimacy, a whole new level of importance and seriousness, to its respective medium.

Even more important, each respective work succeeded in *moving* unprecedentedly large numbers of the American public to feel implicated in the trials and tribulations of the types of persons whose virtues and sufferings had not previously been recognised by the mass audience, the African-American slave in *Uncle Tom's Cabin* and the former slave-owners in *The Birth of a Nation*. Indeed, it would be possible to argue that *Uncle Tom's Cabin* began a process of moving audiences towards a recognition of national guilt about slavery – a process which *The Birth of a Nation*, some sixty years later, served to reverse.

One could cast this relationship between the two works in terms of how a good, anti-racist (though of course still racist), maternal melodrama in which black women were the primary agents of their own rescue comes to be superseded by a bad, paternal, virulently racist, melodrama in which white women were in need of rescue from rapacious black men by white men. Such a formulation would, of course, be shamelessly melodramatic, assigning purely black and white polarities to the good and the bad melodrama.

It would be much more interesting and productive to observe the nexus of shades of grey and shifting polarities – masculine/feminine; paternal/maternal; white/black – operating not so much in two different and distinct works but rather in two works which are part of a larger whole: the long-running melodrama of race and gender that I call in this paper 'Versions of Uncle Tom's Cabin'. That is to say, *Uncle Tom* set the stage, literally and figuratively, for the melodramatic terms in which subsequent conflicts of race and gender would be cast in American popular culture. For if melodrama is the place in popular culture where moral legibility is an issue, as Peter Brooks[3] and Christine Gledhill[4] have so compellingly suggested, and if race and gender are two of the most nagging issues of American moral legibility, then we might learn something about our present situation of ever-intensifying appeals to victimhood by examining the history of these most influential aspects of the melodramatic tradition.

As Gledhill has argued in her own important work on the form, within film studies melodrama has for too long been assigned to a ghetto realm of genre studies – for example woman's film, family melodrama – when its pervasion is actually too broad for any genre to contain. I would suggest that melodrama is not so much a specific genre as a fundamental *mode* of American cinema; not a deviation or excess of a more classical realist narrative, but *the* dominant mode of popular moving pictures. It encompasses most films which ask audiences to feel for, or identify with, an initially powerless and virtuous underdog.

The key questions to ask of melodrama are how the form succeeds in moving people and what it moves them towards. The different stage and screen versions of *Uncle Tom's Cabin* are very interesting in this respect. Therefore, I will first of all trace the chronology of the work and the various transformations which have affected its progression from novel to the theatre to the cinema.

Uncle Tom's Cabin – The Novel

On 20 March 1852 Harriet Beecher Stowe, theologian's wife, daughter of the famous preacher Lyman Beecher, mother of seven children, published the anti-slavery novel *Uncle Tom's Cabin; or, Life among the Lowly*, in two volumes. Stowe's main impetus for writing the novel was to respond to the inclusion of the Fugitive Slave Act in the compromise of 1850. This Act, which was one of the most hated measures passed by the US Congress, provide federal aid to anybody seeking the capture of fugitive slaves in the free states and made it a crime for individuals to refuse to help capture and return the property of Southern slaveholders. While in church, Stowe claims to have had a vision of a black man being beaten to death because he would not deny the existence of his true master, Jesus Christ. That afternoon she began to write.

On publication, *Uncle Tom's Cabin* became an immediate best seller and remains to this day the most popular American novel ever written, despite the fact that it was banned for some time in the South. Of course, Stowe's work has been open to charges of racism. James Baldwin, for example, has argued that Tom is both 'robbed of his humanity and divested of his sex'.[5] While not wishing to defend the contemporary image of an 'Uncle Tom', I do think that the work can be productively analysed by placing it in both the historical context of 1852 and of melodramatic structure.

According to Peter Brooks, classical melodrama both begins and attempts to end in a maternal, domestic space characterised by innocence. For example, Chapter 4 of Stowe's novel, entitled 'An Evening in Uncle Tom's Cabin', posits the cabin as such a space marked by happy domesticity. In fact Stowe treads a fine line in the early chapters of the book, flirting with the minstrel tradition of the happy plantation in order to posit the Kentucky home as the space of innocence. (Stephen Foster's song 'Kentucky Home' was written the very year Stowe was writing the novel.) She needs to posit the happy Kentucky home in order for the melodrama to work, for Tom to feel nostalgia for a lost happiness. However, if this nostalgia is posited too forcefully she risks losing the edge of her anti-slavery critique.

113

Moreover, subsequent theatrical adaptations of *Uncle Tom's Cabin* can be classified in terms of which side of this line they fall. If they play up the happiness aspect of the Kentucky home – and some versions even keep Tom on that home, never selling him down river – they cast too benign an eye on slavery. On the other hand, if they emphasise the evils of slavery from the beginning, then they are unable to establish Tom's humanity as a happy husband and father whose life is ruined by the fact that he is a piece of property to be bought and sold.

The two most famous moments of pathos in the novel are the death of Little Eva, the daughter of St Clare, Tom's second owner, and of course the death of Uncle Tom himself. Jane Tompkins cites the death of Little Eva as being the most commonly derided instance of the novel's excessive sentiment. However, she defends this sentiment with the argument that, in the system of belief that undergirds Stowe's enterprise, 'dying is the supreme form of heroism'.[6] Death in this sense is a victory, bringing an access of power.

However, Tompkins casts the novel too entirely within a New Testament religious paradigm which denies other important features of melodrama even as it tries to validate these Christian aspects. Her emphasis on religious pathos ignores the way it alternates with, and gives validity to, the actions of a remarkably self-sufficient, self-rescuing womanhood. In other words, melodrama needs to be considered not merely in relation to pathos, but as a dialectic between pathos and action. In seeking to show how the novel moved readers to oppose slavery, Tompkins ignores how melodramatic pathos also motivates the dramatic actions of characters who act against it. Readers did not only respond to the pathetic deaths of Little Eva and Uncle Tom; they also responded to exciting moments of conflict and action of which there are several in the novel – for example, the slave Eliza's heroic escape at the beginning when, child in arms, she makes her way across the frozen Ohio river with the slave catchers at her heels; Cassy and Emmeline's even more remarkable escape and attendant revenge on their brutal owner, Simon Legree, at the end of the novel when they pretend to be ghosts come to haunt him.

Tom's death, modelled in part on the martyrdom of Little Eva, is similarly an escape from worldly sorrows to the new Jerusalem. But it is also more challenging to the patriarchal institution of slavery because, unlike Eva's passive fading away, it encompasses a more active defiance of Simon Legree's power. Tom both refuses to beat his fellow slaves and to reveal the whereabouts of Cassy and Emmeline.

Stowe's novel contains two key elements which are either developed or abandoned, for reasons relating to shifts in the national consciousness about the institution and legacy of slavery, by subsequent theatrical adaptations of *Uncle Tom's Cabin*. First, there is the motif of escape and escape-revenge. Three sensational escapes occur in the novel, two by female protagonists entirely under their own steam: Eliza crossing the frozen Ohio river with her child Harry, and Cassy and Emmeline haunting Legree with his own guilt (she spooks him the way the Ku Klux Klan will later spook former slaves) before escaping under a sheet. In addition, the fugitive slave George Harris and his family escaping after a gun battle with slave catchers.

The second element concerns the various configurations of couples which can be organised along racial lines:

White and Black This category includes Simon Legree and Cassy – the lascivious, white slave-owner and his mulatto concubine, an example of the interracial couple of slavery's worst abuses; Tom and Eva – the older black male slave and his young mistress, the good interracial couple, predicated upon an absence of any sexual relationship between them; and Ophelia and Topsy – the older white Yankee woman and the adolescent black girl who comically resists being civilised.

White and White The two examples here are Mr and Mrs Shelby – the well meaning couple who are nevertheless complicitous with slavery; and Marie and St Clare – the selfish, vain Southern woman and the Southern gentleman who no longer loves her. Due to Marie's shortcomings, Eva lacks a good mother, which creates the conditions for Tom to assume this maternal role.

Black and Black (Slave Couples) There are two examples of this category. George Harris and Eliza – the good, loving husband and wife representing the ideal family; and Uncle Tom and Aunt Chloe – representing similar virtues. Both couples contrast with the bad couple, the St Clares.

Uncle Tom's Cabin on Stage
Many of the theatrical versions of *Uncle Tom's Cabin* which were to be staged from 1852 onwards were not only derived from the novel but were also rooted in the context of amateur popular entertainment in America, in particular the tradition of minstrelsy. Minstrelsy (especially black-face minstrelsy) was the predominant popular form of indigenous American music during the heyday of the 'Tom' plays. The performance of appropriated versions of the songs and dances of slaves in elaborate minstrel shows swept the nation in the 1840s and '50s. Consequently, *Uncle Tom's Cabin* cannot be properly understood without seeing it in the context of this musical tradition.

The origins of minstrelsy date back to 1831 when Thomas Rice, a white performer, 'jumped Jim Crow' by imitating the song and dance of a crippled old black man whose clothes he borrowed. This comic performance, in black face, inaugurated the tradition of black-face minstrelsy. The minstrel show facilitated transgressive celebrations of drink, sexuality and other things which Victorian morality did not condone, and which would have not been permitted without the cover of black-face. However, such transgressions were also given a grotesque comic veneer by the stereotyped treatment of blackness. According to Alexander Saxton, black-face minstrelsy ignored the slave spirituals and the more 'moving' or sentimental musical traditions because its caricature was not interested in developing the humanity of slaves. Instead, it developed a kind of slumming identification with the more comic and pornographic illicit pleasures of black bodies as a way for whites to have temporary access to the realm of the forbidden. In an era otherwise marked by cloying romantic sentiment, minstrels sang love songs like this:

My Susy she is handsome
    My Susy she is young
My Susy looms it bery tall
    Wid udder like cow
She'd give nine quarts easy
But white gals don't know how.[7]

So minstrelsy enabled white culture to appropriate a feeling, a mood, a melody, a gesture from African-American culture; to enjoy its transgression, its differences, even its irreverence; but at the same time avoiding ever being trapped within the stereotype. The audience for minstrelsy was predominately the urban Northern whites who were allied to the Southern planters who supported slavery. So in political terms this music was overtly linked to the Democratic Party and served to propagandise this alliance of the Northern working class with planter interests in the south.

The use of such stereotypes in the minstrel tradition helps us to understand why Tom may have been, as Baldwin put it, 'divested of sex'. For to invest the character of a slave, either male or female, with sexuality was, in the 1850s, to place that character automatically in the realm of minstrelsy. Consequently, the only conventional figure available to Stowe was arguably that of the feminised Uncle.

Minstrelsy is commonly regarded as the epitome of the white racist, pro-slavery position. However, what is interesting is that the plantation myth of the happy slave was propagated not only by this comic material but also by the more sentimental songs of longing for an idealised image of the South construed as a symbol of a collective rural past. Saxton assumes that a sentimental song rendered in 'darkey' vernacular and nostalgic for the good old South was automatically contributing to a plantation myth and thus was pro-slavery. He writes that such songs appropriated an 'emotional impact that was logically unrelated to their content – i.e. the bawdy, comic content of minstrelsy'.[8]

Yet this interpretation may be too simplistic. It assigns a too rigorous comic content to minstrelsy and assumes that any sentimental song about the old plantation automatically supports slavery. Take the example of the well-known song, 'Ethiopian Melody: Old Folks at Home', 'written and composed' by E. P. Christy and published in 1851:

Way down upon de Swanee ribber, Far far away
Dere's wha my heart is turning ebber, Dere's wha de old
   folks stay.
All up and down de who creation, Sadly I roam,
Still longing for de old plantation, And for de
   old folks at home.

All de world am sad and dreary, Ebry where I roam,
Oh! darkey how may heart grow weary, Far from de old
   folks at home.

On the minstrel stage it may very well have been used to propagate the plantation myth, but its appearance in Act V, Scene iii, of the abolitionist Aiken-Howard stage version of *Uncle Tom's Cabin* (discussed below) suggests that in another narrative context it could perform a very different function. In this stage version of *Uncle Tom* the scene is 'a rude chamber'. Tom is discovered in old clothes, seated on a stool. He holds in his hand a paper containing a curl of Eva's hair. The scene opens to the symphony of 'Old Folks at Home' and Tom makes the following speech:

I have come to de dark places; I's going through de vale of shadows. My heart sinks at times and feels just like a big lump of lead. Den it gits up in my throat and chokes me til de tears roll out my eyes ... Dere's de bright silver dollar dat Mas'r George Shelby gave me the day I was sold away from old Kentuck, and I've kept it ever since. Mas'r George must have grown to be a man by this time. I wonder if I shall ever see him again.

This theatrical appropriation of a minstrel song suggests how easily one tradition can be borrowed by another. Minstrelsy may have been devoted to burlesquing the slave and its dominant affect may have been comic, but the plantation myth was also sentimental and this

117

sentiment could be put to a new use.

Alongside minstrelsy, melodrama was also a major popular form of entertainment in the America of the 1850s. While these were separate forms, they could, and did, borrow from one another. Until the advent of theatrical versions of *Uncle Tom's Cabin*, there was no tradition of serious, extended melodrama occupying a whole evening or afternoon's entertainment. Stage melodramas were relatively short three-act affairs. Between the acts there were songs, dances, acrobats and ventriloquists – in other words, elements of minstrelsy. Moreover, while controversial subjects were often addressed, as was frequently the case in anti-temperance melodramas, there was no tradition of anti-abolitionist theatre and there was certainly no tradition of a black hero or heroine occupying the central role in a serious play. However, this was soon to change in the adaptation of Stowe's novel for the stage.

The first theatrical version of *Uncle Tom's Cabin*, produced by Charles Western Taylor, opened on 23 August 1852 at the National Theatre in New York. This version of the play, which was not very popular with audiences, ran for eleven nights and ended with the return of Tom to his cabin in what is described by Kessler as a 'Happy Denouement and Grand Finale'.[9] This version, like most popular drama of the day, shared the bill with the usual variety fare: a Herr Cline who executed three costume changes on a tightrope, a romantic Neapolitan dance performed by male and female performers, and, perhaps most interestingly, a 'Burlesque of Otello' in which T. D. Rice (the legendary white inventor of black-face minstrelsy who made famous the song and dance 'Jump Jim Crow') played a comic Othello.

The typicality of the burlesque minstrel mode for all forms of black representation suggests the reason for the happy ending of the Taylor version of Uncle Tom. As there was no precedent for pathos and seriousness in the representation of a black character, many early stage versions, even those produced within a clear context of a moral abhorrence of slavery, chose to rewrite the ending. To do so, of course, automatically entailed softening the pain and suffering of slavery and subscribing to the plantation myth of the happy slave.

The next stage version of *Uncle Tom's Cabin* was produced in November by Henry J. Conway at the Boston Museum. Once again the play began with an evocation of the plantation myth with happy slaves singing and dancing. The structuring of events in this version, as reproduced by Kessler, also indicates a happy ending with George Shelby's rescue of Tom from the hands of Simon Legree[10] – a further indication of how difficult it was for many to countenance a melodrama about a black hero with a sad ending. Conway's production, in a subsequent spectacular adaptation by P. T. Barnum, appears to have influenced some of the later film versions of *Uncle Tom*.

However, in 1852 the abolitionist Aiken-Howard version of the play was also produced. This was to be the most important, longest-running, most socially significant stage version of *Uncle Tom's Cabin*. It was written by a 22-year-old Bostonian playwright, George Aiken, who had already written an anti-slavery play called *Helos, the Helot, or the Revolt of Messene*. Consistent with contemporary conventions, Aiken's first version of the play was in three acts, ending with the death of Little Eva and thus omitting Tom's later ordeal with Simon Legree. The play was thus basically a dramatisation of the first volume of Stowe's novel.

This version proved to be such a success – primarily due to the popularity of Little Cordelia Howard as Little Eva – that George Howard, the producer, decided to stage what amounted to a sequel: a three-act dramatisation of the second volume of the novel, entitled *The Death of Uncle Tom, or Religion of the Lowly*, with many of the same actors taking up the same roles.[11] While this play did not feature the presence of Cordelia Howard, it too was a great success.

What happened next made theatre history. Howard had Aiken combine the two plays into a single 'Grand Combination' which came to be known as the 'complete' *Uncle Tom's Cabin*. It was essentially this version of *Uncle Tom*, of unprecedented length, in six acts, eight tableaux and thirty scenes (later expanded to seven acts and thirty-four scenes), presented on a single bill, with no other attractions, that made history. The play opened in Troy, New York, on 15 November 1852.[12]

There are several significant elements in the Aiken-Howard production which mark if off from the Taylor and Conway stage versions. The play begins with the decision of George Harris to flee – there is no allusion to happy times on the plantation here. The play also remains true to the abolitionist pathos of Stowe's novel, ending with the tragic death of Uncle Tom. In fact, almost all the elements of minstrelsy are resisted in this production. Not only is the happy plantation myth rejected but all the comedy in the play is given over to white characters: to Phineas Fletcher, the lovesick Quaker, and to Marks, the lawyer, with his umbrella.

Howard explained the significance of his production in the following way:

Till the advent of *Uncle Tom* in New York, no evening at the theatre was thought complete without an afterpiece, or a little ballet dancing. When I told the manager *Uncle Tom* must constitute the entire performance, he flouted the idea; said we would have to shut up in a week. People came to the theatre by hundreds, who were never inside its doors before; we raised our prices, which no other theatre in New York could do.[13]

In both Troy and New York City, the play did attract a 'new class of audience'. The National Theatre was situated in a rough neighbourhood where prostitutes were said to solicit customers in the balcony of the theatre. However, *Uncle Tom's Cabin* earned this theatre, and melodramatic theatre in general, a new measure of respectability since, as one critic put it, 'the stigma of entertainment was not so great with just one serious moral drama as with three questionable ones'. The manager of the National Theatre could thus advertise his establishment as a 'temple of Morality', stressing the patronage of refined audiences composed of families, ministers and teachers.

During the run of the play the manager also introduced the, then almost unprecedented, feature of the matinée to encourage women and children to visit the theatre with less fear of the rougher elements who frequented the neighbourhood. Even church groups attended with their pastors. Upper tiers of more expensive seats had, according to one reporter, 'an air of sanctity'. However, another reporter noted something more interesting about the class of people occupying the cheaper seats: 'The gallery was filled with a heroic class of people, many of them in red woollen shirts, with countenances as hardy and rugged as the implements of industry employed by them in the pursuit of their vocation.'[14]

This reporter was puzzled by the silence of the entire audience when Eliza crossed the river. When he turned to look, he was astonished to discover that the whole audience, including the rough men in the gallery, were in tears.[15] This rough group in the gallery, reduced to tears over the sufferings of slaves, seems historically as important as achieving respectable converts to melodrama. A reviewer in the antislavery *New York Tribune* noted: 'No mob would have dared to disturb the Abolition party at the National Theatre', even though the audience for the play was composed predominantly of the sort of people who had previously composed the anti-abolition mobs that had burned down Freeman's Halls, destroyed printing presses and assaulted public speakers. While the material contained in *Uncle Tom's Cabin* was considered volatile enough to start a riot, the drama also succeeded in dissipating any pro-slavery sentiment which might otherwise have provoked a disturbance.

Perhaps even more interesting was a third element of the audience whose reactions were not noted at the time but whose very presence in the theatre was remarkable. For the manager of the National Theatre broke entirely with tradition and admitted blacks in a segregated section by the pit (a situation comparing favourably to churches at the time where blacks, if admitted at all, were given the very worst seats).

Therefore, the adaptation of *Uncle Tom* to the stage was as significant to the theatre as *The Birth of a Nation* proved to be to cinema nearly sixty years later. There are three main aspects to this significance.

First, the theatre achieved a new social importance (largely because it became a legitimate entertainment for a middle-class audience). This was reflected in higher prices, longer shows, greater seriousness, and the relative absence of variety acts and minstrel components. Yet, as we have seen, in its music and appropriation of some aspects of the plantation myth it was never completely severed from that earlier tradition.

Second, the melodramatic stage also became a place for the forging of an emergent national consciousness. In this case consciousness was formed around feelings for the sufferings of slaves who become a repository of American lost innocence and childhood, linked to a sentimentalised, idealised rural past.

Third, in addition to the inclusion of the middle classes, the staging of *Uncle Tom's Cabin* was the occasion of a major shift in the audience composition of the theatre, which now brought together women, children, blacks and middle-class gentlemen with the rougher working-class audiences who had always attended.

Of course, this conversion by which Northern audiences who once laughed at minstrel caricature began to feel implicated in the lives of slaves as embodying something peculiarly American – as opposed to Ethiopian exoticism – was no simple matter of a new-found Northern working-class sympathy for the suffering of slaves. Nor should we forget, of course, that there were no 'real' blacks in these productions. In 99 per cent of cases the roles of Uncle Tom and Topsy were played by white actors in black-face, and those of Eliza, Cassy and George Harris by white actors playing mulatto characters. But it is clear how powerful the melodramatic denouement of this version of *Uncle Tom's Cabin* was in the decade before the Civil War.

In 1854, in addition to the Aiken-Howard version of the play at the National Theatre (billed as the only 'correct version' of the novel), New York City alone had three other competing versions of *Uncle Tom's Cabin*, all of which tended towards minstrelsy. One of these, P. T. Barnum's adaptation of Conway's happy-ending version from 1852, was the biggest commercial challenge to the Aiken-Howard version. Barnum's mounting of *Uncle Tom* at his American Museum Theatre in New York tried to out-spectacle the Aiken competition even as it billed its version as the more realistic representation of slavery. His advertisements read:

It represents the Southern Negro SLAVERY AS IT IS embracing all its abhorrent deformities, its cruelties and barbarities [yet] it exhibits a true picture of Negro life in the South, instead of absurdly representing the ignorant slave as possessed of all the polish of the drawing room, and the refinement of educated whites.

Rather than abolitionist fervour, Barnum offered comedy and spectacle, including a grand panorama of the Mississippi by moonlight, painted by a popular scenarist, which depicted a steamer on its way to New Orleans with real rotating wheels, lights, and puffs of smoke emerging from its smokestack.

Another of the New York productions of the play in 1853 was unambiguously pro-slavery: Christy and Wood's Minstrels performed a burlesque of the Aiken-Howard version in a one-act portion of their variety show entitled, *Uncle Tom's Cabin, or, Life Among the Happy*. The burlesque was so successful that in the spring of 1854 the company developed a full-length 'opera' on the subject. In this version Tom is not even sold away from Kentucky. Instead, returning from a revival camp meeting he criticises the dandified pretensions of 'free Darkies' and expresses his love for 'old Kentuck'. In the last act, George and Eliza are joined in a slave 'wedding' ceremony consisting of 'jumping the broom'.[16]

So by the mid-1850s, five years before the beginning of the Civil War, we see a struggle taking place in popular theatre regarding the appropriate mode, comic or melodramatic, with which to portray the 'life of the lowly'. After the appearance of *Uncle Tom's Cabin*, the tradition of minstrelsy is placed on the defensive, devoting its own full-length show to answer the Stowe/Aiken-Howard assertion that the suffering of slaves is of melodramatic import.

Post-Civil-War 'Tom' Shows

After the Civil War Uncle Tom's Cabin continued to be extremely popular. Touring companies, given over entirely to productions of *Uncle Tom's Cabin*, performed across the nation, now including the Southern states. Indeed, by the 1890s more than five hundred such companies were touring 'Tom', or 'Tommer', shows. The plot and characters were by now so familiar that spectacle often assumed greater importance than the narrative in such shows. In the 1880s, one travelling company had fifty actors, twelve dogs, a mule and an elephant.[17] In 1888 another included a steamboat race, which is possibly the origin of the race between the *Robert E. Lee* and the *Natchez* in Edwin Porter's 1903 film version, discussed below. Also in 1880 the first theatrical use of electric lights was to illuminate the winged figure of Eva, come to take Tom to heaven.[18]

However, the post-war period is marked by a general tendency for *Uncle Tom's Cabin* to slip back into, or at least to rework aspects of, the old minstrel tradition. A 'Tom' show was often an occasion for nostalgia for the 'good old plantation' and an accompanying de-emphasisation of the evils of slavery, especially since audiences could now be reassured that history had corrected the 'error' of slavery. Hence many versions began to allude to the Civil War and to supplement Tom's glimpse of glory (or actual ascension into heaven) at the end of the play with more earthly solutions, such as the inclusion of a tableau depicting Lincoln signing the Emancipation Proclamation or a 'Scene of the Union armies triumphing over the confederates'.[19]

During the Spanish–American war of 1898 Northerners and Southerners were uniting together against Spain rather than engaging in fratricidal war. The patriotic lesson of this satisfying, and healing, union of North and South charging gloriously on horseback against a common enemy (in this case imperial Spain trying to hold on to its colony in Cuba) was not lost on Thomas Dixon, who would later utilise it in his first novel, *The Leopard's Spots*, and later in *The Clansman*.

In 1906 the Kentucky State Legislature passed a law making it illegal to present 'any play that is based upon antagonism between master and slave, or that excites racial prejudice'. This law was specifically aimed at preventing productions of *Uncle Tom's Cabin*.[20] This legislation was most likely aimed at preventing stagings of the Aiken-Howard version of the play, for it is clear that Barnum-style versions flourished in the South.

In some of the more sensational productions it became traditional for Simon Legree to foam with rage and to beat Uncle Tom at length. Tom would have a container of red fluid to smear over himself at such moments.[21] The prizefighter John L. Sullivan played the part of Legree in one touring company: here the attraction was seeing Sullivan's Legree brutally knock out many slaves (this is the same Sullivan who would never deign to fight a black contender in the ring). In these versions Topsy would sometimes be aged up from a child to an adolescent or adult. In some performances her wild, comic wickedness was transformed into sexual wickedness in her songs and dances, especially in performances after the Chicago Exposition of 1893, where Little Egypt made such a sensation.

But in the later post-war period there were also some black troupes touring with the play. In 1902 in Davenport, Iowa, a well-known white actor writes of attending an all-black performance of *Uncle Tom's Cabin* as a joke. 'We went to laugh but remained to pray, for we saw an exquisitely beautiful, dignified and marvellously pathetic

123

and sweet performance given of Uncle Tom by Charles Albins, who afterwards came to New York and played Othello.'[22]

Cinema Versions of *Uncle Tom*

Given the continued popularity of productions of *Uncle Tom* on the stage for fifty years it is unsurprising that it should quickly be appropriated as suitable subject matter for the cinema in the very early years of the new medium.

The first film version of Stowe's creation was Edwin S. Porter's *Uncle Toms Cabin or Slavery Days (sic)*, produced in 1903 for the Edison Company. This production incorporates a fascinating confluence of minstrelsy without actual song, of stage melodrama without dialogue and of early cinema's reliance on its audience's familiarity with the many pre-existing forms of *Uncle Tom's Cabin*, whether novel, stage or pictorial illustrations. Much has been written by film historians about the narrative and spatial-temporal incoherence of this and other Porter films. Some have suggested that pre-1909 cinema audiences had an 'ambivalent' or 'different' sense of temporality and causality from those of later years.[23] However, this argument has been recently demolished by Janet Staiger, who points out that audience familiarity with novel and stage versions of what was after all the best-known story of the second half of the 19th century made a chronological sequence of events unnecessary. Staiger maintains that audiences who saw Porter's tableau could call up a whole 'causal chain of events, fully motivated in the psychologies of characters, and complexly ordered into a story that involved a simultaneity of events as well as a sequentiality'.[24]

I agree with Staiger that we need not seek a romantic 'otherness' in the primitive film-viewer's ability to enjoy a pure, unnarrativised spectacle. It seems obvious, given the remarkable familiarity of this material, that viewers who enjoyed the spectacle also knew 'the story'. But we have also seen that this story was not 'fixed'. It is interesting, therefore, to consider another sort of ambivalence or incoherence in this film version of *Uncle Tom*: its contradictory presentation of slavery as on the one hand a fondly remembered period of innocent childhood and, on the other, a cruel period of human auctions, separations of families and murderous floggings.

It is interesting to consider in some detail the structure of Porter's film version of *Uncle Tom's Cabin* in order to place it within the wider context of the *Uncle Tom* tradition from novel to stage to screen. This film is comprised of 14 scenes. The titles of each scene are given below with a description of the actual action and an indication of the source, if known, in brackets.[25]

124

1. *Eliza Pleads with Tom to Run Away*

Eliza appears in the snow outside Tom's cabin, pleads with him to go, then bids him farewell. (This is the equivalent of Act I Scene iii of the Aiken-Howard stage version except that in the play the scene is played in the cabin.)

2. *Phineas Outwits the Slave Traders*

The comic Quaker Phineas holds Marks and Haley at bay as Eliza escapes through the window of a tavern with her child. (In the Aiken-Howard version, as in Stowe's original, Eliza escapes without help from Phineas. In later versions – such as the unpublished one in the Harvard Theatre Collection, this film version and the 1926 film – Phineas gets more, and Eliza less, credit for the escape.)

3. *The Escape of Eliza*

Eliza jumps onto a papier mâché ice floe and is carried across the river. (Aiken-Howard is substantially the same except that Phineas is seen awaiting Eliza on the opposite shore.)

4. *The Reunion of Eliza and George Harris*

George and Eliza escape the Quaker refuge and fire down on Marks and the slave catchers from the rocky pass above. (This is a condensation of the reunion of George and Eliza in Act II Scenes v and vi of Aiken-Howard.)

5. *Race between the* Robert E. Lee *and the* Natchez

The steamships race. (This is a cut-rate version of the elaborate race in the 1888 stage version.) There is no basis for this scene in the original novel.

6. *The Rescue of Eva*

While disembarking from the steamboat that has carried her home to New Orleans, Eva falls overboard. Tom immediately jumps after her and both are pulled out. St Clare immediately purchases Tom. (This is in Stowe's novel, but not in the Aiken-Howard. It is probably derived from Act II of the Conway version.)

7. *The Welcome Home to St Clare, Eva, Aunt Ophelia and Uncle Tom*

(In neither Stowe, Aiken-Howard nor the Harvard Theatre Collection version do we see anything like these happy, well-dressed, dandified, dancing slaves. This material would seem to be borrowed from the Barnum-style spectacles showing happy times on the plantation. The dancers seem to be African-Americans.)

8. Tom and Eva in the Garden

The first half of this scene is taken up by an elaborate group dance of high-stepping, elegantly dressed 'darkies' (who appear to be actual African-Americans, not white actors in black-face) who dance on, perform, and dance off stage before Tom who, in white tie and tails, reads the Bible to Eva as she sits in his lap. (The minstrel component of this scene is, as above, probably a post-Civil-War addition.)

9. The Death of Eva

Eva dies; a superimposed angel descends and takes up her superimposed body. (This is a more elaborate special-effects version of Aiken-Howard, in which Eva simply dies without the angel.)

10. St Clare Defends Uncle Tom

St Clare is killed defending Uncle Tom against an unnamed man whom we later recognise as Simon Legree. (In Aiken-Howard St Clare simply comes home wounded with no explanation; in the novel he intervenes in an altercation between two men in a bar.)

11. The Auction Sale of St Clare's Slaves

This includes the minstrel convention of gambling and dancing slaves at the beginning of the scene before Emmeline and Tom are sold to Legree. Except for Uncle Tom, the sold slaves are uncommonly well dressed; one even wears a suit and tie. At the end of the scene Legree exults over a kneeling Tom and Emmeline. (Except for the minstrel ingredients, this is narratively faithful to Aiken-Howard.)

12. Tom Refuses to Flog Emmeline

Tom refuses to flog his fellow slave Emmeline and is flogged himself in return. (As in the novel and Aiken-Howard.)

13. Marks Avenges Deaths of St Clare and Uncle Tom

George Shelby enters, speaks to Legree and exits, presumably to find Tom. Then Marks, known by his umbrella, enters, quarrels with Legree and shoots him. Legree falls. (This follows Aiken-Howard, but not Stowe who only has George Shelby strike Legree.)

14. Tableau: Death of Uncle Tom

Tom dies in George Shelby's arms. (Audiences familiar with the play would remember Tom's 'Oh Mas'r George, you're too late. The Lord has bought me, and is going to take me home' (Act VI, Scene vi).) Instead of the play's vision of 'gorgeous clouds' and Eva robed in white on the back of a mild-white dove extending her hands in 'benediction over an image of St Clare and Uncle Tom kneeling and gazing

126

up to her', we see in a balloon on the right side of the screen a succession of five still images: the same angel that came for Eva; a version of the painting *John Brown Going to His Execution* (a famous painting of the legendary martyr who tried to lead a slave revolt at Harpers Ferry federal arsenal in 1859. In this painting, inspired by the journalist Horace Greenly, Brown is depicted pausing on the steps outside his jail on the way to his execution to kiss a black woman's child); an American flag in the field of the Civil War; Lincoln standing with a slave crouching at his feet (an allusion to the Emancipation Proclamation); Confederate and Union soldiers shake hands with a winged figure standing between them (an allusion to the reunion of North and South).

The title of Porter's film, *Uncle Toms Cabin or Slavery Days* (*sic*), is interesting in the replacement of Stowe's (and many stage versions') subtitle, *Life Among the Lowly*, with *Slavery Days*. This seems to reflect many of the crucial changes in the approach to the material since the ante-bellum period. By 1903 slavery days were long gone and in many scenes, particularly 5, 7 and 8, they are fondly pictured in minstrel dances – though not minstrel comedy – evoking the still popular plantation myth. The fact that many of these same scenes are also faithful, if truncated or condensed, versions of the Aiken-Howard play suggests that an audience was presumed to have no difficulty holding the contradictory opinion that slavery days encompassed elegant spectacles of well-dressed happy slaves as a kind of background to the sufferings of Eva and Uncle Tom.

There were several subsequent film versions of *Uncle Tom's Cabin*, but as with the play I will only note those of particular interest.

The 1910 film version, directed by J. Stuart Blackton, is especially interesting in that it keeps some of Stowe's material of the haunting of Legree by Cassy and Emmeline. The film shows Cassy putting a sheet over Emmeline's body and Legree cowering at the sight of it. The two also escape on their own – in a manner constitutive of a kind of proto-*Thelma and Louise*.

In 1914 a 60-minute version, directed by Irving Cummings, was produced. This version was released in the same year in which *The Birth of a Nation* was in production. Like *Birth* it abandons stagy tableaux for more authentic locales, even outdoing Griffith in the authenticity of its plantation scenes. However, its action sequences lack the drama and suspense of those in *The Birth of a Nation*. Tom is represented as an old and decrepit figure but in this version he is actually played by a black actor. There is also an interesting moment in that the slave whom Tom refuses to whip later stalks Legree with the latter's own gun. In the foreground we see a black hand holding the gun and Legree falling after being shot in the distance. This is a very rare moment in which the slave is allowed to kill the slave driver.[26]

In 1926 Universal Studios produced a version of *Uncle Tom's Cabin* directed by Harry Pollard, who had actually played Tom in a 1913 screen version directed by Otis Turner. This was a much touted $2 million production, originally scheduled to star Charles Gilpin, a black actor who had played the lead in *The Emperor Jones* on Broadway. Pollard reportedly instructed Gilpin to be meek and submissive in his interpretation. The latter refused the part and subsequently gave up acting. The role subsequently went to James B. Lowe, the first serious black actor actually promoted by a Hollywood studio in a non-comic starring role. His Tom is a younger and stronger figure than in many of the 'Tommer' shows and also a very dignified and moving character. The film was a great success, being the sixth most popular film at the American box office in 1927.

What is interesting is that by now this familiar melodrama had begun taking its lessons from both Thomas Dixon and D. W. Griffith. A long opening flashback in Pollard's film idealises life on the Shelby Kentucky plantation – as Griffith did in his adaptation of Dixon – in showing the marriage ceremony of George Harris and Eliza. The elegant wedding takes place in a bower with both masters and slaves in attendance (which is pure fantasy, historically speaking). The action which follows is an occasion for both plantation myth gyrations as well as the more genteel dancing of the masters.

Later, when Eliza learns that her child is to be sold, her escape is reminiscent of Griffith's classic *Way Down East* (1920), a film which had itself learned many lessons of melodramatic pathos and action from *Uncle Tom's Cabin*. Like Lillian Gish's character in *Way Down East*, Eliza finds herself on the floes of a river hurtling towards a waterfall. Like Gish, she is rescued at the last minute, in this case by a kindly Quaker (an unnamed Phineas) hanging upside down from a tree. We see here an interesting shift in the narrative from a victim-heroine who rescues herself to a damsel in distress requiring to be rescued by a heroic male. This rescue motif is central to other Griffth films, including *The Birth of a Nation*, as we shall see.

In Pollard's film, Eliza is subsequently recaptured and sold to Legree. In this way, the otherwise diverging narratives of Eliza, George and Uncle Tom are brought together. Eliza is substituted for the character of Emmeline so her narrative is also brought together with that of Cassy. Thus where Stowe's novel contained the melodramatic contrivance that Cassy was Eliza's long-lost mother, Pollard's film version unites mother and daughter in their captivity under Simon Legree.

Another major change in this version is the expansion of Porter's (and many stage versions') allusion to the Civil War and the emancipation of slaves through a narrative elaboration of the convention of the tableaux. Thus we learn that war has broken out soon after Eliza is captured and sold to Legree. In this way history itself becomes the *deus ex machina* for her eventual rescue. Rather than merely reassuring audiences that history would eventually right the wrongs of slavery, Pollard's film has a historical event that occurred long after the events detailed in the novel and the play versions of *Uncle Tom* inserted back into its fiction to 'right' the particular wrongs of these characters. History (and Mas'r George) are still 'too late' to right the wrong of Tom's fatal beating, but it does save Eliza and Cassy. While this change is reassuring, it also has the effect of diminishing the power of Cassy and Eliza to effect their own escape.

Legree is haunted in this version, but not by Cassy's ingenuity. Rather, he sees a ghostly image of Tom which causes his fall from a spire. When Eliza screams, George, passing by with the Union army below, hears her call and rushes upstairs. Their reunion is to the tune of the Battle Hymn of the Republic and then a Jolson song. So in this film version Tom's memory effects a kind of vengeance, George is almost a rescuer and the women are, as in the films of Griffith, placed in need of rescue rather than empowered to rescue themselves.

The Unmaking of *Uncle Tom's Cabin* as the Making of *The Birth of a Nation*

From 1852 through all the versions of *Uncle Tom's Cabin* from the novel to the stage and the cinema, the traditions of melodrama and minstrelsy are co-opted into the struggle over the question of how Americans should feel about slavery and slaves. But, as Leslie Fiedler argued in an essay on Dixon and Griffith,[27] from 1902, with the appearance of Thomas Dixon's first novel, *The Leopard's Spots*, we can see the beginnings not simply of another minstrel revival but of an important refunctioning of elements of the melodrama of race and gender that would find its fullest expression in 1915 with the unprecedented popularity of the film *The Birth of a Nation*. This refunctioning is what Fiedler calls the 'anti-Tom' literary, theatrical and cinematic tradition. In this tradition the moral polarities of *Uncle Tom's Cabin* are reversed: the black female slave whose virtue is threatened by the white slave master – embodied in the Tom material by the lascivious Simon Legree (played most memorably in the Pollard film by George Siegman) – becomes the white daughter of the South whose virtue is threatened by a lascivious former slave, Silas Lynch (portrayed in Griffith's *Birth* by the same George Siegman). But the main point I want to make is not simply that one group of Dixon-Griffth texts reversed the victim–villain configurations of the Uncle Tom texts, but rather how strongly entwined the Dixon-Griffith melodrama is with the Tom tradition.

The Birth of a Nation has been evaluated in a number of ways by film studies: as the beginning of classical film narrative; as the most important advancement of cinematic language; as a realist epic; and, most recently and importantly, by Michael Rogin, as a 'racist epic'.[28] However, what is missing from these evaluations, and indeed from the whole tendency to categorise the film within an epic, realist, novelistic tradition, is the fundamental impact of *The Birth of a Nation* as a melodramatic spectacle eliciting an affective response of sympathy for racist heroes which is as important culturally and politically as the earlier weeping over Uncle Tom. *The Birth of a Nation* thus needs to be understood as a crucial American melodrama featuring white victim heroes.

The white hero of *The Birth of a Nation* suffers the ravages of the Civil War and returns home as powerless and stricken as the slave heroes Uncle Tom and Eliza. Out of this abject virtue – a virtue whose passive suffering inevitably feminises all victims, male and female alike – they gain the 'moral' strength to rise up again. Without this initial feminised powerlessness the victim heroes of melodrama have no moral legibility; consequently the most conventional heroes of classical melodrama have often been women, pets, and men whose manhood has been threatened. Uncle Tom is simply the most important and the most influential example of this. Moreover, we are now so accustomed to regarding the racism in *The Birth of a Nation* as belonging to some bad old nineteenth-century racist tradition that we never consider how the film can actually be regarded as an important regeneration of one form of anti-slavery melodrama into another white supremacist form.

Thomas Dixon was a Southern preacher who undertook to fight melodramatic stereotype on its own turf – in the novel and on the stage. The appearance in *The Leopard's Spots* of a new type of villain – the lustful black rapist preying upon an innocent white virgin – can to some extent be understood as the guilty fantasy of white supremacy seeking to reverse the historical record of centuries of white masters violating female slaves with complete impunity. As many scholars have noted, it was not until after emancipation that the white supremacists began to articulate the 'one drop rule' – a theory of the dangers of 'racial mongrelisation' that had never bothered the planter class during the era of slavery. One important point to bear in mind is that this myth of the black rapist could only be articulated in terms of a specific refutation of Stowe's novel and the Tom plays. *The Leopard's Spots*, whose working title was 'The Rise of Simon Legree', is essentially a tract on the evils of educating former slaves who would aspire to mate with white women. To illustrate this point he included a subplot in the novel following the adventures of George and Eliza Harris's son wandering from north to south.

In 1905, Dixon wrote his second novel, *The Clansman*, in which he reworked his original tract into melodrama, demonstrating in the process that he had learned much from the popular stage versions of *Uncle Tom's Cabin*. The Clan rides at the end of the novel for vengeance against a black man who has raped a white woman, and to rescue Phil Stoneman, the son of liberal senator Austin Stoneman, who has killed a black man and is about to be executed by his father's own law.

In 1907 *The Clansman* was staged as a play and was particularly successful in the South. In the play the Clan rides twice. The first ride is an act of vengeance against Gus, the black rapist. But in the second ride, this time a ride of rescue rather than vengeance, Dixon reverses the gender of the rescued person. Instead of Stoneman's son it is now his daughter, Elsie, who is threatened with forced marriage by the mulatto, Silas Lynch. Thus this time the ride of the Clan achieves the rescue, in the nick of time, of the white virgin.

Dixon's theatrical version of *The Clansman* actually does much the same thing as most post-Civil-War theatrical versions of *Uncle Tom* in rescuing women (remember that Cassy, Emmeline and Eliza were played by white women on stage) from a 'fate worse than death'. The stakes are now the same: saving the innocent virgin from the lustful villain. The only thing that looks different, since the women all *look* white, is the colour of that villain, who is now unequivocally black.

Griffith subsequently appropriated Dixon's reversed version of *Uncle Tom's Cabin* and upped the ante of the rescue, having his Clan first ride in vengeance for the death of Little sister (the rescue that is too late) and then perform what Rogin calls the 'multiple rescue operation': first, to save the father, daughter and the former slaves of the Cameron family as they are besieged in the Union veteran's log cabin by black soldiers who are slowly breaking down its doors (here the rape threat to white womanhood is made clear as the men prepare to kill the women before they themselves are killed); and, second, to save Elsie Stoneman from the same fate threatened by Silas Lynch.

Thus the Clan, which was historically the instrument of terror and vengeance used against former slaves, here becomes a melodramatic instrument of rescue. The spectacle of the endangered, suffering feminine or feminised victim is as crucial to the one melodramatic tradition as to the other. Melodrama constructs the virtue of the suffering victim and the virtue of the rescuer – recalling Master George, who is 'too late' in *Uncle Tom*. While the white master is discredited in the

Tom melodrama, Dixon and Griffith rework the melodramatic tradition to redeem the former masters by endangering their daughters with the same threat they themselves once posed to the former slave women.

In both cases there are structurally similar elements of the melodrama. In *The Birth of a Nation* many of the interracial configurations of *Uncle Tom's Cabin* are morally reversed. For example, in place of the benign couple of the older black male and the young white female – Tom and Little Eva – we have the predatory relationships of Gus, the black rapist, and Flora and of Silas Lynch and Elsie. In place of Legree and Cassy we get the racially parallel couple of Austin Stoneman and his mulatto housekeeper Lydia Brown, the difference being that this time it is the woman who is portrayed as the lascivious partner. While in *Uncle Tom's Cabin* it is the self-rescuing, long-suffering mother who gains moral legitimacy, in *The Birth of a Nation* it is the son who rescues his own 'guilty' father and the white daughter. *Uncle Tom* is predicated on maternal empowerment – the escape of Eliza and Cassy – while *Birth* is about paternal empowerment – the rescue of Elsie and the besieged folks in the cabin. In the former, Legree, the white Northern villain, is to blame; in the latter it is Lynch, the black Northern villain, followed by the figures of Gus and Stoneman. In Uncle Tom it is the patriarchal institution of slavery which is the system at fault; in *Birth* it is the institution of radical reconstruction.

There are also several iconic elements at work in each of the two melodramas.

The Cabin
This is the lost home, the space of innocence, the symbol of humble beginnings. In *Uncle Tom's Cabin* it is what Tom loses and Mas'r George is too late to restore. In *The Birth of a Nation* it reappears this time as an icon of white virtue, via its association with Lincoln's humble beginnings.[29] As it would be unseemly for the former masters to fight to regain the plantation, no real plantation ever appears in *Birth*. Consequently the main set of the Cameron home is portrayed as a house in town and we have to imagine that the fields are the back yard of this house. In the absence of an isolated rural plantation the narrative conspires to make the rescue that of the former slaves and masters in the cabin home of a Union veteran.

Hauntings
In *Uncle Tom*, Cassy and Emmeline use white sheets to haunt Simon Legree (black haunter, white haunted), the ghosts in this instance functioning to activate the guilty conscience of the villain who has

profited from the sufferings of slaves. They are associated with the mother as Legree thinks he is seeing his mother's shroud and he feels guilt towards her – the maternal spirit activating the moral occult of *Uncle Tom's Cabin*. Dixon and Griffith, on the other hand, reverse this function with the KKK wearing sheets to disguise themselves while committing illegal acts of violence (white haunter, black haunted). Instead of hiding those who escape as in *Uncle Tom's Cabin*, the sheets hide the perpetrators of acts of terror. These ghosts are associated with the father, scaring the former slaves back into a servile fear of the master. Stowe will forgive Legree as long as he remembers his mother and cowers before a spectre of feminine power, while Dixon and Griffith will forgive the former slaves as long as they cower before a spectre of vengeful masculine power. In both cases it is the superstitious, weak-minded, childish nature of the haunted that the haunter provokes. This is especially the case in Griffith, who invents a child's inadvertent evocation of the haunting as an 'innocent' inspiration for the KKK.

The Figure of Abraham Lincoln

We have seen how later theatrical and film versions of *Uncle Tom* use Lincoln to bless paternalistically the emancipated slave who kneels before him. Stowe, of course, does not evoke Lincoln. But as the historical figure given the credit for freeing the slaves he is utilised as a means of reassuring post-Civil-War audiences that slaves finally were rescued – effectively by Lincoln himself. In the 1903, 1914, and 1926 film versions of *Uncle Tom's Cabin*, Lincoln is both pictured at the end and quoted in the Emancipation Proclamation. Indeed, in the 1958 reissue of the 1926 Pollard version, the voice of Raymond Massey (famous interpreter of Lincoln) as narrator makes this paternal presence felt throughout – displacing Stowe's motherly narrative voice with that of an empathetic father. So, already within the Tom tradition, we can see the beginnings of this process of revision of the maternal melodrama in the direction of paternal melodrama.

What is fascinating, however, is that Dixon and Griffith's use of Lincoln moves in quite another maternal direction. For both Dixon and Griffith, Lincoln is reinscribed as the feminine, motherly 'great heart', the sorrowing martyr who sheds tears for the sufferings of his white children of the South and who would have rescued them from radical Republican reconstruction had he lived. Thus, while his introduction in the Tom tradition seems to temper its radical celebration of maternal power in a paternal direction, suggesting that the women, children and slaves were rescued by a patriarchal institution – a new America without slavery – Lincoln's presence in the paternal melodrama of the Dixon-Griffith race conflict is softened with a touch of the maternal.

133

If melodrama always requires a 'space of innocence' to be nostalgic for, then a feminised Lincoln (and his cabin) in *The Birth of a Nation* serve the same purpose that Tom (and his cabin) serve in *Uncle Tom's Cabin*. Melodrama, it would seem, cannot function without some element of this 'mothering heart', however briefly invoked.

Escape Versus Rescue
The slave women's escape in *Uncle Tom* is a revolt against the chattel system of slavery that takes human beings as property. But it is also the revolt of a woman against a patriarchal system that regards women as the property of men. Dixon and Griffith obviously can't have their female victim-heroes rescuing themselves; to do so would be to challenge the very patriarchal system they wish to rescue. We saw how Dixon gradually arrived at the solution: not the rescue of the son by the Klan, which he originally performed in the novel of *The Clansman*, but the rescue of the daughter of the North by the Klan. If that rescue cannot occur in the nick of time then these women must die. This is why Griffith includes the image of the gun pressed to Margaret Cameron's head in the cabin. There is no such possibility as even the rescue of the sullied woman in *Way Down East*. If the woman is raped by the black man, she is presumably ruined in a way that she is not if raped by a white.

Dixon's real achievement was not simply to reverse the polarities of victim and villain established by Stowe in *Uncle Tom's Cabin*, but to make them work as a revelation of 'moral legibility' in a dialectic of pathos that operates in a melodramatic, rather than an epic, mode. Griffith's even greater achievement was to make this reversal work as suspense. In other words, if Ben Cameron were simply the heroic epic hero audiences would not have been moved by his final empowerment. Indeed, it is a source of great embarrassment to most audiences of this film that they are still moved by this final explosion into movement in the two-way last-minute rescue.

Both *Uncle Tom's Cabin* and *The Birth of a Nation* have long occupied undeniably important, if highly controversial, positions in American popular culture. Stowe's anti-slavery novel of the mid-19th century would, one hundred years later, begin to be as reviled as much for its racism (in addition to its 'phoney feminine sentimentality') as Griffith's pro-Jim Crow film. But while Griffith's racist film has engendered greater artistic legitimacy within its cinematic terms than Stowe's attempts to counter racism, whether in the novel or the many stage versions of *Uncle Tom*, I would maintain that the most pro-

134

ductive approach to these two 'works' is, as I have attempted here, to see them very much as two sides of the same melodramatic coin.

Coda: The Case of Rodney King

I have noted that in the anti-Tom, white-supremacist tradition an audience could go to see *Uncle Tom's Cabin* to enjoy the beating of Tom by someone like the prizefighter John L. Sullivan. Indeed, many audiences wept and felt morally uplifted at the spectacle. How the audience feels at the sight of a white man beating a black man functions as both the core issue of melodramatic impact of the *Uncle Tom's Cabin* tradition and the starting point of any subsequent unmaking of that tradition.

The two trials in 1992 and 1993 of four Los Angeles police officers accused of beating black motorist Rodney King hark back to this very sensitive issue out of our slave heritage. The videotaped assault on a black man by white men with clubs, taser (stun gun) and boot inevitably recalls this history. And for the jury not to have seen this beating as a crime suggests they were in some way able to regard the policemen as potential victims and Rodney King as a villainous brute. How that happened in the original trial is both appalling and fascinating. If melodrama is essentially about what Peter Brooks calls 'moral legibility', then we would do well to attend to the ways American melodrama continues to engineer such affective response to racial guilt.

In the different outcomes of these two trials – the four officers were acquitted in the first and two were subsequently found guilty in the retrial – we have seen the fickle essence of American melodrama at work – the irony that a dubious, but undeniable, moral power lies in the role of abject victim. For, as much as we may object to the tear-jerking manipulations of melodramatic spectacles of suffering, there seems to be no question that the person who is construed to occupy the role of the victim – the cruelly beaten Uncle Tom – is the person best positioned to to win moral sympathy in the melodramatic contest for justice. That Rodney King, who seemed such an obvious victim to most people who saw his beating on the videotape, was nevertheless successfully positioned in the first trial by the defence as a violent threat 'in total control' of the situation, and therefore as a danger to the four police officers who argued that they were his victim, only proves that audiences can have very different responses to the same melodrama according to the race, class and gender of the protagonists and of themselves. Like the making and unmaking of *Uncle Tom*, the polarities of melodrama are not fixed. What does become clear is the increasing importance, even necessity, of the role of the victim within the functioning of melodrama.

Notes

1. Karl Brown, *Adventures with D. W. Griffith* (London: Secker & Warburg, 1973), p. 64.
2. Ibid., p. 63.
3. Peter Brooks, *The Melodramatic Imagination: Balzac, Henry James, Melodrama and the Mode of Excess* (New Haven, Conn., and London: Yale University Press, 1976).
4. Christine Gledhill, 'The Melodramatic Field: An Investigation', *Home Is Where the Heart Is: Studies in Melodrama and the Woman's Film* (London: British Film Institute, 1987).
5. James Baldwin, 'Everybody's Protest Novel', *Notes of a Native Son* (New York: Bantam, 1955/1964), p. 13.
6. Jane Tompkins: 'Sentimental Power', in *Sensational Designs: The Cultural Work of American Fiction, 1790–1860* (New York: Oxford University Press, 1985), p. 85.
7. Alexander Saxton, *The Rise and Fall of the White Republic: Class, Politics and Mass Culture in Nineteenth Century America* (London: Verso, 1990) p. 178.
8. Ibid., p. 176.
9. William Jackson Kessler II, 'The Early Productions of the Aiken-Howard Versions of Uncle Tom's Cabin', dissertation, University Microfilms Inc., Ann Arbor, Michigan, p. 81.
10. The structuring of events in the Conway version was as follows:

Act I
A Negro's holiday (happy days on the plantation with singing, dancing and celebration); the escape of Eliza and George together; farewell to Tom by Master Shelby; the detainment of Haley by Sam and Andy; the arrival at the inn of George and Eliza in disguise; the escape of the Harrises with the help of Wilson and Drover John; the pursuit by captors and dogs; their fight for freedom at the rocky pass.

Act II
The sale of Tom to St Clare for Eva; the introduction of Aunt Vermont; the rescue of Eva from the river by Tom.

Act III
The arrival of St Clare and part at home; the introduction of Topsy as a gift to Vermont; Chloe's devotion to Tom; St Clare's intention to free slaves; Eva's love for Topsy.

Act IV
Eva's premonition of death; Vermont's problems with Topsy; St Clare's challenge to Vermont; forebodings of Tom; the death of Eva; the reformation of Topsy; the death of St Clare.

Act V
The now married Vermont and Partyside's plans to buy Tom; Eliza and Cassy on Legree's plantation; the crooked sale of Tom to Legree.

Act VI
Harris and George Shelby at the home of Vermont and Partyside; the decision to free Tom and Eliza; Cassy's undermining of Legree's sanity;

the cruelty of Legree, the death of Legree; the arrival of the rescue party; the reunion of Eliza and George; freedom for Uncle Tom.

Quoted in Kessler, pp. 294–6.
11. Ibid., p. 127.
12. The structure of the Aiken-Howard version is as follows:

Act I, Scene   i: The decision of George Harris to flee is told to his wife Eliza. (No happy times on this plantation.)
           ii: Discussion of the sale of Tom and Harry between Shelby and Haley is overheard by Eliza.
          iii. Tom's decision to remain. (Eliza goes to Tom's cabin to say she is escaping.)
          iv: The escape of Eliza from the tavern with the aid of Phineas.
          v: Pursuit of Eliza by three slave catchers (no dogs).
         vi: Eliza's crossing of the river.

Act II, Scene   i: Arrival of St Clare, Eva, Ophelia and Tom at the plantation (the occasion of some minstrel celebration).
          ii: The introduction of Topsy (song and dance 'I'se so Wicked').
         iii: The escape of George from the tavern with the aid of Wilson and Phineas.
         iv: Eva's love for Topsy.
          v: The reunion of Eliza and George Harris.
         vi: Freedom for Eliza, Harry and George.

Act III, Scene   i: St Clare's challenge to Ophelia.
          ii: Eva's premonition.
         iii: Tom's foreboding.
         iv: The death of Eva.

Act IV, Scene   i: Tom's religion; Ophelia's receipt of Topsy; St Clare's bereavement.
          ii: The interference of St Clare.
         iii: Announcement of St Clare's wound.
         iv: The Death of St Clare.

Act V, Scene   i: Sale of Tom and Emmeline to Legree (slave auction).
         ii: Ophelia and Topsy in Vermont.
         iii: The cruelty of Legree.
         iv: The routing of Cute by Topsy.

Act VI, Scene   i: Tom's witness to Cassy.
         ii: The joining of George Shelby, Marks and Cute.
         iii: The guilt of Legree and the plot of Cassy and Emmeline to escape.
         iv: The death of Legree.
         v: The Death of Uncle Tom.

Again quoted in Kessler, pp. 253–62.

13. Quoted in Kessler, p. 153.
14. Quoted in Thomas F. Gossett, *Uncle Tom's Cabin and American Culture* (Dallas, Tex.: Southern Methodist University Press, 1985) p. 270.
15. Quoted in Gossett; see Edward G. Fletcher, 'Illustrations for Uncle Tom', *Texas Quarterly*, 1, 1958.
16. Gossett, p. 276; Robert Toll, *Blacking Up: The Minstrel Show in Nineteenth Century America* (New York: Oxford University Press, 1974) p. 93.
17. Janet Staiger, 'Rethinking "Primitive" Cinema: Intertextuality, the Middle Class Audience, and Reception Studies', in *Interpreting Films: Studies in the Historical Reception of American Cinema* (Princeton, NJ: Princeton University Press, 1992) p. 108.
18. Ibid.
19. Gossett, p. 382.
20. Ibid., p. 371.
21. Ibid. p. 377.
22. Ibid., p. 381.
23. See Noel Burch, 'Porter or Ambivalence', *Screen*, vol. 19, no. 4, Winter 1978–9.
24. Staiger, p. 118.
25. This is a description of the version of Porter's *Uncle Tom* held in the Library of Congress. The version in the National Film and Television Archive has been rearranged into yet another order:

    1. The Rescue of Eva; the sale of Tom to St Clare.
    2. The arrival at the St Clare plantation.
    3. The race between the the *Lee* and the *Natchez*
    4. Tom and Eva in the garden.
    5. Death of Eva.
    6. St Clare defends Tom.
    7. Auction of St Clare's slaves.
    8. Tom refuses to flog Emmeline.
    9. Eliza pleads with Tom.
    10. The escape of Eliza.
    11. Eliza and Phineas.
    12. Legree beats Tom.
    13. The death of Tom – tableau.
    14. Marks kills Legree.

    The major changes are, first, instead of an episodic weaving of the story of Eliza and George (moving to freedom) with the story of Uncle Tom (moving to New Orleans, first to the St Clare plantation, then to Legree's), we have all the Eva–Tom material first and then all the Eliza material placed in relation to the Tom material. So it seems that Eliza is asking Tom to run away from Legree and not Shelby – as if a black slave could run anywhere. This version also ends not with the death of Uncle Tom but with that of Legree.
26. The scene of the slave's revenge on Legree is cut out of the NFTVA's version of the film, probably the consequence of British censorship.

27. Leslie Fielder, *The Inadvertent Epic: From Uncle Tom's Cabin to Roots* (New York: Simon & Schuster, 1979).
28. See Michael Rogin: ' "The Sword Became a Flashing Vision": D. W. Griffith's *The Birth of a Nation'*, *Representations*, 9, Winter 1985.
29. Ibid.

CINEMA AND THE CITY OF THE DEAD
Reel Histories of Pompeii

Maria Wyke

The destruction of the ancient city of Pompeii and the agonising death of many of its citizens, buried by the eruption of Vesuvius in AD 79, have been recreated on screen through the course of this century, from the beginnings of the cinematic art in the 1900s up to a television mini-series of the 1980s. The purpose of this paper is to explore part of the cycle of cinematic reconstructions of the ancient city as a useful point of entry into and interaction with current debates about the relation-ship between cinema and history.

Three films will be considered in detail, *Gli ultimi giorni di Pompei* (Mario Caserini, Ambrosio, 1913), *Gli ultimi giorni di Pompei* (Car-mine Gallone and Amleto Palmeri, Grandi Film, 1926) and *The Last Days of Pompeii* (E. B. Schoedsack, RKO, 1935). All three films are set in the same historical time and place, and were produced and exhibited within some twenty years of each other, yet they evince interesting ruptures and discontinuities in their portrayal of the city's infamous collapse. An exploration of the changing mode of their historical reconstructions engages with a number of pertinent con-cerns both about history in cinema and cinema in history.[1]

History in Cinema

In recent years, film scholarship has elaborated a variety of strategies for interpreting historical films, by means of which more or less weight is attached to the historical period chosen for cinematic realisation. According to Marc Ferro, film, even if it speaks about the past, is always and only a narrative in the present tense.[2] If, in that paradoxi-cal sense, the historical film is always contemporary, it would scarcely seem to matter which historical period has been chosen for cinematic reconstruction. The cinematic representations of Pompeii would then have no common bond at all but be grounded entirely in the specific moment of their production, each operating independently as a pre-text for narratives about the present.

According to Pierre Sorlin, however, the historical film is also a discourse about the past as well as the present. The historical dimension, then, lies not only in the film's relationship to the period of its production but also in its utilisation of a more or less rigorously reconstituted past in which its audience is disposed to take an interest.[3] Film is a medium which initially located itself as an extension of nineteenth-century representational forms. The new technology of the moving image could be seen as a further development of a nineteenth-century technical progression through engraving, lithography and photography towards ever more refined 'realistic' representations, whether of the present or of the resurrected past.[4] One of the most fascinating attractions which the new medium claimed to offer was the possibility of reconstructing the past with a realism superior to that of documentary sources or the historical fictions of painting, theatre and the novel.[5]

Claims to truth and accuracy which have been made for historical films by their promoters and subsequently much debated by their reviewers are, in a sense, a masquerade. Whatever the antiquarian attention paid to accurate reconstruction in a film's surface texture (such as the set design, costumes and props of the 'Pompeian' cycle), all historical films, as Sorlin observes, partake of fiction.[6] One of the first 'reel' histories of Pompeii, *Gli ultimi giorni di Pompei* (Luigi Maggi, Ambrosio, 1908), while drawing on the cultural hold of the ancient city which the twentieth-century excavations constantly stimulated, borrowed its pictorially impressive visual conventions from Victorian classical subject painting and nineteenth-century stage designs, conceived the Pompeian past in the spectacular terms of pyrodramas, and based its melodramatic narrative on a historical novel by Edward Bulwer-Lytton.[7]

In his novel *The Last Days of Pompeii*, published in 1834, Bulwer-Lytton brought the ruins of Pompeii to life by narrating a fictional love story set against the backdrop of the doomed city. Glaucus, an Athenian gentleman living in Pompeii, falls in love with the beautiful Greek girl Ione. Jealous of their love, the evil Egyptian priest Arbaces murders Ione's Christian brother and has Glaucus accused of the crime. When Vesuvius erupts, a blind flower-girl, Nydia, hopelessly in love with Glaucus, rescues him from the lions in the arena and takes the lovers to an escaping ship. She then drowns herself as the lovers sail off to Athens, where they marry and convert to Christianity.

No historical film (in the terms of Stephen Heath) escapes the obligation of a narration. Consequently, in the 'classical' narrative strategies of historical film to which the Pompeian cycle partially conforms, romance is the point of the historical discourse. History is contained within domestic conflict and provided with the perfection of a story,

141

and an end here spectacularly signalled by the eruption of Vesuvius and the burial of the city.[8]

Thus historical film is a discourse about the past as well as the present but, as Sorlin also argues, that discourse is an *imaginative* form of historiography, one component of a culture's historical capital.[9] The cinematic representations of Pompeii then are fictions, but fictions which share the usage of a well defined and limited historical moment that calls up a constellation of specific meanings for its audiences. The cinematic resurrection of Pompeii operates not as a mere substitute for a narrative of present times, but as one attribute of twentieth-century historical consciousness.

If film scholarship has problematised the relationship between the past projected on a cinema screen and the present moment of its production and reception, it seems to utilise a form of discursive slippage between cinema and society which itself requires further interrogation. Ever since the psychoanalytic readings of German cinema offered by Siegfried Kracauer, in which a relationship was posited between Weimar films and Fascism, many critics have justified reading the films of a particular nation as a manifestation of that nation's psychosocial disposition.[10] Such accounts tend to place most emphasis on the social and ideological contexts of production, and to overlook the specificity of the institution of cinema. But only a partial interrogation of the relation between cinema and society can be achieved if any sociological or psychoanalytic investigation of film texts is separated from the study of the technical and economic conditions of their production, the formation and development of their representational conventions, and the processes of constructing and consuming their aesthetic pleasures.[11]

To say this much, however, is not to abandon the proposition that historical film is an attribute of twentieth-century historical and national consciousness. Since the 1910s, an array of institutions including governments and film industries themselves have recognised and attempted to exploit the potential function of historical film as a national discourse. In a recent study of British cinema of the 1930s and 1940s, for example, Sue Harper has argued that the 'costume' films of the period were held to be vitally concerned with cultural politics and frequently marshalled into discourses of British national interest with a view to deploying them as agents of social influence and control.[12]

One way, therefore, of interrogating history in cinema, and the Pompeian films in particular, is to examine the intersection between historical films and the national, political, economic and cultural identity of the community in which they are produced. While at the same time exploring the ways in which the films reformulate that

142

identity in specifically cinematic terms, building up their own historiographic conventions of style, narration, space, time, performance, aesthetic pleasure, address and regulation of audience knowledge.[13]

'Reel' Pompeii, Nationalism and the Italian Film Industry

The thirty to forty years which preceded the First World War (and witnessed the birth of motion pictures) assiduously created an array of 'invented traditions'. By 'invented traditions', in the terminology of the historian Eric Hobsbawn, I refer to those discursive practices which attempted to establish for a community a continuity with a suitable historical past. The purpose of these traditions was to cement group cohesion and legitimate action through the use of history, and the communities whose institutions, policies and social relations were being established, symbolised or legitimated historically were more often than not the newly formed nation states.[14]

After the unification of Italy in 1861, for example, the problem of assimilating its disparate peoples into a single nation was summarised by Massimo d'Azeglio thus: 'We have made Italy: now we must make Italians.'[15] Needing to justify itself historically, Italy was able to find a major justification in the invented tradition of *romanità*, whereby the origins and legitimacy of the new Italian body politic were found to reside in the ancient civic virtues and military glories of the Roman republic and empire.[16] The invented tradition of *romanità* gave to the heterogeneous Italians a piece of common national history.[17]

In the years preceding the First World War, there was a substantial increase of capital investment in the production of Italian feature-length films. Bound to the dictates of high finance, and to the bourgeois values of its financial backers, Italian cinema began to prosper as an instrument of cultural hegemony. In the logic of its producers, it was thought capable of becoming a means of shaping the cultural horizons of its mass, largely illiterate audience and a privileged instrument for transmitting to them the symbols of Italy's recently constituted national identity. 'Reel' history, the display of Italy's past on screen, became another mechanism for the production and consumption of *romanità*.[18]

What relationship then did reconstructions of Pompeii have to Italian cinema's nationalistic agenda in the period preceding the First World War? Since the unification of Italy, the excavation of the buried city of Pompeii had itself become a part of Italy's nationalistic imperatives. For the preceding century and a half, the city had been treated as a quarry for works of classical art by the various dynasties that had ruled Naples. Under the occupation of the Austrian, Spanish and French administrations, Pompeii had provided prestigious archaeological treasures for royal residences and foreign museums.[19] At the time of unification, the new king, Vittorio Emanuele II, appointed an Italian to oversee future excavations in order to reclaim Pompeii as the cultural property of Italy. The king's visit in 1869 further supplied much-needed publicity and international recognition for a site that could supply a strikingly tangible historical legitimacy for his new kingdom.[20] From the end of the 19th century, the rediscovery and restoration of Pompeii's ancient monuments had taken on a nationalistic, proprietorial imprint.[21]

The technologies of film production employed in *Gli ultimi giorni di Pompei* (Caserini, 1913) offered the film's Italian spectators, therefore, a unique visual pleasure. For audiences were able to witness not only the repairing of the Pompeian ruins and the reanimation of its corpses, but also the replacement of famous ancient artefacts (which were by now dispersed throughout European and American museums) in their 'rightful' locations – that is, in the houses and hands of the Pompeian citizens themselves. In viewing and recognising the film's careful reconstructions of the city's architecture and domestic furnishings, and in identifying with the point of view of the film's hero and heroine, Italian spectators could enact the reclamation of Pompeii and its people as part of their own national heritage.

Such a cultural appropriation of Pompeii through 'reel' history, however, was not without its paradoxes. For the ancient city which was being reclaimed for the Italian nation had, from the very moment of its catastrophic destruction, been locked into narratives which read its burial as a sign of divine vengeance on a sinful people. Various repressions and alterations of Bulwer-Lytton's novel were needed for *Gli ultimi giorni di Pompei* to mesh more comfortably with the cultural identity that was being formulated for the Italian nation in the period around 1913. Thus Christianity has no place in the film as a set of values to be esteemed above those of its pagan persecutors. Nor are sensitive, democratic Athenians set against avaricious, decadent Romans. Instead Pompeii is represented as a community corrupted by a *foreign* evil that the eruption of Vesuvius must expunge.

Once the central characters have been introduced in the opening sequences of the film, it is the priest Arbaces who initiates the narrative proper. He is visually demarcated as Other, a non-Roman. His elaborate head-dress and costume and the architecture and religious artefacts of the temple of Isis within which he attempts to initiate his disciple into the foreign cult identify the priest within the terms of Orientalism as belonging to the racially inferior, decadent East, to the older superseded culture of the Pharaohs.[22] Constantly framed on screen by black slaves, Arbaces is described in the intertitles as a bird of prey who sweeps down on the innocent dove Ione. The priest thus conforms to Western stereotypes of Egyptian savagery, deceitfulness, immorality, animality and perverse sexual dominance. Such devices for the construction of a cinematic Orientalism had particular potency in the period around 1913, for, only a few years previously, audiences in Italian cinemas had watched documentaries on the history and habits of Egypt such as *Paesaggi egiziani* and *Regno dei Faraoni*, in the context of Italy's imperialistic ambitions to conquer territories in North Africa. The death of Arbaces which occurs in the climactic moments of *Gli ultimi giorni* thus conforms with the racist sentiments of Italian imperial policy in the early 1910s.[23]

Gli ultimi giorni di Pompei (1913) simplifies and reshapes the narrative of Bulwer-Lytton's novel to offer its spectators a 'reel' history of Pompeii that takes its audience on a voyage of purification from Oriental contamination. Within this new filmic narrative, the eruption of Vesuvius functions to cleanse a degenerate Italian community which has been degraded by external agencies. The spectacular movement of the Pompeian crowds through the collapsing fabric of their city communicates cinematographically the collective racial fears generated by Italy's pre-war imperial ambitions.[24] Only those can attain salvation who have escaped the corrupting influence of the East.[25] On its release, *Gli ultimi giorni di Pompei* was received very favourably in Italy.

After the First World War, the Italian film industry was beset by crisis. Faced with a European-wide economic recession, the industry's own disorganisation, a substantial increase in costs, an invasion of imported American films and a consequent decrease in the numbers of consumers of the national product, the Italian film industry attempted to monopolise production and the control of its own market through the formation, in 1919, of the Unione Cinematografica Italiana (UCI).[26]

In its attempts to reverse the disintegration of indigenous production, the Italian film industry looked back to the critical and economic success of its earlier 'reel' histories, particularly those exploring the concept of *romanità* . However, it is precisely to this form of cinematic conservatism that much of the subsequent failure of the industry during the 1920s has been imputed. Italian spectators were now far more attracted to the allure of Hollywood imports. Comparison between the products of the Italian and the American film industries exposed the poverty and the provincialism of the Italian 'reel' histories of the 1920s, which manifested scarcely any aesthetic or technical advance over the cinema of the 1910s. From the end of the First World War, Italian 'reel' histories were also of considerably less interest to their own public because they were less subject to the ideological predisposition towards nationalistic readings which had accompanied the genesis and growth of the genre.[27]

It was in this context of the stagnation and collapse of the Italian film industry that yet another *Gli ultimi giorni di Pompei* was produced in 1926 through the assistance of UCI, for Grandi Film at Rome and under the direction of Carmine Gallone and Amleto Palermi. The opening sequences of the film explicitly direct its audience to read this reconstruction of the Pompeian past as having considerable bearing on the present. The camera tracks through the excavations at Pompeii as they would have looked to the tourist of the 1920s. All the monumental public architecture that was destroyed in the eruption appears in fragmented ruins before the gaze of the Italian spectator – the temples, the forum, the amphitheatre, the court-house, and the baths. An intertitle ascribes a moral purpose to the resurrection of the ancient city with which the film is subsequently concerned:

> Pompeii. City of joy for imperial Rome, in the year 79 after Christ was buried beneath a hail of ashes and fire. After 19 centuries, it rises again today, a marvel and a warning to men of the alternations in the human condition.[28]

The visual resurrection of Pompeii which follows is evidently marvellous. The reconstructions of the public monuments and the private dwellings which the film displays demonstrate an extraordinarily fine archaeological exactitude, and the *mise en scène* is littered with recognisable reproductions of famous Pompeian artefacts. This pleasurably authentic reproduction of the ancient city, achieved through the magic of moving images, was frequently commented upon in reviews at the time of the film's launch.[29] What is less evident is the nature of the moral warning which the film proceeds to disclose.

According to the film historian Mira Liehm, this 'reel' history of Pompeii, like the earlier historical films of the 1910s, exalts Italian nationalistic feelings, is permeated with 'the glorification of the Roman superpower' and establishes a 'continuity between the Rome of Caesar and that of Mussolini'.[30] Certainly the film continues and enlarges on the Orientalist strategies of Caserini's *Ultimi giorni*, where West is pitted against East, innocence against evil, the archaeologically detailed replication of the hero's small Pompeian house against the gloriously Egyptianised, vast art deco palace of Arbaces.

The grandeur of Rome's authority also receives momentary tribute when a Roman soldier is seen still on guard duty by a gateway of the crumbling city. The two intertitles at this point read: 'Pompeii is abandoned. Only the legionary stays immobile beneath the fury of the fire and ash, faithful to duty, symbol of the majesty ... of the Roman empire.' Between the two intertitles, the screen is filled with a drawing of those symbols of Roman authority which were to be taken up so potently for the legitimation of the Fascist regime – the eagle and the *fasces*.

146

The dutiful soldier, however, represents only a passing moment of glorification of Rome's majesty. The innocents who achieve salvation are identified unequivocally as Athenian or Christian. Those who die are marked out as Roman aristocrats and attributed with the vices of decadence, effeminacy, cruelty, and avarice. Moreover, within the course of the film's narrative progression to the final catastrophe, the Christian proselytiser Olinthus calls the eruption 'a warning from God to the idolators who live in corruption'. *Gli ultimi giorni* (1926), therefore, can only offer a highly qualified glorification of Rome. The warning to which the opening sequences of the film refers is that any city dedicated to pleasure is bound to be punished in an inferno, in the manner of Sodom and Gomorrah.

If Italian spectators are given the opportunity to identify briefly with the stoic heroism of a Roman soldier, or to assimilate themselves to the moral purity of the first Christians, they are also allowed to revel in the brutality and sensuality of the cultural patrimony of which they are the inheritors.[31] The conception of *romanità* which *Gli ultimi giorni* (1926) offers its audience is doubly ambiguous, for it is through that very brutality and sensuality – the production values of violence and eroticism – that the film attempted to obtain box-office success. Spectacular displays of naked women painting their toenails in the Roman baths, dancing at orgiastic banquets, being flagellated or sexually violated, all these were the visual ingredients employed to sell the film and other 'reel' histories of the 1920s in the absence of any decisive nationalistic imperative by which their narratives might be driven or to which they could appeal.

Having lost the unidirectional nationalistic drive that pertained to many Italian historical films of the 1910s, the 'reel' history of Pompeii produced in the 1920s did not achieve the commercial success of its immediate predecessor. Reviewers, at any rate, were scandalised by the employment of foreign actors as some of the film's principals, a move which had been necessitated by the commercial need to seek foreign financial backing.[32] On its release, *Gli ultimi giorni di Pompei* (1926) even won for itself the deprecatory title of 'the last days of Italian cinema'.[33]

'Reel' Pompeii, the Depression and the Hollywood Studios

The only 'reel' history of Pompeii to be produced in the United States to date was directed by E. B. Schoedsack for the RKO studio in 1935. Although set in the same historical time and place as the Italian versions of the 1910s and the 1920s, Hollywood's *The Last Days of Pompeii* evinces a considerable rupture from the earlier Italian cinematic conventions for the portrayal of the ancient city.

The United States had had recourse to an invented tradition much like that of the Italian nationalistic conception of *romanità* in the early years of the nation's foundation. American national identity had had to be forged out of the mass of its heterogeneous immigrants who were encouraged to participate in a whole host of rituals and historical discourses which commemorated the history of the new nation and rooted it in a more remote past.[34] America was created according to the model of an ideally conceived Roman republic whose civic virtues and conception of liberty were evoked as precedent for and validation of the new republic during the course of the American revolution and thereafter.[35] In particular, George Washington became a focal point of efforts to Romanise American history. In pictures and statues, he was to be seen draped in a Roman toga. In the literature of the period, the 'father of his country' was hailed as another heroic symbol of republican virtues along the lines of the Roman leaders Cincinnatus or Fabius. Such assimilations to Rome then continued to surface in the representational forms of the 19th century, in novels, plays, paintings and pyrodramas.[36]

The American formulation of its relationship to ancient Rome, however, was far more ambiguous, less intimate and ultimately less pressing than the Italian conception of *romanità*. For the Roman empire was almost always conceived of as decadent, enslaving, irreligious and 'Other', and such negative assessments could seep back into and undermine the positive assessments of Roman republican virtue. A certain confusion reigned over the relevance of both republican and imperial Rome to America because America's place within history, unlike that of European nations, was not clearly demarcated. Tangible remains of the past did not litter America's landscape. Furthermore, Americans were very conscious of the uses to which ancient Rome had been put by the European nations in their own cultural and national self-definition. England, too, had constructed itself as inheritor of a Roman cultural patrimony, yet it was from England that America most needed to differentiate itself. Allusions to Rome thus could assume a contradictory quality, and their value as markers of nationhood diminished as America began, in the course of the 19th century, to develop its own more locally rooted sense of history.[37]

By the time of the release of *The Last Days of Pompeii* in 1935, a vast gulf lay between this cinematic reconstruction of antiquity and the earlier urgency with which Rome had been pressed into the service of America's self-definition. Nor could the resurrection on screen of Pompeii's architecture and artefacts constitute the collective reclamation of a cultural heritage viewed as utterly America's own. Looking at visual images of Pompeii was unlikely to generate the intense pleasures of ownership which the Italian 'reel' histories were capable of providing for their own national audience. In the America of the 1930s,

148

therefore, archaeologically detailed 'reel' histories of Pompeii would not have had the same grip on American historical consciousness as their earlier Italian counterparts had had in Italy and would not have been received by the American public with quite the same degree of interest or familiarity. In crossing the Atlantic, not only had the cultural force of Pompeii radically altered but so had the mode of its cinematic reconstruction. Whereas *Gli ultimi giorni di Pompeii* (1926) had harked back to the representational forms of the Italian 'reel' histories of the 1910s, *The Last Days of Pompeii* (1935) was constructed according to a substantially different set of cinematic aesthetics that had been developed and perfected in the United States after the First World War and had gained a wide ascendancy in other markets – a formal system now known customarily as 'the classical Hollywood style'.

Thus, while the educational guide published to accompany the release of the film in the United States makes grand claims to authenticity, accuracy and truth for the film's architectural backgrounds and its displays of ancient costumes and customs, the film offers its own historical authentication through the replication of only two Pompeian public monuments – the amphitheatre and the temple of Jupiter at the north end of the forum. *Last Days* also abandons the earlier Italian films' melodramatic tale of love locked into and beset by a doomed, Orientalised community, in favour of a narrative that concerns individual self-discovery, familial responsibility and personal redemption. Marcus, a hard-working blacksmith, is embittered after the death of his wife and son, and takes up the more profitable, if morally suspect, professions of gladiator and slave trader, but at the moment of Vesuvius's eruption he learns the Christian values of human life and liberty, and sacrifices himself to aid the escape of his adopted son and some runaway slaves, dying finally in the comforting glow of a visitation from Christ himself.

By 1930 the standardisation of Hollywood's products, at which the studios aimed to ensure cost-effective production, involved the modified repetition of popular narratives. Film genres, cycles and serials were institutionalised and 'reel' histories were often structured in ways that corresponded to and gained some of their appeal from narrative genres set in the present.[38] Thus DeMille's *Cleopatra* drew on the success of the director's earlier social comedies and Schoedsack's *Last Days* borrowed from the narrative strategies of a film genre grounded in the era of the Depression, namely the gangster film.

The intertextual pleasures of *Last Days* reside less in a familiarity with current excavations of Pompeii, or with the nineteenth-century representational systems for resurrecting the city, than in the narrational codes of the contemporary gangster film. Especially in its opening

149

sequences, the film reflects the hardships of the Depression era. Initially, Marcus the poor but honest blacksmith proudly declares: 'I have a wife who loves me and a baby son. I work hard, eat heartily and sleep sound. What more could I have?' But he is cruelly robbed of his faith in rewards for hard work and the fairness of the social system when he loses both wife and son in his inability to pay a doctor's fees. Marcus learns from his bereavement that 'money is all that matters and to get it all you have to do is kill'.

Lured by money and its gain through the violent means of the arena and an illicit trade in horses and slaves, the 'Pompeian' Marcus thus takes on the recognisable features of Hollywood's gangsters who are lured into criminality through their desire for wealth and power, but soon learn the futility of their materialistic values and end up punished for their violence. In its dialogue, visual style and narrative development, *Last Days* draws deeply on cinematic rather than historical knowledge. Prominence is everywhere given to its presentist strategies of restaging in the past the hardships of the Depression and in reproducing a contemporary moral tale like that of *Little Caesar*.[39]

By 1930 a revised version of the film industry's Production Code had already proposed that criminals and sinners should not be portrayed sympathetically on screen and that narratives might close with happy endings only if wrongdoers were seen to reform. After the Catholic Legion of Decency was founded in 1934 to campaign against 'immorality' in cinema, the board of the Motion Picture Producers and Distributors of America (MPPDA) immediately endowed the Production Code administrators with greater powers to police the film industry. No film could now be screened by members of the MPPDA unless it carried the Production Code seal of approval.[40] As a highly moralistic gangster film dressed in classical costume, *The Last Days of Pompeii* clearly met the stringent requirements of the new Production Code. But, in conforming to the Code, it offered a historicised moralism without a display of the supposedly pagan eroticism that had marked *Gli ultimi giorni di Pompei* (1926) or the 'reel' histories of antiquity directed by DeMille – *Sign of the Cross* (1932) and *Cleopatra* (1934).

Although *Last Days* drew on *Sign of the Cross* for its representation of arena fighting and the persecution of innocents, it forsook the visual riches offered by DeMille's hugely elaborate imperial sets, costumes and props, and the director's infamous displays of extravagant and sensual consumption. It further jettisoned the use of a visually seductive female character like those played by Claudette Colbert in *Sign* and *Cleopatra*. The women of *Last Days* are humble, homely and pure, not power-hungry, exotic temptresses. Any grandeur which the historical setting of Pompeii might have bestowed on the presentist plot of *Last Days* is undercut by the extraordinary manipulation of past events which was undertaken by the film's makers in pursuit of a crudely constructed moralism – the hero Marcus witnesses both the crucifixion of Christ and the eruption of Vesuvius in a time span which was clearly perceived as totally implausible by the film's reviewers.

Is it appropriate, then, to say of *The Last Days of Pompeii* that it is a historical film written entirely in the present tense? Is the past which it erects on screen arbitrary, a Pompeian 'veneer' which can be chipped away to reveal the Depression lying beneath? Or can a Hollywoodian history of the ancient city have an integrative relationship to American historical consciousness?

It was within the cultural competence of American spectators to read the decadent and doomed Pompeian city as a metaphor for the perceived decadence of modern Europe, precisely because European nations had long since defined themselves in terms of *romanità*. Such an analysis of *Last Days* as wilfully turning the tradition of *romanità* against the very communities which had invented it is supported by a question that was posed to school students in the educational guide which accompanied the release of the film. It reads: 'What form of salute was used by the Romans? In what countries are similar salutes now demanded by the government?'

Such a question requires of the respondent an acknowledgement of the continuity between imperial Rome and Fascist Italy or Nazi Germany and opens up the possibility of extending that sense of historical continuity beyond the moments in the film where Pompeians salute. In *Last Days*, it is not the fear of Orientalism that is buried by Vesuvius's eruption, but the fear of Fascism – metonymically represented by the huge statue of a militant male athlete in the Pompeian arena.

Furthermore, at one significant moment in *Last Days*, Marcus's adopted son, Flavius, speaks to fugitive Pompeian slaves of his vision of escape from the city to an unspoiled world which is still free, where the people are not enslaved, or subject to torture, because they are out of reach of the Roman empire. A reading of that 'unspoiled', 'free' world as a reference to modern-day America was also within the cultural competence of the film's spectators because America had invented a historical tradition in which it dissociated itself from the evils of imperial Rome and aligned itself with the virtues of the Roman republic. Given that, from 1933, large numbers of Jewish émigrés were arriving in the United States from Nazi-occupied Europe, the circumstances of the film's release would have provided further encouragement to read the historiography of *Last Days* as an integrative aspect of the historical text America was then writing about itself and its relationship to the violent conflicts now surfacing on the European continent. Pompeii's cinematic reconstruction was capable of reminding a heterogeneous national audience of the security of being an American.

The Last Days of Pompeii was a commercial flop. The setting of the film could not draw American audiences as successfully as had the Roman imperial courts and Egyptian boudoirs of DeMille's earlier 'Roman' films. The lack of famous historical figures associated with Pompeii may have partially necessitated the film's implausible importation into the city of Pontius Pilate (played by Basil Rathbone as the film's only star of any note). The attention and the expenditure of the RKO studio seems to have been focused largely on the drawing power of the film's special effects – the miniatures, glass paintings, double exposures and stop-motion techniques directed at the realistic display of the volcanic eruption and the collapse of the ancient city. But even here reviewers compared the effects of *Last Days* unfavourably with the earlier work of the same RKO team (Meriam C. Cooper, Ernest B. Schoedsack and Willis H. O'Brien) on the enormously successful film *King Kong* (1933).[41]

Cinema in History

According to the historian David Lowenthal:

> The past remains integral to us all, individually and collectively. We must concede the ancients their place ... But their place is not simply back there, in a separate and foreign country; it is assimilated in ourselves, and resurrected into an ever-changing present.[42]

The aim of this paper has been to explore, through the consideration of three cinematic representations of Pompeii, the place of the past in the ever-changing production and reception of 'reel' histories. It is clear from the preceding analysis that within the institution of cinema the past performs its own specific operations and that those operations are not uniform. The three Pompeian films demonstrate a considerable variety and discontinuity in the rapport they establish between the ancient city of Pompeii and the present moment of its cinematic reconstruction, in the cultural competences on which the films draw, and in the aesthetic pleasures of historical reconstruction which they offer their disparate audiences.

But the project of focusing upon the past–present axis in historical films, the cultural resonance of the historical period selected for cinematic representation and the interaction of that cultural resonance with other discourses that work towards the production of history in cinema, is only one mode of analysis of historical films which has here been favoured over other possible approaches. Even where critics have held in common the project of examining how films have functioned in a culture, their approaches manifest significant differences. To take just two recent examples: an article on early American cinema focuses on the analysis of a single film – *Julius Caesar* (Vitagraph, 1908) – in the context of the wider cultural circulation not of the represented figure 'Julius Caesar' but of the Shakespearean source material;[43] while Sue Harper's book on British costume films of the 1930s and 1940s omits much discussion of the cultural resonance of the various historical settings of the costume films in order to focus predominantly on the general debates then circulating in the press concerning cinema's function as a representation of national history and culture, and on the public institutions of the period which sought to influence the production of historical film.[44] Both studies also pay some attention to the intersection of historical films with issues of race, class or gender. The writing of the history of cinema is thus as diversified as the histories which cinema itself has 'written' on the screen.

Debates about history in cinema inevitably interlock with debates about cinema in history. Both explore how the discourses of history – whether they be film texts or film theories – establish and order their subject. The study of historical film has sensitised film critics to the rhetorical strategies of historiographic discourses more generally. As the writing of the history of cinema has moved away from teleological accounts of cause–effect chains, so critics have noted that earlier theories of film history operated in a manner similar to the strategies of 'classical' historical films – that is, they channelled historical phenomena into neatly bounded narratives.[45]

While historical film has helped to pose questions about the direction to be taken in theories of film history, so those theories now pose further questions for the study of historical film. In particular, critics such as Geoffrey Nowell-Smith have argued first for the need to establish 'a history of subjectivities' through the exploration of specifically cinematic practices, and second to examine the cinematic representation of history in the process of subject formation. In the case of the study of the Pompeian cycle of films, this would necessitate further work on how the films solicit, construct and interpellate spectators into their historical narratives, what cultural repertoires different spectators draw on to make sense of and gain pleasure from the Pompeian reconstructions, and how the films themselves take part in the process whereby traces of the past shape subjects.[46] Thus, in the study of the relationship between cinema and history, we need to hold any analysis of historical film in constant productive tension with an analysis of cinema in history.

Notes

1. *The Last Days of Pompeii* is available for viewing at the British Film Institute, London. The two Italian films in the Pompeian cycle can be seen at the Cineteca Nazionale, Rome. This paper forms part of a larger, book-

length project to examine representations of Roman history (in particular, narratives concerning Spartacus, Cleopatra, Nero and Pompeii) in Italian and American cinema. The book, entitled *Projecting the Past: Ancient Rome, Cinema and History*, will be published by Routledge. As part of this larger project, the British Academy, the British School at Rome and the Wingate Foundation generously provided me with research funding to examine archive materials held at the Cineteca Nazionale, Rome, and to visit the excavations at Pompeii.

2. Marc Ferro quoted in Gianfranco Miro Gori, *Patria diva: La storia d'Italia nei film del ventennio* (Florence: La casa Usher, 1988), pp. 9–10; and cf. Marc Ferro, *Cinema and History* (Detroit, Mich.: Wayne State University Press, 1988), p. 84.

3. See Sorlin quoted in Gori, *Patria diva*, p. 10, and Pierre Sorlin, *The Film in History: Restaging the Past* (Blackwell: Oxford, 1980), p. 44.

4. Stephen Bann, *The Clothing of Clio: A Study of the Representation of History in Nineteenth-Century Britain and France* (Cambridge: Cambridge University Press, 1984).

5. Antonio Costa, 'La traduzione filmica di un romanzo storico: "Il Gattopardo" da Lampedusa a Visconti', *Cinema e storia* (Venice: Quaderni di circuitocinema 34, 1989), p. 3; David Williams, 'Medieval Movies', *The Yearbook of English Studies*, vol. 20, 1990, p. 4; Geoffrey Nowell-Smith, 'On History and the Cinema', *Screen*, vol. 31, no. 2, 1990, p. 163.

6. Cf. Williams, 'Medieval Movies', p. 4, and Nowell-Smith, 'On History and the Cinema', pp. 163–5.

7. Cf. Maria Wyke, 'Make Like Nero!: The Appeal of a Cinematic Emperor', in J. Elsner and J. Masters (eds), *Reflections of Nero* (London: Duckworth, 1994), on the reel histories that centre on the emperor Nero.

8. Stephen Heath, 'Contexts', *Edinburgh Magazine*, no. 2, 1977, pp. 37–43; Philip Rosen, 'Securing the Historical: Historiography and the Classical Cinema', in Patricia Mellencamp and Philip Rosen (eds), *Cinema Histories, Cinema Practices* (American Film Institute Monograph Series Vol. 4, 1984), pp. 17–34.

9. Sorlin, *The Film in History*, p. 21; Gori, *Patria diva*, p. 10. Cf. Denys Arcand, 'The Historical Film: Actual and Virtual', *Cultures*, vol. 2, no. 1, 1974, pp. 24–5.

10. See the discussion of Kracauer's readings in Thomas Elsaesser, 'Film History and Visual Pleasure: Weimar Cinema', in Mellencamp and Rosen, *Cinema Histories*, pp. 47–84. See also Robert C. Allen and Douglas Gomery, *Film History: Theory and Practice* (New York: McGraw-Hill, 1985), pp. 159–60, and Terry Christensen, *Reel Politics: American Political Movies from Birth of a Nation to Platoon* (Oxford: Basil Blackwell 1987), pp. 6–7.

11. See, for example, Arcand, 'The Historical Film', p. 22; Allen and Gomery, *Film History*, pp. 166–7. For a detailed critique of Kracauer see Elsaesser, 'Film History'.

12. Sue Harper, *Picturing the Past: The Rise and Fall of the British Costume Film* (London: British Film Institute, 1994). Cf. Costa, 'La traduzione', p. 3, and Gori, *Patria diva*, on Italian historical films.

13. See Andrew Higson, 'The Concept of National Cinema', *Screen*, vol. 30, no. 4, 1989, pp. 42–3, on 'national' cinema.

14. Eric Hobsbawn and Terence Ranger (eds), *The Invention of Tradition* (Cambridge: Cambridge University Press, 1983). Cf. David Lowenthal, *The Past Is a Foreign Country* (Cambridge: Cambridge University Press, 1985), pp. 44 and 53.
15. Quoted in Hobsbawn, *The Invention of Tradition*, p. 267.
16. Giovanni Calendoli, ' "Cabiria" e il film della "Romanità" ', in *Materiali per una storia del cinema italiano* (Parma: Edizioni Maccari, 1967), p. 108.
17. Gori, *Patria diva*, p. 12.
18. Gian Piero Brunetta, *Storia del cinema italiano 1895–1945* (Rome: Editori Riuniti, 1979), pp. 133–4; Aldo Bernardini, *Cinema muto italiano: arte, divismo e mercato Rome 1910–1914* (Rome: Editori Laterza, 1982), p. 34; Aldo Bernardini, 'Le cinéma muet italien, étapes et tendances', in Bernardini and J. A. Gili *Le cinéma italien de La Prise de Rome (1905) à Rome ville ouverte (1945)* (Paris: Centre Georges Pompidou, 1986), pp. 192–3; Gian Piero Brunetta, *Cent'anni di cinema italiano* (Rome: Editori Laterza, 1991), p. 62.
19. Paul Mackendrick, *The Mute Stone Speaks: The Story of Archaeology in Italy* (London: Methuen, 1962), p. 197; Wolfgang Leppman, *Pompeii in Fact and Fiction* (London: Elek Books, 1966), pp. 49–55; Raleigh Trevelyan, *The Shadow of Vesuvius: Pompeii AD 79* (London: Michael Joseph, 1976), pp. 39–44.
20. Trevelyan, *The Shadow of Vesuvius*, p. 85.
21. Giorgio de Vincenti, 'Il kolossal storico-romano nell'immaginario del primo novecento', *Bianco e Nero*, vol. 49, no. 1, 1988, pp. 16–20.
22. For the discourse of Orientalism generally, see Edward W. Said, *Orientalism* (London: Penguin, 1978).
23. de Vincenti, 'Il kolossal storico-romano', pp. 25–6.
24. Brunetta, *Storia del cinema italiano*, pp. 149–50, and Brunetta, *Cent'anni di cinema italiano*, pp. 67–8.
25. Calendoli, 'Cabiria', p. 78.
26. Bernardini, *Cinema muto italiano*, pp. 26–7; James Hay, *Popular Film Culture in Fascist Italy: The Passing of the Rex* (Bloomington: Indiana University Press, 1987), p. 68; Brunetta, *Cent'anni di cinema italiano*, pp. 128–36.
27. Hay, *Popular Film Culture*, p. 152; Brunetta, *Storia del cinema italiano*, pp. 195 and 270–1; Bernardini, *Cinema muto italiano*, pp. 26–7; Brunetta, *Cent'anni di cinema italiano*, pp. 93–4 and 145–6.
28. See also the account of Gori, *Patria diva*, p. 18.
29. Cf. Jon Solomon, *The Ancient World in the Cinema* (South Brunswick: A. S. Barnes, 1978), p. 54. *La rassegna del teatro e del cinematografo* (Milan, 2 February 1926) spoke of the 'grandiose reconstruction of Pompeii' and the 'perfect architectural reproduction of the city', while *L'Impero* (Rome, 13 February 1926) referred to the 'powerful recollection' of the classical world.
30. Mira Liehm, *Passion and Defiance: Film in Italy from 1942 to the Present* (Berkeley: University of California Press, 1984), p. 10.
31. J. A. Gili, *L'Italie de Mussolini et son cinéma* (Paris: Editions Henri Veyrier, 1985), pp. 24–5; Gori, *Patria diva*, p. 18.
32. See, for example, *L'Impero*, Rome, 13 February 1926.

33. See Solomon, *The Ancient World*, p. 54.
34. Hobsbawn and Ranger, *The Invention of Tradition*, pp. 279–80.
35. Maxwell L. Anderson, 'Pompeii and America', in *Rediscovering Pompeii* (IBM Exhibition Catalogue, Rome: 'L'erma' di Bretschneider, 1992), p. 95.
36. Lowenthal, *The Past Is a Foreign Country*, pp. 112 and 321; William L. Vance, *America's Rome*, Vol. 1, *Classical Rome* (New Haven, Conn.: Yale University Press, 1989), pp. 12–20.
37. Lowenthal, *The Past is a Foreign Country*, pp. 112–16; Vance, *America's Rome*, pp. xix–xx, 30–5 and 62. See also David Mayer, *Playing Out the Empire: Ben-Hur and Other Toga Plays and Films. A Critical Anthology* (Oxford: Clarendon Press, 1994), pp. 1–20.
38. Neil McDonald, 'Portrayals of Capitalism, Class and Crime in the Early American Sound Film', in Anne Hutton (ed.), *The First Australian History and Film Conference Papers* (North Ryde, N.S.W.: Australian Film and Television School, 1982), p. 109; Christensen, *Reel Politics*, p. 27.
39. Derek Elley, *The Epic Film: Myth and History* (London: Routledge, 1984), pp. 20 and 124. For the gangster films of the 1930s see Jack Shadoian, *Dreams and Dead Ends: the American Gangster/Crime Film* (Cambridge, Mass.: MIT Press, 1977) and McDonald, 'Portrayals of Capitalism'.
40. Christensen, *Reel Politics*, pp. 39–40; Izod, *Hollywood and the Box Office*, pp. 105–6; Brian Neve, *Film and Politics in America: a Social Tradition* (London: Routledge, 1992), p. 2.
41. See, for example, *The New Yorker*, 26 October 1935.
42. Lowenthal, *The Past is a Foreign Country*, p. 412.
43. Roberta E. Pearson and William Uricchio, 'How Many Times Shall Caesar Bleed in Sport: Shakespeare and the Cultural Debate about Moving Pictures', *Screen*, vol. 31., no. 3, 1990.
44. Harper, *Picturing the Past*.
45. Heath, 'Contexts', pp. 37–43; Allen and Gomery, *Film History*, pp. 43–7; Rosen, 'Securing the Historical'; Nowell Smith, 'On History and the Cinema'.
46. See in particular Nowell-Smith, 'On History and the Cinema', pp. 168–171, concerning Gramsci's call to construct an inventory of the traces of the past which have been deposited in individuals. Harper, *Picturing the Past*, p. 4, also refers in passing to Gramsci's argument.

FILM AND FEMALE IDENTITY
Questions of Method in Investigating
Representations of Women in Popular Cinema

Janet Thumim

Introduction: Film and Female Identity

In this paper I present the methods I developed for my doctoral thesis, 'Methodological and Critical Problems Arising from the Question of Popular Cinema's Contribution to the Ideology of the Feminine in Britain between 1945 and 1965', which was published as *Celluloid Sisters* by Macmillan in 1992. This work dealt with what are, essentially, questions of identity formation. On the assumption that 'femininity' is a cultural construct I was interested in examining the operation of one important contributor to the social field in which such construction takes place – the cinema. Consequently my focus was on the representations of women in popular cinema, defined by success at the British box office during the post-war period when cinema was the dominant form of mass culture. Before detailing the various elements of the methodology I developed for constructing and analysing my sample set of films, I want briefly to outline some key elements to the question of female identity formation.

My research was concerned with those fictional representations of identity (group identity, individual identities) which appeared to have satisfied their readers and audiences to a significantly greater extent than other available contemporary representations. I was interested in the relation between the individual and the social group or groups in which he or she participates and in particular how this concerned women. This included fictional women, women as individual readers and women as audience members, and entailed looking at the interaction between the two terms – the (fictional) proposition and the (real) addressee and at its consequences for the continuous process of the social construction of gender. This brought me to my specific interest: a discovery of the construction of the 'feminine' in post-war Western society.

Such a concern with the 'feminine' led me immediately in what seemed to be very different directions. Put simply, these are, on the one hand, the sociological and political issue of the subservient position allotted to women in the social power structures and, on the other hand, the psychic and unconscious processes entailed in the formation of each individual woman's subjectivity. It is here, suspended between these two apparently contradictory directions, that the psychically organised 'feminine' becomes the 'feminine other' against which patriarchy's norm, the masculine, is defined. But this separation is, of course, an artificial one, and it is the space where the two meet, where the individual female takes up, refuses or subverts the 'feminine' position allotted to her in the social group, which was my intended focus. This endeavour was important for a feminist analysis of patriarchal culture and its hegemonic work because the 'zone'[1] of mass culture is, for dominant social groups, a privileged space where 'authority does not need to speak politically in order to act politically'.[2]

In order for me to speak, though, I had to separate, to disentangle, the terms on which my questions depended, and here there were pitfalls. I wanted to insist on the multiplicity of discourses informing my approach to empirical materials, to affirm my wariness of the apparent simplicities of empiricism. In the attempt to hold a plurality of thought systems in play simultaneously I risked, of course, overly superficial accounts of these discourses. This risk always accompanies interdisciplinary study, however, and must be taken if the results of scholarly activity are to be of any use in illuminating the confusing web of experience, language, fantasy and desire within which the individual subject has her existence and on which the dominant social group continuously attempts to impose its order. Moreover, it is the point of both critical and scholarly activity, as far as I'm concerned. For female subjects it is a political matter: hence a central objective of feminist scholarship is to uncover the operations by means of which patriarchal hegemony is maintained. In pursuit of this objective feminist critics have turned to psychoanalytic theory, particularly in its explications of the operation of fantasy and desire, both of which play a crucial role not only in the identity formation of the individual subject but also in the conscious and public operation of the culture industries. The usefulness of psychoanalytic theory, flawed though it is, to feminist analyses of identity and of the social construction of gender and other value-laden social structures is in its ability to reveal these processes.

Psychoanalysis proposes that the formation of identity is a radically different process for the masculine and feminine subject because the whole edifice of psychoanalytic theory concerns masculine subjectivity: the feminine is accounted for as difference. But it is invaluable in that it shows how the individual subject internalises the social, reproducing it as the subjective. According to psychoanalytic theory, then, the female subject, taking her place in the social edifice, does so by equating 'I am' with 'I have not'.[3] But the social edifice is a system of interrelated structures of power, language, kinship and property relations all requiring this act of negation on the part of the female subject. It is constructed on the equation penis–phallus, where the phallus, in patriarchal order at least, is not only the 'object of desire' (subjective identity requires the assertion 'I am', wants – desires – the power to know and to say 'I am') but is also equivalent to authority: possession of phallic power confers the right to know, to speak, to name. In this way social unity is mapped over psychic unity. We can consequently picture social unity as a façade constructed in order to meet the hegemonic requirements of patriarchal ideology, a façade which covers up both psychic and social divisions. No matter how perfect, how convincing is the unity of the façade, the divisions it conceals remain active ones in both the psychic and the social edifices. For feminists, the act of negation which patriarchal social structure requires of its female subjects is a fundamental problem. Psychoanalytic propositions explain the mechanics of this negation, as well as revealing its centrality to the inarticulate structures of fantasy and desire which fuel the experience of all subjects. The theory is invaluable in its ability to reveal the psychic divisions on which cultural unity depends, but at the same time unacceptable because it stops short of an explication of the feminine as anything other than the boundary of the masculine. Female subjectivity is denied. Feminist theory therefore attempts to refuse this misrecognition and to remedy this lack.

A major problem for feminist scholars researching the formation of feminine subjectivity is that in drawing, as we must, on the established disciplines of psychology, psychoanalysis and linguistics, we continually threaten to undermine our propositions as they are made by revealing the partisan role played by language itself in the formulation of both questions and answers.[4] But it is not enough just to recognise the repressive functions performed by the languages we necessarily employ in both communication and speculation; neither is it sufficient simply to accept the 'data' of experience as constituting an unproblematic reality to be measured, described, organised.

What is required is constant reference to both these poles, to the repressions of language and to the experience of reality. We mustn't forget that our exploration of the cultural data which describes and orders our identities and our social positioning is in itself a process of meaning production. Toril Moi's warning should be engraved on every computer terminal, every television receiver, over the entrance to every library: 'The real is not only something we construct, but a controversial construct at that.'[5]

My own research nevertheless remains, subject to a conception of reality as a 'controversial construct', an unashamedly empirical piece of work. The concept of empiricism is, in this context, a decidedly shady if not an entirely disreputable one. However, I have used it to signal my attention to tangible traces of cultural activity – popular films and the published discussion which accompanied them.

I approached the 'zone of mass culture' in a historical period, tracing the contours of a small section but remaining aware that the mechanisms I was attempting to uncover were equally likely to be operative in other periods – such as the present. By 'mechanisms' I mean the various ways in which any woman in the audience 'zone' may deal with the meanings proposed in and surrounding the cultural object, because, as Foucault reminds us, 'though membership of a social group can always explain why such and such a person chose one system of thought rather than another, the condition enabling that system to be thought never resides in the existence of the group'.[6]

The interaction between the audience and the cultural object is generally designated as 'reading',[7] but in the terms of feminist work on the politics of gender even the apparently innocent phrase 'any woman in the audience zone' is a far from simple concept. Does the notion 'any woman', for example, imply the legitimacy of considering women in general as a homogeneous and coherent grouping? How, in such a formulation, can other differences between individual women such as those of age, race, class, sexual orientation, wealth, education, occupation be accounted for?

This problem has long exercised feminists since, though it is of course true that all women are not-men, such a generalisation has mischievous consequences, whether discussion centres on the exclusion of women from patriarchal language, or on the organisation of key social institutions such as the family, the relation between capital and labour, and so on. Biologism and essentialism are reductive positions which not only inhibit recognition of the special position of (any) woman but also, through this inhibition, serve to 'naturalise' the inequities of patriarchal social order which rest on biologist or essentialist premises. It is in the day-to-day usage of the terms 'femininity' and 'the feminine' that the complex psychic and social processes of gender construction are conflated to offer a simple and serviceable way of aligning the modes of existence against which the masculine can define itself, since the feminine becomes, within the social, that crucial boundary allowing the form of masculine order. Being a man, a masculine being, can thus be clarified, and the inexplicable feminine can be relegated to the murky regions beyond the boundaries. Hence the ubiquitous cultural and social oppositions – light and dark, sun and moon, public and private – which are mapped onto the primary

160

opposition of the masculine and the feminine. A spurious equality is suggested, 'you can't have one without the other', and the primacy of one term – light, sun, public, masculine – in the social arena is masked.

Rosalind Coward shows how terms relating to sexuality are frequently conflated, with deleterious consequences for the adequate theorisation of any of them. She proposes definitions of sex, sexuality, sexual identity, sexual divisions, and sexual relations, concluding that 'in our society there is an ideological investment to effect the equation between anatomical division and sexual identity. This equation, with its consequences for the lived subjective experiences of sexuality, is the mechanism by which women are subordinated to men.'[8]

The relation between 'lived experience' and language, which lies at the centre of feminist semiotics, is one suggested in the anthropological work of Lévi-Strauss.[9] He conceived of kinship as a system of communication analogous to language. In both cases the elements are the same: these are systems of difference, signs, relations of exchange. The concept 'communication' promises reciprocity, and thus suggests the possibility of integration between the self and others. But in the communications enacted in kinship it is *women* who are exchanged as signs. When this kinship model informs linguistic communication there is a problem for female readers, who must always be confronted with woman-as-sign at the same time (in the same image) as woman-as-woman (like herself). To say 'I am' for the female subject means also to say 'I have (am) not'. It is through close analyses of texts (films, paintings, writing) that it becomes possible to view this finely balanced equation between the representation, woman-as-sign, and the reader, woman-as-person, or, in Coward's phrase, 'between anatomical division and sexual identity', at work. The precariousness of the equation, too, requires that it be continually reconstructed, reasserted. In my attention to popular film texts purveying, as they do, the 'controversial construct of the real' this is precisely what I aim to elucidate.

But the 'audience zone' is also a complex term, exercising both feminist theorists and cultural critics. What does it mean, for example, to refer to 'the female audience'? Is there such a thing? It appears to indicate those members of the collective audience who are female, but it also implies both an entirely female audience, a grouping composed exclusively of women, and a form of spectatorship peculiar to feminine subjects. Both propositions are problematic. In late capitalist society, how can we conceive of the audience, with its implicit suggestion of large-scale groupings, when so much of the audience's primary activity, spectatorship, now takes place, if not entirely in private, certainly in small-scale domestic contexts. Here is the field of sociological and political inquiry, the larger canvas on which the relations of individuals to the state, of workers to employers, of consumption to

161

production, are played out. This is where the semiotic equation is operative in hegemonic struggles which have practical consequences for the lived experience of subjects – men and women. Foucault, excavating thought in the early stages of capitalism (from the 17th to the 19th century), formulates a useful analogy between those paradoxically abstract forms which so dominate us, money and words:

> Money, like words, has the role of designating, yet never ceases to fluctuate around that vertical axis: variations of price are to the initial establishment of the relation between metal and wealth what rhetorical displacements are to the original value of the verbal signs.[10]

The fluctuations of rhetorical displacements are the stuff of hegemonic struggle, and are at their most visible in the public arena of cultural discourses. But for the female subject there is a double displacement, one that Foucault – even in his *History of Sexuality*[11] – makes no attempt to account for. For Foucault sexuality, identity and 'the self' are matters of concern to the individual male subject. Here again is the ideological investment to which Coward draws our attention, the mischievous elision between the multiple terms pertaining to sexuality, which allows the subordination of women to men, and which, within 'the social', assigns to the feminine the task of offering, by a constant negation of self, a constant reassurance to the masculine of its existence. I *am*, he can say (masculine), because I *am not* (feminine). Thus, although the subordination of labour to capital, of consumption to production, of the needs of Third World economies to the exigencies of the Western banking system are all issues with which, in my 'lived experience', I am constantly confronted, it is the subordination of women to men *within* this coterminous set of power relations that concerned me. The audience zone is the space where authority – the dominant group – does not need to speak politically in order to act politically.

These concerns translated into three distinct practical tasks, each requiring a specific and appropriate methodology. I will now give an account of the methods developed in relation to my research on cinematic representations of women, in the hope that they may prove adaptable to other questions concerning popular culture's instrumentality in the maintenance of patriarchal power or, indeed, in other forms of hegemonic struggle. Broadly the tasks entailed selecting a sample group of films, analysing their representations of women and the feminine, and, finally, collecting sufficient contextual material to arrive at a sense of the discursive field within which the

162

filmic representations were consumed at the time of their original release.

Correlating Annual Assessments of Success at the British Box Office

In order to pursue my exploration of popular cinema's routine representations of women in the post-war period, I needed to know which were the most popular films at the box office. There is no simple answer to this question: the popular is not exactly equivalent to the financially successful; neither can it be said to conform to the requirements of any discrete social grouping. Popularity, in the field of mass culture where the popular objects are the product of more or less industrialised processes, is the result of temporary congruences of taste, and the economic success of the product is itself the consequence of these congruences. Drawing general conclusions, making broad assessments of the developments and changes in the popularity of films over an appreciable historical period, as my question required, inevitably involved some method of sampling the possible range of available material. In arriving at a sampling method it is clearly imperative to keep the purposes of the investigation in mind because a method appropriate to one purpose might be meaningless for another. Bordwell, Staiger and Thompson employed random sampling as the basis for their analyses.[12] They took the list published in *The 1961 Film Daily Yearbook* of 29,998 titles released in the United States between 1915 and 1960, and, after 'eliminating all titles not from an American studio', used a random number table to select 851 titles, of which they located 100 for detailed study. They claimed:

> Our selection procedures represent the closest a researcher can come to random sampling when dealing with historical artifacts. The point remains that our choices were not biased by personal preferences or conceptions of influential or masterful films.

Since their project was to define and describe the cultural product loosely referred to as the 'classical Hollywood picture' it clearly made sense for them to develop a sampling method which could remain independent of evaluative judgments and theoretical constructs both contemporary with and subsequent to the production of the films themselves. This is in stark contrast to the claim in the 1986 publicity for the then forthcoming Firethorn Press *International Dictionary of Films and Film-Makers*:

> The selection in this volume has been made by an international advisory board of notable film scholars, critics and archivists.

163

Entries in Films have been selected on the basis of each film's importance in cinematic history and its broad cultural significance.

The work contained a mere 500 entries and could therefore hardly avoid representing a distillation of already existing historical and cultural prejudices about cinema likely to reinforce hegemonic discourse. Charles Barr, in his *Ealing Studios*,[13] avoided the problem of sampling altogether by dealing with the entire output of a particular studio for the whole of its productive life; an appendix lists the credits of all the films produced at Ealing and synopsises most of them. Clearly this was not an option available to Bordwell, Staiger and Thompson, whose object of study comprised some 30,000 films, nor to publishers of the various 'encyclopedias' of films in their attempts to delineate a substantially larger field. Barr's object of study – the exploration of an already defined product – was coherent enough to be susceptible to this degree of thoroughness. Other more general studies tend on the whole to be unashamedly idiosyncratic in their dependence on their author's assumptions. Arthur Knight in his *The Liveliest Art*,[14] for example, assumes that film is indeed an 'art' and proceeds to describe its evolution in terms such as 'style' and 'movement' which are directly borrowed from the histories of the 'high' arts of painting, music, literature and architecture: 'Consequently I have centred this book on what I consider to be key films, pictures that are important not only in themselves but also that seem to summarise a whole style or movement in film history.'[15]

A little earlier, in 1937, Gilbert Seldes asserted the peculiar features of the cinema audience: 'The movie is mass entertainment – and both these words are important because the feeling that a large crowd is sharing one's experience is cherished by almost all human beings.'[16] He characterised his book as a 'guide' for the filmgoer, purporting to distinguish between 'good' and 'bad' products and thus essentially conforming to the paternalist model of culture prevalent in the 1930s and 1940s.

My position was a different one. Like Bordwell, Staiger and Thompson, I wished to explore, as untrammelled as possible by prejudice and assumption, some familiar and well worked terrain. Unlike them, my emphasis was not so much on the product itself – in their case the 'Hollywood' film – but on consumption of the product. My sampling method was therefore required to privilege contemporary assessments of audience preferences. Fortunately, there were further relevant constraints: I was interested in the British audience and, though this inevitably implied attention to the American product, assessments of the American audience were of marginal interest. Therefore, though I noted successes at the US box office, I did not include these in my calculations. Similarly, I noted but did not include the assessments of critics and professional peer groups as evidenced in the American Academy's 'Oscar' awards and the British Academy awards since I found that these had a fairly low correlation with box-office success.[17]

An important issue in all the polls, assessments and top-ten listings published during the period was the state of British production, and the categories employed for assessment purposes often assumed particular attention to this. Since I was concerned with the British audience rather than with the production histories or origins of the films my interest, however, cut across this preoccupation. The evident concern with British production was symptomatic of more general worries about the economic health of the British industry in general during two crucial phases – the immediate post-war period of economic reconstruction and the mid-1950s expansion of broadcast television. Such worries are most evident in *Kinematograph Weekly*'s categories, which varied markedly, hindering a consistent evaluation of the period as a whole. In the interests of such an evaluation I ignored all but the most consistently used categories for the purposes of generating a sample of films for analysis.[18] I was, however, obliged to take account of assessments of popularity expressed in terms of particular stars since these were one of the most consistent categories in all sources. Wherever possible I have recorded the particular film for which an actor/star's performance was cited, and the scoring system I devised takes account of star names in ascertaining the relative popularity of the most frequently cited titles.

I correlated the two annual awards of the fan magazine *Picturegoer*, 'Best Actor' and 'Best Actress'; three of the most consistent categories in *Kinematograph Weekly*, 'Biggest Box Office Attraction', 'Most Popular and Consistent Stars' and 'Best Individual Performance'; and two of the categories in the American *Motion Picture Almanac* attending specifically to the British box office, 'Top Ten Stars' and 'Top Ten Pictures'. All these three sources gave annual accounts of the industry in terms of film titles and stars' names, sometimes, though not always, linked. Given this material there were twelve different ways of calculating the relative popularity of films at the British box office in each year. I tested these methods on one year, 1954, selecting a method which excluded all American listings except those of *Motion Picture Almanac* concerned with the British box office, and all critics' evaluations and awards, but took account of the popularity of named stars at the British box office. I then applied a numerical calculation to each of the years from 1945 to 1965 to yield a small group of markedly more popular films for each year.

The method I used was as follows. Each mention of a film title was recorded as a point on a table for that year. The total number of points for each film was the film's 'score'. A similar process, on a separate table, was undertaken in respect of stars' names. The top-scoring films were then listed and the score for the star(s) appearing in the film, if any, added to the film's score. In practice, the addition of the star score to the film score made little difference in the top two films in each year, but was helpful in distinguishing between the rest of the films recording multiple points on the table for their year of release. Clearly some films and stars achieved duplicated points by this method, because of citations recorded twice, such as *Kinematograph Weekly*'s 'Most Popular and Consistent Star', for which a point was recorded against both the film cited and against the star's named cited in connection with the film. The consequence of this duplication, however, was a magnification rather than a distortion of an already existing difference, and the effect was potentially available to all titles. In practice this method allowed clarification of rather small differences and took account of the important factor of the stars' box-office drawing power – their significance in bringing audiences in to a particular film. A more serious problem concerned the scoring for successful films which were released late in the year, and which therefore tended to appear in adjacent years in different listings. In the year I tested with different scoring methods, 1954, the inclusion of adjacent year's listings made a difference when US box-office listings were included, but not when I restricted my calculations to UK data only. The inclusion of critics' awards, such as those of the American Academy – the 'Oscars' – the British Academy, the Golden Globe, and so on, also made a difference. However, since the method selected excludes both critics' awards and US box-office data it seemed reasonable to ignore listings of adjacent years.

One further problem was the changing context of my sources. The marked decline in cinema audiences in the latter part of the period is evidenced in the 1959 demise of the fan magazine *Picturegoer*. The machiavellian relations between British and American sources of production finance in the declining industry of the later 1950s may well be a factor in the non-appearance of the *Motion Picture Almanac* listings specifically related to the British box office between 1957 and 1962. However, my sample sets of films for analysis were drawn from periods when there were at least two different sources of data available: thus for 1945/6 I used *Picturegoer*, *Kinematograph Weekly*, and *Motion Picture Almanac* (star listings only); for 1955/6 *Picturegoer*, *Kinematograph Weekly*, and *Motion Picture Almanac* (stars and films); and for 1963/5 *Kinematograph Weekly* and *Motion Picture Almanac* (stars and films).

The top-scoring films in each period are therefore, by definition, those which appeared in listings from all possible sources (though not

166

necessarily in all possible categories employed by the sources) relating to their year of initial release. Finally I selected a set of six titles from each of three points in the period, namely 1945/6, 1955/6, 1963/5, from amongst those which appeared in my calculations to be the most popular. The final selection was determined partly by availability and partly by my wish to achieve as much generic diversity as possible in my sample of eighteen films.[19]

I am satisfied that these results represented an adequate assessment of the contemporary box-office popularity of the films listed, in relation to each other, and were thus a sufficiently useful answer to my first question: what were the most popular films at the British box office during the period 1945–1965?

Analysing the Representation of Women

My central questions concerned the operation of popular culture in respect of the social positioning of women. In order to pursue these questions it was necessary to develop methods of analysis which privileged the text, because there is a crucial difference between using texts as evidence with which to substantiate a set of propositions already in existence and drawing propositions from the texts themselves, which thus maintain a primary position in the research. This primary position is justified by the careful and systematic sampling method outlined above.

Each of the eighteen films in the sample was the subject of a discrete and detailed analysis in which a relatively discursive essay was accompanied by a list of all characters, male and female, in their order of appearance, following which the characters were assigned to one of four groups as indicated below. Once this task had been completed for a set of six films, the relative disposition of characters in their groups was compared. Finally, taking all the three sets of six films, the detailed analysis of all female characters in all the films was tabulated according to the schema outlined below, allowing observations about the typical and changeable features of the filmic construction of women and the feminine over the twenty-year period. These observations were the subject of discussion in the main text of my dissertation and *Celluloid Sisters*.

The methods deployed for these sequential analyses were developed apropos another set of six films popular at the British box office in 1954, and it is these methods and their rationale which I want to present here. The six films popular at the British box office in 1954, according to the correlation outlined above, were *The Glenn Miller Story* (Anthony Mann, US, 1954); *Doctor in the House* (Ralph Thomas, UK, 1954); *On the Waterfront* (Elia Kazan, US, 1954); *Hobson's Choice* (David Lean, UK, 1953); *Rob Roy the Highland*

Rogue (Harold French, UK, 1953); and *The Million Pound Note* (Ronald Neame, UK, 1954).[20]

I approached the films in turn, considering no methodological schema for the set as a whole until certain analytic tasks had been completed for each one. These tasks were as follows. I viewed the film, noting its narrative content and development and paying particular attention to all representations of, or utterances about, women. Following the viewing I made a brief synopsis summarising the film and referencing its underlying themes. Then, using my viewing notes, I identified and numbered all the female characters in order of appearance, and wrote an outline of each character recording her initial presentation, her diegetic experience and the extent to which audience complicity with her point of view was constructed through the narrative and *mise en scène*. It became clear during the course of this work that in each film the characters fell quite neatly into clearly defined groups as far as their narrative functions were concerned.

A discussion of characters drawn from a set of films entails the development of a method of differentiation between various characters in one film which makes sense in terms of all the other films in the set. The method cannot, clearly, depend on a generic classification since the films are not all drawn from one genre, nor can it have anything to do with star personae since all the characters are performed by different actors, some well known, some obscure. The directors, studios and national sources of the films are no more consistent. The differentiation must be in terms of the *narrative function* of the character – the work of the character in the unfolding of the narrative – and also in terms of the audience access to the character. It is, after all, the relation between the film and the audience which is at issue: the basis for selection of the sample of films for analysis was their popularity with contemporary audiences as expressed at the box office and via fan magazines. The general inquiry is, precisely, concerned with the dynamic relation between fictional and actual conventions concerning female behaviour – with the social positioning of women and the ideological construction of the feminine. By comparing the narrative functions of characters in all the six films I was able to define four groups by means of which the narrative functioning of all the characters might be described. In the subsequent work with the main sample of eighteen films I also numbered and allocated to groups all male characters, thus enabling recognition of the relative frequency with which male and female characters appeared. I want now to outline the characteristics of each group and then to offer an example from each group to demonstrate how the classification works in practice.

Group 1 characters are central to the film. They are named, they develop or change in some way during the course of the narrative, they are affected by the narrative resolution, and audience access to their point of view *vis-à-vis* their diegetic experience is clearly invited.

Group 2 characters are major though not central. They are named, they are developed during the narrative but they do not essentially change as a consequence of narrative events, they are affected by the narrative resolution and there is some audience access to their point of view.

Group 3 characters are minor. They may or may not be named, they are presented rather than developed and do not change as a consequence of narrative events, they may motivate the narrative but are not affected by its resolution, and there is no audience access to their diegetic experience constructed in the film – the audience is never invited to share their point of view.

Group 4 comprises not so much characters as 'figures'. These are representations either of the category 'women' conceived in general terms – simply as not-men – or of particular groups of women identifiable within this general category. These figures are rarely named, do not participate in narrative events beyond their simple presence and are not affected by the narrative resolution. There is, clearly, no audience access to their point of view. This group also contains those figures who, though they have a diegetic existence in that they are spoken of by other characters, never appear on the screen – the most widespread example being dead mothers.

The 1954 set of films all contained female characters in Groups 3 and 4, and in either Group I or Group 2, with only *Hobson's Choice* having characters in both Group I (Maggie (Brenda da Banzie)) and Group 2 (Vicky and Alice, her sisters).

Group 1: Helen (June Allyson) in The Glenn Miller Story
Helen is a central character. The film documents her marriage to and life with Glenn Miller (James Stewart). We first hear of her during the opening scene, and the final image is of her. At the opening she is young, single, living with her parents and going out with Ed, whom, it is implied, she will marry chiefly because of his dependability in conventional terms – 'I want a man like Ed who's got a factory or something solid. Certainly not a wandering nomad like Glenn Miller.'

Despite this assertion she marries Miller fairly early in the narrative and proceeds to devote herself to him, her care and support being shown to be instrumental in his success. She makes 'something solid' out of the 'wandering nomad'. She both acts and changes during the course of the narrative and she is affected by its closure. This is defined by Miller's death; Helen is left a widow and to some extent custodian of his creation, his 'new sound'. Audience access is constructed to her

169

point of view, though initially modified by Miller's definition of her. When we first see her on the screen answering his telephone call we share *her* response to the call: unlike Miller himself we know that at first she has no idea who he is, and we stay with her after the conversation is over, seeing and participating in her slightly irritated, slightly intrigued response to his insistent invitation. He wants to see her that very evening despite the fact that they haven't met for two years and that she has another date. Throughout the film we have similar access to her own understanding of events as they unfold; we share knowledge with her that other characters do not have. Thus our complicity with her actions is invited. At the end of the last scene a close-up allows us a view of her tears denied to other characters and the film closes with an emblematic shot of her face. She is looking out of a window through which daylight floods onto a photograph of Miller which stands on a small table. Against her cheek she holds the little brown jug he had given her on their tenth wedding anniversary and she listens, with us, to the band broadcasting his new song live from Paris despite his death. At the end of the story the audience is with Glenn Miller's widow.

Group 2: Joy Gibson (Muriel Pavlow) in Doctor in the House
Joy is a major character, certainly the most developed female character in the film, and is frequently on screen. Her character is not developed in the sense that her diegetic experience is explored, but the audience has sufficient access to her to know much more about her by the end of the film. In this sense, then, she is developed. We first see her fairly early in the film when Simon Sparrow (Dirk Bogarde), as a new medical student, is trying to find his way to the lecture theatre. This is the sequence in which the world of the hospital is laid out for Simon's and the audience's inspection, many moments of comedy being based on his misfortunes during his journey to the lecture theatre. Joy Gibson is one of a group of three nurses of whom he asks directions. Their replies are so peppered with medical jargon – here the obscure discourse of the medical profession is offered for our amusement – that he ends up even more confused. In leaving, he drops his suitcase, the contents spill out and the three nurses laugh. It is Joy who good-naturedly helps him to retrieve his belongings. However, despite this suggestion that she differs from the rest of the inhabitants of this hospital world in her helpfulness, neither Simon nor the audience, firmly locked into his point of view, notice her much at this early stage. Later she becomes his girlfriend and during the second half of the film the audience often shares her view of Simon's exasperating naiveté and single-mindedness. An example is in a scene near the end of the film where she and Simon are sitting on a balcony on a moonlit summer's

night. The film cuts straight in to a medium-close-up of the two of them as Simon says earnestly, 'Tell me the answer, please,' and Joy responds, 'Can't you guess?' The location and the story so far encourages the audience to assume that he has just proposed marriage, but this is yet another comic moment: she is in fact testing him in preparation for his final exams. The audience, however, is alerted to her point of view and invited to sympathise with her in the dialogue which immediately follows:

Simon: Joy, I've been thinking. If I do qualify, I shan't be seeing so much of you, will I?
Joy: No, I suppose you won't.
Simon: Are you always going to be a nurse? Be funny if we met some time and you were a Matron and I was a Harley Street specialist.
Joy: Yes.

Her response is accompanied by an eloquent look of resigned exasperation, seen in a medium-close-up, which can be read by the audience but not by Simon. Thus we have a moment of complicity between Joy and the audience, of which there are several during the course of the film. Such moments are, it must be noted, exclusively concerned with Joy's response to and understandings and expectations of the hero of the film, Simon. There are no invitations to explore the life she might enjoy when he is not there. She has the final words of the film, and again these are ambiguous, allowing the audience to savour for the last time the pleasure of a double entendre. Simon has passed his exams and they are all celebrating in the pub when he is called to Casualty – his first assignment as a qualified doctor.

Simon: Will you wait for me?
Joy: Yes, I'll wait.

Whether she is waiting for him to return to the merry-making or whether she is waiting to marry him is unclear but the audience's satisfaction at the narrative's close requires the latter interpretation. It's all right for Joy to wait, for ever.

Group 3: Mrs Hepworth (Helen Haye) in Hobson's Choice
Mrs Hepworth is a minor character, appearing in two scenes. She is an old, authoritative and upper-class woman who commands respect by virtue of both her wealth and her judgment. She is opposed, within the diegesis, to Mrs Figgin, Will Mossop's (John Mills) landlady and mother of Ada Figgin, to whom he is apparently 'promised'. Will's

171

choice is between Ada and Maggie (Brenda da Banzie); if Ada will become like her unkempt and foul-tongued mother perhaps, the film suggests, Maggie will become like Mrs Hepworth. In both of the scenes in which she appears she motivates ensuing narrative development. In the first she visits the shoe shop, demands to know who made her boots, and congratulates Will Mossop on his craftsmanship. Her recognition of Will's exceptional skill, offered to the Hobson family and to the audience, motivates Maggie's choice of him for her husband (and business partner). In Mrs Hepworth's second scene Maggie and Will have visited her at her sumptuous home to ask for a loan to set up their business. Despite the unsuitability of their proposed marriage in class terms, Mrs Hepworth recognises the strengths of their bargain and gives them both her congratulations and the loan. There is no audience access to her point of view but through her presence in these scenes, and implicitly when she is referred to in dialogue at other points in the film, she enables the audience to evaluate the actions of other characters within the terms of the diegesis.

Group 4: The Female Guests at the Lansdowne Reception in The Million Pound Note
This reception is the scene where Henry Adams (Gregory Peck), an American alone in London enjoying temporary possession of the million pound note, is introduced to 'London society'. Without exception the guests are late-middle-aged couples with young adult daughters, and Henry Adams is introduced to and whisked away from them all in turn. The elderly mothers do most of the talking and their subject matter is the special qualities of their daughters. This group of characters, or figures, represents the avaricious English aristocracy anxious to get their hands on American money, and the desire of elderly women to 'settle' their daughters in marriage. Some of these figures may reappear in a subsequent scene, a charity affair, but it is immaterial to the unfolding of the narrative whether or not they are the same people. Apart from their representation of the two diegetic assumptions suggested above, they also act as a foil for another female character, Portia Lansdowne, their collective similarities enabling her difference.

This classification of characters across the six films into four groups allowed for detailed questions concerning the definitions of and assumptions about women as these are structured into the narratives and *mise en scène,* and thence about their possible consequences for contemporary audiences. Three sets of questions followed. I could speculate about contemporary audiences' responses, their readings, by considering audience pleasure and point of view, drawing on theoretical propositions about the reading process. This question entailed consideration of contemporary published material. Secondly, I could ask how many female characters in each film were developed, constructed to invite audience access to their point of view, and affected by the narrative closure: how often, in short, and in what ways female experience was imbricated in the satisfactions the audience was invited to experience as a consequence of the resolution of the narrative. The answer to this question was of particular interest in comparison with sets of films from different moments in my period, since I was in a position to say whether the representation of women in film was more or less consistent or whether there were appreciable changes over time, and what these changes were. The numerical relation of male and female characters on screen was also of interest. Finally, I could ask detailed questions about the particular ways in which women were represented in the sample group of films. I framed these questions as follows. What female roles are represented? How are women presented on screen and what is the narrative significance of various modes of presentation? In what ways are female characters affected by the resolutions of the narratives? This third group of questions required another stage to my analysis, for which I now offer the rationale, again in relation to the 1954 set of films.

Female Characters and Definitions of Women

Articulating the ways in which women are defined in popular film entails, inevitably, drawing on the plurality of discourses by means of which the world outside the cinema is habitually negotiated. I refer to the variety of strategies which enable recognition, more or less successfully, of the heterogeneous social positioning of individuals. This variety can be succinctly reduced to the following main terms: gender, age, class, race, nationality, occupation – and these are indeed the categories routinely called on in representing the self or the other in many discursive modes, including fiction.

In this set of films from 1954 the issue of race did not occur. While this fact was clearly of interest in itself and the absence of definition by race noted, the issue did not concern me further with respect to this group of films. I maintained it, however, as one of the queries in my analyses of the major sample. For this analysis there were three terms – age, class and occupation – to be used in examining characters in these films.

These three terms, 'modes of definition', were all drawn upon in establishing characters in each of the four groups, but their importance varied: the characters in Groups 1 and 2 were defined in more complex ways than those in Groups 3 and 4. I consider next how these different definitive modes were deployed in the four groups, and then I show how they contributed to the development of the narratives.

Female Roles: Occupation and Aims
There were two questions to be considered here. First, how frequently are female characters defined by their aims and/or occupations? I considered the character to be so defined if at any point in the narrative the audience could know what her occupation is or what, if any, her aims or ambitions are. Second, what occupations are represented in this group of films – in other words, when women are seen working on screen, in what kinds of work are they engaged?

Of the ten characters in Groups 1 and 2, four had no apparent occupation. These were Helen (June Allyson) in *The Glenn Miller Story*, Helen Mary (Glynis Johns) in *Rob Roy*, Portia in *The Million Pound Note*, and Stella in *Doctor in the House*. In addition, the occupations of two more characters in these groups were only tenuously defined. Margaret in *Rob Roy* is the mother of the clan chief and maintains the large house which symbolises this position. Crucially and by virtue of her class position she also engages in a limited amount of political intrigue on behalf of her class – defined in the film as the aristocracy of the general group 'Highlanders' opposed to the general group 'English'. Edie Doyle (Eve Marie Saint) in *On the Waterfront* is home on holiday, for the duration of the film's action, from the residential college where she is training to be a teacher. At the end of the film she decides not to return to her studies, thus implicitly giving up her future career. This leaves four characters whose occupations are clearly defined. Three of these are Maggie Hobson (Brenda da Banzie) and her sisters Vicky and Alice, in *Hobson's Choice*, and they all work in the family shoe business. Maggie manages the shop and her two sisters are sales assistants, both emphatically defined by their reluctance to work. The fourth character is Joy Gibson in *Doctor in the House*, who is a nurse. The question of the characters' aims or ambitions was of minimal significance in this set of films, though it was of interest in films in the main sample, where I took account of it in considering the narrative resolutions of characters in Groups 1 and 2.[21] The question is not relevant to characters in Groups 3 and 4 because the audience is not privy to their point of view.

In Group 3 definition by occupation is a factor for about half the characters. Examples are the wife of the restaurateur in *The Million Pound Note* and Mrs Croaker, the landlady in *Doctor in the House*. In Group 4, the most generalised group, about a third of the characters were defined by occupation. Examples are the nurses in *Doctor in the House* and the singers and dancers in *The Glenn Miller Story*.

The second question about occupation concerned the range of occupations represented: when women work, what do they do? Apart from forms of domestic work such as cooking, ironing, and so on, which, it is interesting to note, were seen quite rarely, there were two main forms of work represented. One is managing or participating in a business, such as Maggie's work in *Hobson's Choice*. The other is still broadly domestic but in the guise of paid employment outside the home: here there were landlady, cleaner, maid, hotel staff and, the most frequently occurring category, nurse. Apart from Edie Doyle in *On the Waterfront*, who is training to be a teacher but who we never actually see at work on the screen, the Group 1 and 2 characters whose occupations are defined come into these two categories. So does the majority of work done by the Group 3 characters, the only exceptions being the female examiner and the female medical students in *Doctor in the House* and the absent sisters (we hear about, but never see, them) in *On the Waterfront*, all of whom could be subsumed under the general term 'teacher/student'. In addition to these in Group 4 there were one or two singers and dancers in *The Glenn Miller Story*, one young girl milking a cow and one street pedlar, both in *Rob Roy*.

Generally, therefore, I could say that on the basis of the forms of work represented in this group of films women work in shops, as nurses, as teachers and as performers – in addition to various specialised forms of domestic work.

Class, Race and Nationality

The nuances of class distinction vary, clearly, between different diegetic worlds. In recognising this mode of character definition I called on the class oppositions set up within the diegesis, such as that between Maggie and Will in *Hobson's Choice*, and also on stereotypical representations referring to the extra-cinematic experiential world such as the difference between the duke (representing the aristocracy) and Reddy the hotel maid (representing the working class) in *The Million Pound Note*. The point is that the character is offered to the audience (partly) in terms of her social status, summarised by her class position. The audience is made aware of the class position of both the characters in Group 1: both Maggie in *Hobson's Choice* and Helen in *The Glenn Miller Story* are middle-class within the terms of their respective diegeses, as well as conforming to stereotypical representations of the middle class evident in other cultural forms. In Group 2 we are aware of the class position of six of the eight characters: of the other two, one – Stella, in *Doctor in the House* – is 'foreign', having an unspecified European accent which renders her class position unreadable. John Hill references a similar effect in his discussion of the character played by Simone Signoret in a later film, *Room at the Top* (Jack Clayton, UK, 1958), in which he notes the use of a foreign actor to represent a character whose class position needs to be ambiguous for narrative purposes.[22] The other Group 2 character, Joy Gibson in the same film, is primarily defined by her occupation. Her accent and her implied future marriage to the newly qualified doctor do situate her in the middle class but this fact is subordinated, I would argue, to her classification as 'nurse'. Definition by class in Groups 3 and 4 tends to be an alternative to definition by occupation. We are aware of the class position of half the characters in Group 3 and only one-fifth of those in Group 4. Race, as I have noted, is not an issue in any of these films and nationality, similarly, is barely at issue, with the exception of the 'foreign' Stella in *Doctor in the House*, noted above. This is to say that in British films all the characters are British or, in the case of *Rob Roy*, English and Highland Scottish – and in the case of the American films all the characters are American. This may well include 'Irish American', as in some characters in *On the Waterfront*, but the point is that no characters, within the respective dieceses, are considered to be of another nationality, or 'foreign'.

Age and Sexual Status
This was both a more complex and a more interesting question. The first observation to be made regarding the representation of women is that in most cases not only their age but also their sexual and/or familial status were major factors contributing to the definition of individual characters. For all the characters in all groups are defined by either their age or their sexual status, many being defined by both these terms. The interdependence of these terms, moreover, requires that they be discussed together.

Apart from Maggie in *Hobson's Choice*, whom we know to be thirty, who is defined by her father as an 'old maid', and who marries during the course of the film, thus becoming a bride/wife, all the characters in Groups 1, 2 and 3 are single young adults, married mothers of young adults, or unmarried women of similar age fulfilling a comparable function in respect of young adults (Sister Virtue in *Doctor in the House* is an example of the latter) or they are old, or dead. The only exception to this rule in this set of films is Helen in *The Glenn Miller Story*. She begins as a single young adult defined as a daughter, and ends after the fifteen years covered by the narrative as a married woman with small children. But it is interesting to note also that June Allyson does not 'age' in the part: though we know by inference that she is fifteen years older at the end of the film, we do not see this. Her clothes and dress style change, but she looks the same at the opening and close of the narrative. By contrast James Stewart and other male actors do look convincingly older by the end of the film.

Group 4 characters, despite being generalised representations –

176

'figures' – rather than characters, were still primarily defined in two-thirds of cases by either sexual status or age, with age predominating as the defining characteristic. The absence of developed characters aged between, roughly, the mid-twenties and the mid-fifties was striking.

Modes of Presentation and Narrative Significance
There were five identifiably different ways in which characters were initially presented. First among these is the *appearance* of the character, her dress, her bearing, physical condition, and so on, and this is the mode most affected by the audience's possible recognition of a well-known actor, or a star. If a star is recognised it seems probable that the star persona will become an important element in the audience's understanding and expectations of the character. Second, there was the *location* of the character. The surroundings in which the character is situated will suggest certain readings of the character which may or may not be (but generally were) substantiated as the narrative unfolds. These two modes, the appearance and location of the characters, both depend on the audience's coding of their visual perceptions. Third, characters were presented in terms of their *actions*, and, fourth, via their *speech*. I do not wish to enter into a semantic discussion about whether or not speech could be said to be a form of action, merely to assert that in practice, as my analyses showed, this was a useful division since one or other generally predominates. Both these modes entail the fictional character's own presentation of herself to the audience. Finally, characters were frequently offered to the audience initially by means of the *utterance of another character*. In this case the audience's understanding of the new character will be modified by their positioning *vis-à-vis* the already known character, subject as this will have been to all the same modes of presentation outlined here.

To summarise, I found that five different ways in which characters are initially perceived by the audience, on which audience readings and expectations initially depend, can be subsumed into three. These are the *appearance and/or location*, the *self-presentation by action and/or speech*, and the *introduction by another character*.

The characters in Groups 1 and 2 were of particular interest since these are the ones to whom some audience insight is constructed – we may have access to their private moments, their motivations and the consequences for them of the narrative's unfolding. The two Group 1 characters, Maggie in *Hobson's Choice* and Helen in *The Glenn Miller Story*, were offered to the audience predominantly through their appearance and location, but also through their introduction by another character. They do also both speak at their first appearance on screen but I would argue that their speech is subordinate to the other two modes as far as the audience's initial understanding of their characters is concerned.

We first meet Maggie early in the film when her father, played by Charles Laughton, returns drunk to their home above the shoe store. We share his point of view, looking up at Maggie standing in a long white nightgown, her hair in plaits, a shawl around her shoulders, halfway down the staircase which leads to the showroom he has just entered, noisily, from the street. She scolds him for his drunkenness, but she is defined *by* him for the audience when he responds with 'You're a proper old maid, Maggie.' In *The Glenn Miller Story* the central female character Helen is introduced to the audience by Glenn Miller (James Stewart) some time before we actually see her. In the pawnshop at the opening of the narrative he asks about a string of pearls which he would like as 'a present for my girlfriend'. We soon learn that despite this appellation he has not seen her for two years. Slightly later in the narrative we see him in a phone booth and the film then cuts directly to a shot of a young woman running down the stairs in the home where she lives with her parents, to answer the phone. This introduction invites us, the audience, to privilege Glenn Miller's definition of her as 'his girl' despite the fact that she does not, at first, remember who he is and is also, as we soon discover, engaged to someone else. Group 2 characters are all offered through their appearance and/or location, but in several cases this is importantly modified by their self-presentation through action and/or speech. It is also important to note that without exception the characters in this group, considerably larger than Group 1, are all initially defined for the audience either at their first introduction or soon afterwards by another (male) character. Edie Doyle (Eve Marie Saint) in *On the Waterfront* is first seen in a rear-view medium shot at night outside the tenement building where she lives, crouching over the body of her dead brother. Her loose blonde hair stands out strikingly amid the general confusion and darkness of the image, and the film cuts to a medium-close-up of her and the priest (Karl Malden): she refuses to be comforted by him and accuses him of 'hiding' in the church. It is she herself who announces to us the question that will drive her through the narrative, 'Who killed my brother?', a question to which the audience already knows the answer. But it is her father's angry speech in the following scene at the morning hiring session which tells the audience who Edie is:

to Edie: Now get back to the Sisters where you belong.
to the Priest: I'm surprised at you Father, letting her see things that ain't fit for the eyes of a decent girl.

178

Edie, her father tells us, is a 'decent girl', which means that certain events familiar to the community are not 'fit' for her eyes. In other words, because she is 'decent' she must be protected from knowledge of some of the more problematic aspects of daily life as experienced by the men of the community.

Helen Mary (Glynis Johns) in *Rob Roy the Highland Rogue* is initially seen as one of the many Highlanders in the second scene where the men are returning from battle. It is only her star persona that enables the audience to single her out from the others as a character to whom they should pay special attention. Before the scene at her parents' inn, in which she presents herself to the audience by enacting a swashbuckling story and then by helping her mother in the kitchen, we have already been alerted to her narrative significance by the conversation between the hero, Rob Roy (Richard Todd), and his mother, Margaret (Jean Taylor Smith), about 'settling down'. The film cuts from this exchange to Helen Mary's performance at the inn, which is completed by Rob's arrival. Thus both Edie Doyle and Helen Mary are offered to the audience in relation to the male heroes of the film. The same is true of all other characters in this group.

In Group 3 the principal mode of presentation was through appearance and location, though location tended to predominate over appearance in so far as these can be separated. Only about half the characters offered themselves via their speech, and none by their actions. None of the characters in this group was qualified by definitions given by other characters. This absence is also true of the figures in Group 4, where, once again, the primary mode of definition was through appearance and location, a small minority being also defined by their action – for example the cleaner and many nurses in *Doctor in the House* and the performers in *The Glenn Miller Story*.

Narrative Development and Narrative Resolution
The striking absence of developed characters between the ages of the mid-twenties and the mid-fifties, noted above, becomes even more significant in terms of the definitions of women offered in these characterisations once the diegetic experience of central and major characters (Groups 1 and 2), to whose point of view audience access is constructed, is considered. For all except one of the ten characters in these two groups narrative development entails a change in sexual status: that is to say that they are initially represented as single young adults and by the close of the narratives they are either married or promised to – committed to marry – a particular man. In seven out of ten cases the man is a central male character, usually the 'hero' of the film. The exception is Margaret in *Rob Roy*, who is Rob Roy's mother and who dies during the course of the narrative. Thus, in these six

179

films, the central and major female characters end up married or dead. In addition, of the five Group 1 and 2 characters who are defined as having an occupation, only two maintained their occupation beyond the point of marriage. One of these is Maggie in *Hobson's Choice*, who began the film as the single daughter managing her father's business and ended it the married partner managing the same business, now jointly owned by her husband and her father. The other is Joy Gibson in *Doctor in the House*, a nurse, who is still a nurse at the close of the narrative, though by now her definition as a future doctor's wife predominates.

Summary
How are these analytic terms useful in summarising the representation of women in films popular at the British box office in 1954? In this set of six films women are typically defined as follows: not only do they act in relation to a particular male character, typically in serving the interests of the male, but also professional female occupations can be largely subsumed under the general heading 'service'. Women either manage or assist in shops and businesses, they are nurses, teachers, or entertainers. Women never change their occupation or their class position, and they are always either young or old. Narrative resolutions offer only marriage or death for women. The central thirty years of women's lives are not represented on screen.

There were some additional observations to be made about the representations in this set of films: given the central presence of women's domestic functions it is remarkable how limited these appeared to be from the evidence of their depiction on screen. We see female characters preparing and serving food, such as Helen in *The Glenn Miller Story*, Vicky and Alice in *Hobson's Choice*, and Helen Mary and her mother in *Rob Roy*. Less frequently we see some of them ironing, and once – Margaret in *Rob Roy* – we see curtains being hung. Occasionally we see them having care of children. Childcare, however, was simply shown in terms of holding the child's hand, pushing a pram, or merely being in the same space as the child: none of the very varied activities which this form of work actually entails was represented.

There were almost no representations of any significance of relationships between women. The exceptions to this are Margaret and Helen Mary in *Rob Roy*, and Maggie, Vicky and Alice in *Hobson's Choice*, both of which can be subsumed under the general term 'family'. Margaret is Helen Mary's mother-in-law, Rob having entrusted her to his mother's care when he is taken prisoner during his wedding feast. Maggie is elder sister to Vicky and Alice and in addition is explicitly required by their father to occupy the position of

180

mother to them since she is not only the eldest but also, as he says, the one with the most sense. Reference to popular film from other periods shows how striking is this absence of any female camaraderie in films from the 1950s: the support and affection existing between Mildred (Joan Crawford) and Ida (Eve Arden) in *Mildred Pierce* (Michael Curtiz, US, 1945) being one example.[23]

A final observation remains to be made. Of the six films in this 'pilot' study four take place in the past: *Hobson's Choice* in nineteenth-century Salford; *The Million Pound Note* in Edwardian London; *Rob Roy the Highland Rogue* in eighteenth-century Scotland; *The Glenn Miller Story* during the fifteen years preceding Miller's death during the Second World War. The period of *On the Waterfront* is slightly ambiguous but can be understood to be contemporary, and *Doctor in the House* is unambiguously contemporary. The conflict over value structures which is the unifying thematic factor of these films was represented, then, in contexts explicitly defined as *other* than that of the audience; in the one film taking place in contemporary Britain, *Doctor in the House*, representation of the path of the hero from student to qualified doctor predominated over that of social conflicts. Innocence and experience are opposed here rather than 'them' and 'us', or good and bad. All the oppositions constituting the thematic centres of these films, however, were played out through male rather than female characters.

A Note about Discursive Contexts

The third and final procedure was the collection and collation of discursive materials.[24] I collected reviews from a range of sources, including specialised trade papers, film journals and fan magazines, national press and women's magazines. Though the greater part of the material was British I did also look at some American and French publications in order to get a sense of the discursive 'climate' in a period when there was considerable traffic between these three countries both of films and of publications relating to the cinema. By surveying the language and content of reviews or related discussion of my sample films I was able to get some sense of what aspects of the films – their themes, their resolutions, their characterisations – were admired or thought contentious and, further, whether there was any unanimity on these points. Admiration, it seemed to me, signified agreement with the appropriateness of the issue in question and might be expressed through praise of a performance.[25] Conversely, denigration of performance frequently masked disapproval of a narrative trajectory, of the aims or experiences of a character.[26] Where there was widespread agreement among different sources regarding the critical assessments of film and performance I took the points in question to be the subject of widely held assumptions undisturbed by their filmic portrayal, but where I found radical disagreement it seemed to me that I had evidence of something which was currently under scrutiny, the subject of debate or unease, something in flux in society as a whole.

Conclusion
Through the tasks outlined here I was able to move from the fine detail of particular films – even of scenes or images within one film – to speculation about the significance of such details to the audiences who found them pleasurable and therefore, I would argue, useful. Having completed the research, I was in a position to compare the dominant thematic concerns of the three decades, among which there were some intriguing differences. The 1940s films typically dealt with the moral problems experienced by female protagonists in their relation to contemporary social structures. There were markedly more central female characters in these films, which also had in common their narrative assertion of the primacy of the family as the fundamental social structure. By implication, therefore, the women on whose moral dilemmas the narratives centred were deemed responsible for the maintenance of the family. Central to the 1950s films, in stark contrast, was an exploration of the various groupings within society, often perceived as existing in uneasy alliance, but nevertheless constituting the nation through their necessary unity. Unlike the 1940s films these individuals, invariably male, served primarily to exemplify discrete social groups or ethical positions, and were of interest in such terms rather than as a consequence of their individual dilemmas. Another change is evident in the common themes of the 1960s films, in which there was a general emphasis on playfulness and innocent pleasure of various kinds and the established structures of society were represented as repressive constraints on the all-important freedom of the individual. The acceptability of such constraints was measured by their authenticity – the degree to which they could be understood to be 'real' in terms of the emotions and desires of the (invariably young) individual protagonist. The personal was opposed to the collective, and tradition usually impeded the proper expression of the new: in general this conflict was expressed as a conflict of generations.

Looking in more detail at female characters, I noted the hegemonic models of gender relations in each of the three decades and was also able to observe both shifts and consistencies in the typical representations of women from central protagonists to the 'diegetic furniture' peopling the screen. It was striking that in these popular film texts there was a far narrower view of women than a panoramic study of social history might be expected to yield. Even on a simple numerical level I found a remarkable imbalance in representations of men and women in the eighteen films, which would seem to detract seriously from any claims the popular cinema may make for verisimilitude.[27] On this score, at least, these popular texts did not conform to the realities of the world outside the cinema. Definitions of characters, gradually built up through the course of the film, were more likely to refer to class position than to race or nationality, and, until the mid-1960s, when a wider range of social classes was routinely represented, the middle class predominated. A far more crucial indicator of the social positioning of the female characters than class, however, turned out to be their age and sexual status. Here there was an overwhelming preponderance of the young adult age group, with such older women as did appear being generally represented as inherently problematic and often disruptive. The sexual status of female characters was almost always carefully delineated and the conventional path from virgin to bride to mother was the happy lot of characters with whom the audience was invited to sympathise. Those few characters who attempted either sexual or economic independence were usually compromised in the narrative closure, if not before. There were three main aims expressed by the various central and major characters: seclusion, power or marriage. The first two were implicitly condemned in the preferred reading urged on the audience through the construction of the narrative and the last affirmed as an appropriate and praiseworthy goal for a woman.

Most interesting of all, in comparing the narrative resolutions of female characters in the eighteen films, I was able to explore in detail the mechanics entailed in the cinematic operation of patriarchal hegemony, particularly those narrative and visual strategies used in securing the collusion of female subjects in their subordination to the masculine. The range of narrative closures deployed to resolve female characters was limited and, moreover, invariably related more to gender, to the fact of being a woman, than to the particular contours of each diegesis. Thus, whether the tale is set in the Britain of the seventeenth century or in the United States of the nineteenth century, in Edwardian London or in contemporary America, it seems that the denouement, for female characters, must always turn on the degree to which they can be shown to have conformed to specific meanings of the signifier 'woman' in patriarchal discourse.

While I might simply have discovered what was obvious in the first place – that women are charged with the maintenance of the family, that marriage is patriarchy's preferred goal for women, that transgressive women will be/must be punished – it *was*, nevertheless, a discovery, because I had arrived there by a systematic process attending first to structure and only then to the qualitative and contestable material constituting the field of interpretation. I am confident that such an approach helps to demonstrate how apposite are both Toril Moi's remarks about 'the controversial construct of the real' and Michele Mattelart's suggestions concerning the 'zone' of mass culture where, as she says, authority – in this case patriarchal authority – does not have to speak politically in order for its utterances to be politically effective. My scrupulously careful pursuit of the obvious, the methodology of which I have outlined here, seems to me to have been justified because it has revealed the ubiquitous processes through which the seemingly innocent, 'entertaining' material of popular culture is engaged in policing the boundaries of the masculine and maintaining the subordination of women.

Notes

1. Michele Mattelart, *Women, Media and Crisis: Femininity and Disorder* (London: Comedia, 1986), p. 24.
2. Ibid.
3. Freud postulated a psychic development which depended heavily on the opposition presence–absence, or possession–lack (of the penis, though not, simultaneously, the phallus) in the subject's earliest recognition of his or her position in the primary social division by gender. Thus the very notion of desire (and of fantasy in its work of imagining satisfaction) was dependent on the curious assertion that the little girl, on perceiving the penis, experiences herself as incomplete, and that concomitantly the little boy on perceiving the little girl's (or his mother's) more discrete genitalia experiences the sight as a threat since he assumes that she must have lost her penis – hence its loss is a horrific possibility. Whereas for the boy 'I am' means 'I have', for the girl 'I am' is required to mean 'I have not'.
4. Foucault suggests that the consciousness of self, the 'self-consciousness', which lies behind the development of the human sciences in the 19th century is 'an event in the order of knowledge', that is, a radical epistemological break, and he points directly to the major problem which must eventually be the consequence of such a self-conscious inquiry: 'They [psychoanalysis and ethnology] ceaselessly "unmake" that very man who is creating and recreating his positivity in the human sciences' (*The Order of Things*, London: Tavistock and Routledge, 1989, pp. 345 and 379).
5. Toril Moi, *Sexual/Textual Politics: Feminist Literary Theory*, (London: Methuen, 1985), p. 45.
6. Foucault: *The Order of Things*, p. 200.
7. See Volume 1 of my dissertation and also Janet Thumim, *Celluloid Sisters* (London: Macmillan, 1992).
8. Rosalind Coward, *Patriarchal Precedents* (London: Routledge & Kegan Paul, 1983), p. 286.
9. Claude Lévi-Strauss, *Structural Anthropology* (London: Penguin, 1968).
10. Foucault, *The Order of Things*, pp. 202–3.
11. Michel Foucault, *The History of Sexuality*, Vol. 1, *An Introduction* (London: Allen Lane, 1978); Vol. 2, *The Use of Pleasure* (London: Pen-

guin, 1987); Vol. 3, *The Care of the Self* (London: Penguin, 1990). Foucault's assumption that the self is male is clear in the titles of the second and third volumes, both of which are exclusively concerned with the problem of the masculine in the social.

12. David Bordwell, Janet Staiger and Kristin Thompson, *The Classical Hollywood Cinema: Film Style and Mode of Production to 1960* (London: Routledge & Kegan Paul, 1985).
13. Charles Barr, *Ealing Studios* (London: Cameron & Tayleur, 1977).
14. Arthur Knight, *The Liveliest Art* (New York: Mentor, 1959).
15. Ibid., p. vi.
16. Gilbert Seldes, *Movies for the Millions* (London: Batsford, 1937), p. 9.
17. See Janet Thumim: 'The "Popular", Cash and Culture in the Post-war British Cinema Industry', *Screen*, vol. 32, no. 3, Autumn 1991, for a fuller discussion.
18. Ibid.
19. *The Bells of St Mary's* (Leo McCarey, RKO, 1946) US; *Brief Encounter* (David Lean, Cineguild, 1946) UK; *Madonna of the Seven Moons* (Arthur Crabtree, Gainsborough, 1945) UK; *Piccadilly Incident* (Herbert Wilcox, ABP, 1946) UK; *The Seventh Veil* (Compton Bennett, Theatrecraft, 1945) UK; *The Wicked Lady* (Leslie Arliss, Gainsborough, 1946) UK.

    The Dam Busters (Michael Anderson, ABPC, 1955) UK; *Doctor At Sea* (Ralph Thomas, Rank, 1955) UK; *East of Eden* (Elia Kazan, Warner Bros., 1955) US; *Reach for the Sky* (Lewis Gilbert, Rank, 1956) UK; *Rebel without a Cause* (Nicholas Ray, Warner Bros., 1956) US; *The Searchers* (John Ford, Warner Bros., 1956).

    Goldfinger (Guy Hamilton, UA/Eon, 1964) UK; *A Hard Day's Night* (Richard Lester, UA/Proscenium, 1964) UK; *Marnie* (Alfred Hitchcock, Universal, 1964) US; *Mary Poppins* (Robert Stevenson, Disney, 1965) US; *Summer Holiday* (Peter Yates, ABP, 1963) UK; *Tom Jones* (Tony Richardson, UA/Woodfall, 1963) UK.

20. The set included lower-scoring titles than those in the main sample to ensure that my analytic methods should be appropriate to as wide a range of films as possible.
21. See Thumim, *Celluloid Sisters*, chapter 5.
22. John Hill: *Sex Class and Realism: British Cinema 1956–1963* (London: BFI, 1986).
23. There are, of course, many exceptions to this broad generalisation among the popular titles of the 1950s. *Calamity Jane* (David Butler, 1953) is typical of these in that the narrative constructs the central female friendship as clearly subordinate to heterosexual romance.
24. I did this only for the main sample of eighteen films. The 1954 set was used to derive the methods of textual analysis outlined in this paper.
25. For example Kate (Jo Van Fleet) in *East of Eden* (Elia Kazan, 1955), whose unsatisfactory mothering was suggested to be a prime cause of the hero Cal's (James Dean) distress, came to a sad end: her performance was widely praised, suggesting that her fate was thought to be deserved.
26. For example Barbara (Margaret Lockwood) in *The Wicked Lady* (Leslie Arliss, 1945), and Marnie (Tippi Hedren) in *Marnie* (Alfred Hitchcock, 1964).

27. Having counted all male and female characters, as outlined above, I found that in the mid-1940s the gender balance was even, in the mid-1950s male characters outnumbered females by 2:1 and in the mid-1960s the proportion was 3:2, male to female.

RESEARCHING AFRICAN TELEVISION

Claire Monk

Prologue: Four Discourses about TV in African Countries

National TV stations were established by most of the African countries after independence, who began in the main to design and
determine their own media institutions ... These new national
assets ... were regarded generally as the 'voice of the nation' and
would be harnessed in the cause of autonomous development.
Needless to say, as in every country around the world, the organisation of the TV medium reflects [the nation's] political and economic philosophy. This is often reflected in the extent to which the
medium is state-controlled and to which there is scope for independent commercial access to 'the masses' via television. However,
these similarities belie a range of differences that become apparent
when one begins to focus on the experiences of the development of
TV in individual countries ... (June I. Givanni, 1992)[1]

In N'Zikpli, a small village without electricity in central Côte
d'Ivoire, the elders of the community were asked what they had
learned from the battery-powered television the government had
installed in the local school in 1974. After explaining, through an
interpreter, that they had learned a lot about life outside the village,
the men were asked if they had any questions about what they had
seen. The chief was the first to speak: 'Is it true that the white man
can fly without wings?' 'Why are whites always stabbing, punching
and shooting each other?' another man asked. (Iain McLellan,
1986)[2]

Are you going to show programmes that are copies of western
programmes, or programmes where the set is falling down?
(Concerned media development academic, April 1994)[3]

Basically what we're looking for is clips for Clive to turn into a joke.
(Anonymous BBC employee on the Clive James programmes when

asked about their selection criteria for the TV clips from other cultures used in the series, May 1994)[4]

Introduction

This paper is derived from research I conducted at the BFI for the purpose of programming 'Adjust Your Sets', a season of African television held at the National Film Theatre in London in October 1995 as a part of the Africa 95 festival of African arts and culture. While my primary aim here is to consider what we actually mean by 'African Television' and to subsequently examine debates about the role of television in developing countries, I will also touch upon some of the ethical and practical problems entailed in programming such a season.

The initial problem I faced was not, as I had anticipated, that in Britain we have only negative images of African television, but rather that most of us have no images of it at all. It hardly needs stating that the exposure of British audiences to TV from African countries is virtually non-existent. With the exception of the recent interest in the South African media shown by the BBC and Channel Four in their coverage of the run-up to South Africa's first all-race elections,[5] the sole example of television from an African country which I (or anyone I spoke to) can recall ever seeing on British television was a clip showing the supposedly meagre prizes on offer in the Nigerian quiz show *Take a Trip* used on LWT's *Clive James on TV* in 1982.[6]

While this 'blank screen' placed a heavy responsibility on the season, it was also an important opportunity to think about African television in terms of its hybridity, diversity and unexpectedness rather than its 'problems'. During my research I encountered many examples of African programming, some stodgily propagandist, studio-bound and turgidly acted, but others creative and resilient, producing professional, engaging and culturally distinctive work on a tight budget. While a few programmes featured trailing microphone leads and visible cameramen, I didn't see any sets falling down. And the only show I saw which could be classed as an outright copy of a First World format – *Caméra Caché*, Tunisia's version of *Candid Camera* – nevertheless asserted its local cultural specificity when it was interrupted without warning by the call to prayer.

I also quickly became aware that African TV had been as marginal an interest for First World media academics and commentators as it was for First World audiences. My research uncovered only ten articles published on the subject in the major European and North American media journals and trade papers since 1977.[7] Of these, two focus on African countries solely as an export market for First World programmes, one demonstrates a similarly hegemonic interest in the arrival of TV in Swaziland, Namibia and Bophuthatswana, and one is purely statistical. In addition, in contrast with the range of recent publishing on African and black diasporic film, no English-language book on TV and the mass media in African countries has been published since 1986.

While the public-service broadcasting model – government-funded or subsidised, and in many countries closely government-controlled without the distantiation or 'impartiality' written into the BBC's charter – was universal among African television institutions by the mid-1980s, these institutions have undergone substantial changes over the past decade. Most commonly, diminishing government funds and sometimes increasingly loose government control have brought shifts from state to 'parastatal' structures and pushed broadcasters into finding commercial funding through programme sponsorship or advertising, with variable success. The most widespread change (and challenge) for African state broadcasters has been the need to respond for the the first time in their history to competition in the form of the new – and expansionist – private satellite and pay-TV operators on the continent.[8] Clearly then, my research had to address the question of African television's changing institutions as well as examining programmes.

Definitional Difficulties: What Do We Mean by 'African television'?
The term 'African television', while serving as a useful piece of shorthand, is problematic in several respects. Though the extent and limits of 'African television' for the purposes of the season were to some extent demarcated for me at the outset of my research,[9] the vast cultural differences between African countries and the realities of programming and programme production *in practice* make it necessary to interrogate the term further.

National Cultures: Historical Similarities, Local Differences
On one level, to collapse the TV institutions and programme production of forty-five culturally, linguistically, politically and religiously diverse countries[10] in a geographically vast continent into a single entity called 'African television' is not only obviously absurd, but could also be argued to perpetuate the First World tendency to think and talk about Africa in precisely this undifferentiated way. At the same time, the *similarities* of history and experience among television institutions in different African countries (for example, the role of colonial powers in establishing TV institutions modelled on their own broadcasting systems and needs, resulting in a legacy of 'inappropriate' technology and training and related difficulties in evolving authentically local television cultures) *are* as important to our understanding of their functioning and problems – and hence their

189

programmes – as national and regional differences. Then again, more detailed attention reveals post-independence African television institutions as the sites of very *different* (and, one could argue, culturally distinctive) responses to or reactions against their 'common' colonial experiences.[11]

The necessity to acknowledge difference as well as similarity raises in turn the complicating question of whether all *geographically* African countries can be considered as *culturally* African. Are TV programmes from the culturally and ethnically distinct Maghreb countries (Algeria, Morocco, Tunisia, Libya, Egypt), which identify more as 'Arab' than 'African' and (in many cases) politically and economically look increasingly to the Middle East, 'African television'? Optimism about the future of the 'new' democratic South Africa notwithstanding, is South African state television – not long ago a white-controlled bastion of National Party hegemony – 'African television'?[12] If the answer to this last question is 'not yet', this throws us back into issues of democracy of address, access and institutional control, cultural 'authenticity' and 'true' reflection of local needs.

The group of countries I concentrated on in my core research embody a *culturally* inclusive conception of 'African television' embracing Saharan as well as sub-Saharan Africa, 'Arab' as well as 'black African' cultures, a diversity of religion (and of religiosity), and in theory a diversity of broadcast languages from English, French and Arabic to Zulu, Hausa and Wolof. What they do not reflect, however, are the continent's full geographical spread (east, central and most of north-west Africa are utterly unrepresented) or (more problematically) the programme output of its newer and poorer TV nations.

The list included Nigeria, Ghana, Egypt, Senegal, South Africa, Mozambique and Tunisia – a selection largely dictated by the need to concentrate on countries believed to be accomplished and prolific programme-makers, which in practice meant those with well established and well developed TV structures. With the exception of South Africa (broadcasting since 1976) and Mozambique (since 1979), the countries chosen had all been TV broadcasters since the early-to-mid 1960s (1959 in the case of Nigeria, the continent's first TV broadcaster).[13] Since these veteran national TV institutions were in most cases established shortly after independence (in Nigeria's case, slightly before), frequently financed and equipped by the former colonists and modelled on their own TV institutions, it could be argued that the selection of material would be limited to programmes in which colonial values and conceptions of quality had been internalised at the expense of those produced within newer TV organisations which had more truly been born out of independence and the desire for cultural autonomy.

190

However, my viewing of actual programmes proved to be a more complex (and less reductive) experience, in which such preconceptions were often radically contradicted. The common criticism that the legacy of colonially supplied equipment, training, and the like, has stymied the emergence of a distinctively 'African' televisual *aesthetic* ignores the fact that African programme genres and formats which may *seem* familiar to British audiences (and academics) will be very different from British programmes in their cultural and political content. Indeed, I would suggest that the tendency to explain or dismiss the programme genres of African countries as 'copies' of British or American ones arises largely because the cultural specificity of their *content* may be so disorienting to an uninitiated First World viewer that the only 'way into' the programme on a first viewing is to seize on what does seem familiar. It should also be mentioned that the potential for 'misreading' a programme in terms of its own culture in such circumstances is considerable, and this may contribute to overinterpretation of the extent to which some programmes 'internalise' culturally imperialist/culturally inauthentic values and perspectives.

A far more serious setback has been the inappropriateness of this colonial technology and training for African economic and climatic conditions, so that African broadcasters have faced the additional hurdles of unlearning inappropriate practices and improvising more locally relevant (and less costly) alternatives, often perpetuating dependency on First World 'help' rather than self-determination. Some of the examples of this cited by broadcasters in Africa make depressing reading.

Barra Yeggo *or* The Love Boat? *Imports and Cultural Imperialism*
Another factor contributing to the ambiguity of 'African television' as a category, and to its broadcasters' problems in serving their populations' needs, is the high proportion of imported First World programmes to be found in many African countries' terrestrial (public) as well as satellite (private) TV schedules. The late Sid Ahmed Nugdalla, former Director of the Extra-Mural Department of the University of Khartoum, Sudan, observed that 'the tragedy in our developing societies is partly reflected in ... the imported *pattern* of broadcasting' (my italics)[14] – a pattern which, in George Wedell's words, 'conceives of broadcasting as a non-stop supply of programmes guaranteed during operating hours. It means that "slots" have to be filled whether or not there is anything worthwhile to transmit.'[15]

The 'demand' for imported programming can thus be seen as something created by the export of inappropriate broadcasting patterns and attitudes by First World countries wishing to promote their own interests; or, to put it another way, the programmes are there in the first place not to meet African audiences' demands for 'high'-quality but culturally irrelevant and educationally void programming but to meet First World demand for expanding economic and ideological markets. Packages of American TV programmes, in particular, change hands at the annual international television market, MIPCOM, at special 'Third World' prices which make it possible for African countries to fill their schedules with First World drama and light entertainment at an hourly cost which is a fraction of the lowest-budget (that is, studio-bound) domestic productions. It is commonly claimed that the hourly cost of domestically made programmes is ten times that of these cheap imports. An article in the Nairobi *Weekly Review* (13 March 1981) estimated that 'low-quality' imported series such as *The Stooges* would cost the Voice of Kenya (the name of the KBC's 1964–89 incarnation) around $2,000, while a 'quality' series such as *Roots* would cost $10,000 upwards. Wedell adds that a single half-hour programme made by the VOK to celebrate the tenth anniversary of independence cost $3,000 to make in 1973.[16]

The pattern is repeated in countries with a recent history of white rule: the proportion of imported programming on the Namibian Broadcasting Corporation (set up in 1990 when Namibia gained independence from South Africa) is estimated at 90 per cent; and the daytime, early-evening and late-night mix of Australian and US soaps and serials on the South African SABC's TV1 (still regarded by commentators as its 'white' channel) is virtually indistinguishable from scheduling in the UK (*Santa Barbara*, ITV network *Home and Away*, *Murder, She Wrote*, *Columbo*, *Street Legal*, and so on).

While few African TV organisations are in a position to supply hard data on which programmes are most popular with audiences[17] – and despite the fact that the upper-class and expatriate urban élites whom African 'public-service' television is often accused of exclusively serving are often claimed to prefer European and US programmes – there is also much anecdotal evidence that, given the opportunity, the wider TV audiences in African countries prefer programmes which reflect their own cultures and lives. Wedell quotes a reader's letter from the Nairobi *Standard* headed 'More boring television', complaining about *The Love Boat*'s overextended mooring on Kenyan TV.[18] *Barra Yeggo*, the first-ever Senegalese TV comedy to be scripted specifically for TV and shot as a 'telefilm',[19] was originally intended as a one-off but proved so popular that three sequels have been made. In 1980s Zimbabwe, a weekly improvised Shona-language drama regularly drew a larger audience than *Dallas*, though the broadcaster ZBC had problems convincing advertisers of this.[20]

The desire (and need) to see highly local and specific self-images on TV seems particularly strong among rural populations. McLellan reports of rural dwellers in Côte d'Ivoire walking up to 100km to the village of Kouassi Blikro, where a communal battery-powered TV set had been installed by the government in the local school, to watch Télévision Ivoirienne's *Télé Pour Tous*, an educational programme for rural audiences conceived by Côte d'Ivoire's education ministry, 80 per cent of which was filmed in remote rural areas.[21]

What is really striking is the fierce commitment to domestic production which is shown by many African TV broadcasters. Given that most of Mozambique's energies are currently absorbed in repairing the devastation left by sixteen years of civil war (after a peace agreement between the Frelimo government and Renamo rebels was reached in October 1992), it is remarkable that indigenously made programmes fill 45 per cent of the country's TV broadcast hours. The Nigerian NTA's figure of 90 per cent of weekly broadcast hours taken up by Nigerian-made programmes is extraordinary by world as well as African standards, comparing favourably with all four UK channels.

Pay TV and Satellite – More of the Same?
In the days before satellite and pay TV, the total absence of competition in TV broadcasting in most African nations was perceived as a major factor in its unresponsiveness to audience demand or needs.[22] However, the arrival of such competitors on the continent – often financially powerful and non-African-owned – and the competitive, commercialised and ultimately deregulated TV climate that will result seem likely to increase rather than decrease the pressure on African state broadcasters to screen cheap imported First World programming (in order to compete with the 'pure entertainment' offered by the new players). This will also exacerbate rather than alleviate the tendency in African countries to predominantly address their most prosperous and 'westernised' citizens, since to compete with private TV broadcasters for advertising and sponsorship revenue the state broadcasters must give the impression that they too have captured Africa's minority audience of 'consumers'. Such effects have been exacerbated by recent cuts in state subsidies for television in many countries (including Nigeria and Senegal).

Another effect of the arrival of satellite and pay TV has been to blur boundaries between locally produced and imported programmes at the reception end of the broadcasting process. Those who can afford a satellite dish have access, in theory, to channels from across Europe, the Middle East and even Russia. CNN and the BBC's World Service Television are available in an increasing number of African countries. National state television services may *include* relays of foreign channels, not always as a pay service: for example, Tunisia's ERTT relays France 2 and Italy's RAI Uno in addition to its national channel,

Channel 2, and recent satellite launch, Channel 7.

The increasing range of 'global' TV programming available to (some) African audiences – perhaps at the expense of the local – has certain major implications for my research. First, it complicates the question of programme origins. For example, when the commercial attaché at the Senegalese embassy in London lent me his own videos of music clips – some from the state RTS channel, others from the French-owned satellite service Canal Horizons – neither he nor I knew whether the Senegalese musicians on the various clips had been filmed by Senegal's RTS, by France's Canal Plus, or by independent video-makers who might have been financed by either. Similarly, the Tunisian embassy staff in London had no more idea than I had whether a drama taped from the state broadcaster ERTT's overseas satellite service was Tunisian or Egyptian. The whole notion that 'African television' refers to programmes made and screened terrestrially in African countries is further thrown into question when one considers that there are Egyptian programme-makers escaping high taxes at home by working in London making (culturally) Egyptian programmes which they can then opt to sell to the Egyptian Radio and Television Union, to the ERTU's (satellite) Space Channel, to the same export markets as the ERTU in the Middle East, or to the London-based satellite broadcaster MBC (Middle East Broadcasting Centre), which since 1992 has beamed Arabic-language programming (including much Egyptian drama) across an area bordered by Zaire, India and Sweden.

But if one considers those satellite broadcasters which do have African ownership and fund (some) domestic production, this becomes a highly political question given the sharp inequalities of resources between profit-motivated satellite and pay-TV companies and Africa's public-service broadcasters. In practice, the only example to fall into my sphere of research was South Africa's commercially successful and expansionist satellite channel M-Net, set up in 1986. Given the specific South African situation – the historical position of the SABC (the state broadcaster) as an undemocratic National Party mouthpiece, and many commentators' dissatisfaction with the seeming entrenchment of its old power structures in the new post-apartheid state – the arrival of a competitor (albeit one whose licence forbids it from broadcasting 'news') could be viewed as a democratising development. Furthermore, some strong-sounding (and independently produced) locally made programmes – such as *Egoli*, a daily soap which is one of the few non-imports with high audience figures on any South African channel – bore out this positive impression. The channel has also been putting some (highly publicised) money into developing and producing *New Directions*, a series of four short films by multiracial teams of (as they put it) 'formerly disadvantaged scriptwriters and directors'.

But despite the PR efforts surrounding M-Net's investment in local talent, only 9–13 per cent of their total programming is locally produced. And none of *New Directions*' new directors is black – though a black 'trainee director' gets a credit on *Come See the Bioscope*, a charming film about ANC co-founder Solomon Plaatje and the travelling film show he took around black populations in the 1920s, which makes *Cinema Paradiso* look politicised. And, while the two hardest-hitting of the 1994 *New Directions* dramas are scripted by young black writers, all four finished films offer images of multiracial South Africa which seem more calculated to reassure prejudiced white viewers than to offer anything positive to black ones.[23] This did not, however, rule out their potential inclusion in the 'Adjust Your Sets' season as interesting exemplars of the contradictory ideologies that result when white-controlled broadcasting bodies in a former apartheid state try their hand at 'multiracial' programming.

Entertainment or Education? Debates about Television and Development

The provision of satellite and pay-TV services is underpinned by assumptions about the existence of a market in entertainment. By contrast, the literature about African television written from a development perspective – that is, from a position of concern about intensifying global and national inequalities and the need for autonomous economic and technological development in African countries – talks about it in terms of education and needs. These two contrasting perspectives are positioned at opposing (and seemingly irreconcilable) poles of the debate about what television in African countries is, what it should be, and what it is for.

For someone researching African television this debate translates into questions of value. Which TV programmes do we value and why? Do we value programmes which are thought to be popular with local audiences, or those which seek to educate them? Those which give local populations a 'window on the world', or those which reflect local cultures, depict local lives and address local problems? I have held off from discussing 'value' as an abstract concept in this paper precisely in order to demonstrate its roots in material and cultural conditions – in this case, the conditions of African countries. Such a line of argument does not necessarily imply cultural relativism, however, since the criteria of value being argued about above might equally be applied to television in the UK. For instance, the proliferation of global cultural imperialism – the increasing domination of multinational-owned media and US cinema product across the globe – means that struggles

195

for the self-determined televisual and cinematic expression of national or regional cultures and concerns from a local perspective are now a problem shared by the 'First' and former 'Second' Worlds as well as the 'Third'.[24]

But, conversely, if we were to transpose development studies assumptions about whether African television's role is to educate or entertain into a current UK media or or media studies context – as if it *were* a straightforward either/or question – their terms of debate would not only be dismissed as unsophisticated but would be identified as a patronising and outmoded exemplar of Reithian top-down paternalism. The interest – and difficulties – of the discussions of African television which have emerged out of development studies as an academic discipline lie precisely in this tacit espousal of Reithian assumptions and hopes about television and its effects. But it should be remembered also that many African public television broadcasters continue to see their own role in Reithian, top-down, paternalistic terms. Re-viewed in this light, the anti-Reithian stance of First World media studies can be seen in part as a symptom of its origins outside Third World contexts in which top-down tactics may be perceived as necessary for transmitting authoritative messages about economic development and national unity. The interest of drawing on development studies perspectives in a media studies context therefore lies in the potential for *mutual* interrogation between the two approaches.[25]

Questions of Effect
The charge against television in poor countries made by commentators working within development studies and development organisations is blunt: it is an unnecessary and disastrously expensive luxury which eats up resources desperately needed elsewhere. As Dietrich Berwanger puts it:

> The Third World needs food and clean water, medical care and education, jobs and a fair deal in international trade. It does not need electronic gadgets for passing the time. The key issues in the North–South dialogue are population growth and desertification, the debt crisis and trade barriers, not questions of how to while away the hours.[26]

Berwanger's own work in fact departs substantially from the negative perspective he quotes, noting that 'the Third World [has not] shared the doubts of its western friends and consultants'[27] and questioning the applicability of existing development theory (in particular, perspectives that stress Third World dependency) to the rapid development of Third World television as 'a medium for the masses'. But it can easily be seen how such accounts lead to the view that television in poor countries is only justifiable at all as a *tool of development* – that is, of education which will further development goals. Furthermore, the expensiveness of television and various problems of reception – the cost of a TV set, the fact that the majority of potential viewers live in villages without electricity which are often not reached by TV signals[28] and the special difficulties of broadcasting for highly multilingual populations – lead many to argue that, if a mass communication medium is required, radio is cheaper and more effective.

Iain McLellan's 'Television for Development: The African Experience', a report concerned with practical strategies for TV in African countries to function more effectively in the service of development, typifies the theoretical problems which remain unaddressed in development studies approaches. Asserting that 'any efforts to use television to communicate development messages beyond the most general of outlines have been spotty, erratic, and have had, for the most part, little impact', McLellan's suggested solutions repeatedly come up against unacknowledged problems of *effect*. The mix of imported material and locally made programming which concentrates on 'political speeches, reports on visits of foreign dignitaries, development "experts" speaking over the heads of the average viewer in European languages ... [and] dramas featuring upper-class characters dealing with typically western problems'[29] is held to have detrimental effects on local culture, self-image, empowerment and development. But it is clear from McLellan's account that those who see television as an educational and developmental tool repeatedly face the paradoxical problem that its effects – in terms of getting populations to absorb its messages about agricultural, health care, birth control, and the like, and put them into practice – are too weak.

McLellan concludes that TV programmes are only effective in 'educating' relevant sectors of the population to change their behaviour (for example, in persuading farmers to switch to a high-yield variety of a staple crop) when they are used as part of targeted face-to-face training by fieldworkers and/or an equally targeted multi-media campaign. Moreover, narrowcasting, community broadcasting and video may have more of a role to play in such direct education than national TV networks – or, at least, the national TV networks as currently conceived by African governments. McLellan also advocates training marginalised populations to use video as a tool of democracy and empowerment which can convey their views and conditions back to governments.

These findings raise serious questions about the wisdom of treating African television as if it 'ought' to be a 'pure' development and educational medium since its extant *reality* as an impure hybrid of education and entertainment, mixed cultures and mixed messages is clearly something very different, and since it appears that other (perhaps cheaper) media such as video might do that particular job more effectively. They also point to the wrong-headedness of expecting or wanting its messages to have a direct, controllable effect on audience behaviour. For all McLellan's apparent commitment to democratising African television to enable it to serve the needs of those groups marginalised or ignored by urban-oriented programming, many of his recommendations rest on precisely the same top-down, paternalistic assumptions (in this case, that the development educator always knows best and that the viewer's resistance to the message is there to be broken down) as the élitist and undemocratic practices in African public television which he attacks.[30]

Perhaps such tactics are necessary to convey 'modernising' messages to resistant traditional populations. All the same, it is disturbing that the question of *whose* message is being conveyed and the contradictions of using undemocratic means to achieve supposedly democratic ends and centralised means to achieve decentralised solutions are never acknowledged by McLellan. Given African television's imperfect and hybrid nature, its apparent weakness in terms of effect on viewers' actions and their resistance to some of its messages – which a development studies perspective such as McLellan's regards as a problem – actually seem to me to be readable as healthy signs of an active and sceptical audience. It is also evidence that presumed negative effects, too (of First World imports and the 'wrong' kinds of domestic programming), are unlikely to be as monolithic as opponents of cultural imperialism and promoters of autonomous development fear.

This is confirmed by other sources. The Nigerian media academic Luke Uka Uche, for instance, wrote in 1985:

The current research finds the audiences of the Nigerian mass media in crisis situations to be extraordinarily independently opinionated, suspicious of the media contents, active rather than passive audiences of the media, and intelligently questioning the legitimacy of any new leadership and the contents of the media ... [The audience] knows when it is being manipulated.[31]

Dietrich Berwanger argues:

Not even a perfected police state is able to suppress all the [to it] undesired effects of television. When the government of South Africa reluctantly gave in to the insistence of the white population and business world, and introduced television in 1976, it was almost the last country in Africa to do so. Two channels were supposed to be for the white population; another two broadcast programmes in Zulu, Xhosa and Tswana for the black population. The organisational set-ups of white and black television were also strictly separated to allow for 'segregated development' in television as well.

In the meantime, 25% of the viewers of one of the 'white' channels are blacks, and the most popular programme on television among both blacks and whites is *The Cosby Show*, starring a black entertainer from the United States ... The government's mistrust had been well-founded: television is not good for apartheid.[32]

Television for Whom? Problems of Democracy

To apply a purist development studies approach to the study of African television would therefore be theoretically and politically inadequate in several respects. At the same time, development-related *programmes* remain a crucially important part of African television programming, and need to be treated as such. Where development-oriented literature such as McLellan's remains helpful is in focusing on problems of lack of democracy of access and unrepresentativeness of address, and in critiquing African television's marginalisation of majority social groups who not only ought to be central to the sense of post-colonial national identity and cultural renewal it aspires to foster but whose participation is vital if autonomous and equitable development is ever to be achieved. Specifically, this means rural populations: women (particularly rural women) and, in sub-Saharan countries especially, local-language speakers who can neither understand the 'official' (usually ex-colonial) language which dominates broadcasting nor read and write.

While this shortage of rural images or images of African women which reflect the realities of their lives can be seen as a problem of attitudes and power imbalances within the broadcasting organisations (Berwanger points out, for instance, that 'production centres are located in the cities and programmes are generally made by city dwellers for city dwellers'),[33] broadcasters in countries with a large number of local languages (such as Ghana, which is estimated to have forty-four or more) clearly find it a practical as much as a political problem to provide a semblance of democratic broadcasting. Language politics in multilingual sub-Saharan countries is a sensitive issue, and governments (and therefore TV broadcasters) may retain the ex-colonial language as their official language precisely to avoid accusations of favouring one local language group over another. Nigeria's NTA and Ghana's GBC, for example, both broadcast primarily in English but with a substantial number of slots devoted to the most widespread local languages. By broadcasting in six local languages,[34] the GBC is able to reach 75 per cent of the population who speak one or more of these languages as a first or second language.

However, Paul A. V. Ansah suggests that, in Ghana at least, the range of languages chosen has as much to do with local-language politics as with maximising the democracy of television's address: while English is understood by only 25 per cent of Ghana's population, Akan, the most widely-spoken local-language group, is a first or second language for 65 per cent of the population. Yet, after decades of discussion, English remains the official, and major broadcast, language, while Akan is allocated only the same percentage of broadcast time as five less widely spoken local languages. While Ghana is perhaps an extreme case, the lesson is that the presence of local – as opposed to European – language programming on a country's TV schedules is not such a straightforward badge of democratic broadcasting as it initially appears.[35]

Turning to the question of the representation of women, a large number of the programmes I did see – whether from Egypt, Nigeria or Senegal – portrayed women as leisured housewives whose main energies were channelled into gossip and their emotional lives. Often dramas depicted women as having careers, but on a modern, westernised, urban model; more tellingly, their work had little bearing on the narratives. Egyptian dramas were particularly adept at placing westernised 'career women' who *appeared* to have high-powered jobs (businesswomen, TV presenters) in highly traditional narratives about (say) bourgeois marriage preparations (the title of one TV movie, *The Ormolu Lounge Suite*, says it all) or problems with in-laws.

On the other hand, programmes conveying such mixed messages about traditional and modern values undoubtedly demonstrate something of the attitudes and aspirations of the cultures that produce them, however retrograde their treatment of women may appear. Similarly, the preponderance of dramas and comedies depicting urban life (from Senegal's *Barra Yeggo* to the Nigerian Lagos-based soap *Mirror in the Sun*) and even *Dallas*-style backstabbing, corruption and contested paternity among the rich (the Nigerian mini-series *Assets* is one example of this popular genre) challenged my preconceptions about programmes from African countries – and contradicted the images of Africa we see on UK television – far more radically than any documentary about rural poverty or traditional rituals could have done. I could not help feeling that the very urbanity of these programmes might radically shift a UK audience's perceptions of the aspirations and self-images of the people of Africa towards seeing them as active agents rather than passive, dependent victims.

Alongside questions of unrepresentativeness in African television there are other issues of democracy of expression – in particular, those relating to top-down institutional structures headed by western-educated and trained personnel, and the political and Islamic censorship and consequent self-censorship in many countries. Of course, these two problems are in no way unique to African countries; attempts by governments to censor or influence the mass media are more of a rule than an exception around the world. Furthermore, the fact that censorship and centralised control of the media are fallible, and that those who repress or control television's contents nevertheless cannot control its *effects*, means that television from highly censored countries can be extremely interesting, extremely boring – and sometimes both.

A good example is Egyptian television, which is not only heavily censored by the government but functions in a climate in which Al-Azhar, the international Islamic university in Cairo, now has powers of political and moral as well as religious censorship over cultural expression in the country. This censorship is evident in, for example, the limited, domestic, trivial subject-matter of many TV dramas. However, the Cairo-based film-maker Mohammed Shebl reports a shift in 1994's Ramadan TV programming which can be read as a move in the Egyptian government's struggle against the Islamic fundamentalists. Where in recent years US soaps and other 'corrupting' imports have been banished from the screen during Ramadan, in 1994 US series were shown regardless. More significantly, three Egyptian-made soaps or mini-series screened during Ramadan that year contained open criticism of fundamentalism and (in the case of one, *The Family*) other aspects of Egyptian society.[36]

Furthermore, Nigeria, a nation with one of the liveliest and most productive TV cultures in Africa, is far from being an uncensored society. One Nigerian press report implied that the failure of the extremely popular independently produced sitcom *Basi and Company*, which ceased production in 1991, to obtain sponsorship (in contrast with amiable but blander comedies such as *The New Masquerade*) was due to its content being *too* sharply socially critical. This was despite the fact that its satire on Lagos's 'get rich quick' society fitted in perfectly with the government's War Against Indiscipline, a campaign whose messages permeated the NTA's 1980s programming from mini-series to children's programmes. Nor was *Basi and Company* (which in my view was far ahead not only of the other Nigerian comedies I saw but also of many current UK sitcoms in terms of script quality and ideas) mentioned in the list of programme recommendations for the season sent to me by the NTA.[37]

Conclusion: Implications for Programming Criteria

In interrogating the complex mesh of political and ethical questions discussed above and trying to feed them into my actual research and (provisional) programming practice, I repeatedly came up against one tension above all others: the tension between *valorising the desirable* and *reflecting the typical*. If I decided to select for the season programmes that were 'desirable' – in that they addressed the rural mass of a country's population – above programmes which were aimed at its urban élites, I would not be reflecting the reality that access to television among the rural masses is very limited and that most programming in African countries does, in practice, address the wealthier urban viewers who make up the its core audience. On the other hand, selecting urban-oriented programmes because they were popular and 'typical' would neglect the failure of much African television to speak to rural populations, the poor and the dispossessed.

However, this distinction between the 'desirable' and the 'typical' itself raised questions which in turn pointed towards a practical – if less theoretically clear-cut – programming solution. First and most crucially, how could I – a white Londoner viewing or reading synopses of programmes far outside their cultural and economic context – judge whether a programme which appeared to me to meet 'desirability' criteria (for example by taking rural and development issues as its subject) had succeeded in its home setting in reaching those whom it appeared to address? Given that we (and for that matter the bulk of African broadcasters) have no way of measuring the effectiveness of African programmes in helping achieve wider local goals, how meaningful would it be to select programmes whose subject-matter *appeared to us* to be relevant to local needs?

The short answer is, of course, that this is all we *can* do. But the job of such a season of programmes is to show the surprising and the exceptional (and perhaps therefore the unrepresentative) as well as the typical. And this aspiration functions to break down the opposition between 'desirable' and 'typical' programmes, since truly exceptional programmes are precisely those which transcend boundaries between 'entertainment' and 'education', the 'popular' and the 'improving'. The enormously popular Nigerian drama series *Cock Crow at Dawn* was commissioned to encourage Nigerians who leave the countryside to seek work in the overcrowded cities of the benefits of returning to rural areas to take up mechanised farming, and to spread the message that Nigeria's banks (one of which sponsored the series) were willing to give financial help. The lead actor from the Nigerian sitcom *Basi and Company*, Albert Egbe, declared in 1986 that the series's 'main aim is to lift the level of spoken English by Nigerian children'.[38] However, one can easily make the argument that *Cock Crow at Dawn* and *Basi and Company* are no more typical of 'average' Nigerian TV than *Edge of Darkness* or *Rising Damp* are of 'average' British TV.

Two further programmes I stumbled across during my research underlined the point that some programmes which were hardly 'typical' and failed dismally on the 'desirability' criterion could nevertheless be fascinating television. *The Evil Will Cease*, an Egyptian TV-movie melodrama about an airline steward brought low by drug addiction and eventually saved by Islam, was gripping, highly entertaining, and stood out among the blur of Egyptian romantic comedies and family melodramas I viewed. Another example, which I was unfortunately unable to see, was an episode of Ghana's *Weekend Rendezvous* variety series featuring GeMann, a young London-based Ghanaian singer-dancer and winner of the Superstar Michael Jackson Imitation Contest.

The overall conclusion I drew was that any general criteria of programme selection would have to be strictly minimal if they were to be both theoretically consistent and workable in practice. I decided to attempt a balance between the desirable and the typical, however fraught with difficulty this might be. Thus programmes addressing development needs, rural needs, women's needs, and the like, would be included in the season alongside entertainment (or at least entertaining) programmes. The principle of 'balance' also gestured towards the need to balance the different marginalised constituencies and socially important topics represented: rural development programming should not be included to the exclusion of programmes about women's lives or conditions in the 'new' South Africa, for example.

My second criterion was that programmes should on some level express, reflect or address the cultural and social conditions of their country of origin. This echoed the aspirations of the Third Cinema theorists for cultural (in this case, televisual) expression which is locally relevant and culturally 'authentic'. It implied programmes which aspire towards autonomous, independent, distinctive post-colonial television cultures rather than those which internalise colonial values – while also trying to allow for the fact that there is no way of 'objectively' measuring this. Thus it sought programmes which are 'linked with national culture', as the Cuban theorist and film-maker Fernando Solanas once put it,[39] but interpreted this as broadly as possible, deliberately refusing to be prescriptive about what constitutes authentic 'national culture'.

In stressing local cultures rather than national culture, this second principle both recognises and valorises cultural diversity, implying the representation/expression of a nation's marginal or 'peripheral' (for example, rural and regional) cultures as well as 'central' (for example, urban) ones. It also signals a refusal to define national culture in *any* essentialist terms, whether of traditional values untainted by colonial influences or fundamentalist Islamic values untainted by western capitalist decadence. Rather, it leaves space for a broader view that an African TV programme 'linked with national culture' might be one in which tradition and modernity, colonial and post-colonial values, or 'messages' and entertainment coexist in a more complex relationship.

Notes
1. June I. Givanni, 'Television in Nigeria and Kenya: A Brief Overview of Its Organisation', unpublished report, 1992.
2. Iain McLellan, 'Television for Development: The African Experience', manuscript report, International Development Research Centre, Ottawa, January 1986, p. 2.
3. From a conversation I had with one UK media development academic in the course of my research.
4. Phone conversation, 4 May 1994.
5. BBC2's *The Late Show* reported on the attempts of the state broadcaster SABC to reinvent itself as 'a new SABC for the new South Africa' (tx BBC 2 26/4/94); Channel Four screened the three-part drama *In a Time of Violence* (tx C4 10–24/4/94), the first-ever international co-production with a wholly South African cast and crew and to be co-funded by the SABC.
6. Only a small handful of TV clips from African (including Maghreb) countries have been used in the various ITV and BBC variants on the 'comic TV clips' genre first fronted by Dennis Norden in 1980. The reasons for this given by Colin Putney, Associate Editor of *Tarrant on TV*, and Jane Mercer of the Clive James programmes range from the severe practical difficulties of communicating and negotiating with African (and other 'Third World') TV institutions – which are likely to be under-resourced, with overburdened or inadequate telecommunication systems, and (with the exceptions of Egypt, which is probably the biggest TV programme producer and exporter in the Arab world, and to some extent Nigeria) contain no structure for programme permissions or sales – to a sensitivity to the unethical and racist implications of encouraging audiences to laugh at programmes in which the shortage of material and training resources is often visible on screen. The increasing homogeneity and US domination of TV *worldwide*, accelerated by the spread of satellite and pay TV, were also cited as problems for such programmes.
7. Information derived from the SIFT database in the BFI library.
8. Pay TV or satellite TV are now available, to those who can afford a decoder or dish, in major cities and sometimes beyond, in at least eleven African countries. Few are African-owned; most broadcast a huge proportion (usually quoted as 80–90 per cent) of imported (usually US) programming. Three important examples are: (i) Canal Horizons, a French-language 'African-oriented' variant on France's Canal Plus launched in Senegal's capital, Dakar, in late 1991, in Tunisia's capital, Tunis, in late 1992, and planning to transmit in Gabon (whose capital, Libreville, already has a private station, Canal Liberté, owned by an opposition politician) and Côte d'Ivoire's capital, Abidjan, from late

1993; (ii) the Egyptian Space Channel (ESC), a satellite channel set up in late 1990 by Egypt's state TV broadcaster, ERTU, to build on its success as a leading programme exporter to North Africa and the Middle East, beamed throughout North Africa, the Middle East and Europe (programming aimed at non-Arabic speakers was planned from October 1993 – outcome unconfirmed); (iii) South Africa's thriving and aggressive M-Net, which has been broadcasting since 1986, and is targeting other nations to the north for expansion.

9. A shortlist of countries on which I should concentrate my research was drawn up by the Africa 95 editorial board, the criteria being that they had well established and well developed television services, were known or thought to produce 'good' or 'interesting' programmes, and were (to an imperfect extent) representative of the continent's cultural, linguistic and political diversity (and by implication the countries' different colonial histories).

10. By the start of 1994, forty-five of the fifty-one mainland African countries were TV broadcasters.

11. For instance, while one state broadcaster in a former French colony, Senegal's RTS, on which French is still substantially used as a broadcast language (although local-language programming is increasing), ended up with the French-designed SECAM colour system (though after rumoured pressure from France to turn down a West German offer of German-designed PAL equipment), the Algerian ENTV's choice of PAL in 1974 (after a year's trial of both systems) was undoubtedly connected with the low ebb reached by Algerian–French relations at that time.

12. South African media academics Lynette Steenveld and Larry Strelitz argue that the ideological project of the establishment of SABC-TV in 1976 was precisely 'to limit the boundaries of political debate to those set by the ideology of the [then] ruling Afrikaner National Party' (see L. Steenveld and L. Strelitz, '1922 and South African television', Screen, vol. 35, no. 1, Spring 1994, p. 36). In the course of my research I encountered vastly differing views on the extent to which the real power in the SABC remains in white hands and the extent to which black producers and directors have been able to make more than token inroads.

13. Though by no means necessarily to the whole nation. The dates given for the inauguration of public television broadcasts in African countries need to be approached with care, and not only because different sources are occasionally inconsistent. It is important to remember that in many countries early broadcasts were or are 'experimental' – for example, 2–3 hours a day in the capital city only, or broadcasting an important event such as a trade fair or the Olympics – or were limited to a single province or to schools broadcasts. Given the economics of broadcasting in African countries, 'experimental' status can linger; alternatively, the public demand whetted by experimental broadcasting can push governments into extending transmission hours to provide a nominally 'national' service when they are not really ready.

14. S. A. Nugdalla, 'Broadcasting and Cultural Change', in G. Wedell (ed.), *Making Broadcasting Useful: The Development of Radio and Television in Africa in the 1980s* (Manchester: Manchester University Press, 1986), p. 96.

15. G. Wedell, 'Broadcasting in the Developing Commonwealth: Help or Hindrance?', *Journal of the Royal Society of Arts*, March 1980, p. 222.
16. G. Wedell, 'Three Priorities for Action', in G. Wedell (ed.), *Making Broadcasting Useful*, p. 292.
17. Aside from a lack of resources to apportion to audience research, African broadcasters face special research difficulties in, for example, gaining access to audiences in remote rural locations with no electricity or communications, poor roads, and so on, to carrying out field research. Neither Ghana nor Nigeria had any audience data which they felt was recent enough to pass on to me, and only South Africa was able to supply weekly audience ratings.
18. Wedell (ed.), *Making Broadcasting Useful*, p. 292.
19. That is to say that it was the first to look like a location-shot UK sitcom. Before that, TV comedy in Senegal would have followed a format which continues to be common in low-budget African television: simply videoing a live (and usually improvised) studio or outdoor performance by comedians who are already popular as *live* entertainers. Televised 'traditional theatre', in which traditional stage dramas acted by eminent stage actors are simply filmed, and 'traditional variety', in which tribal dances and rituals are re-enacted indoors in a TV studio, are also very typical and distinctive TV genres in many African countries.
20. McLellan, 'Television for Development', p. 38.
21. Ibid., p. 16.
22. See Wedell, 'Three Priorities for Action', in *Making Broadcasting Useful*, p. 286.
23. One, *The Apology*, allegorically portrays the nation as a culturally white élite private school whose privileges 'deserving' (and suitably grateful) blacks may now share (without presenting any threat to white hegemony) but which must acknowledge its past mistakes. Another, *Learning the Hard Way*, depicts townships as sites of black-on-black exploitation in which black male lust and greed prey on 'coloured' female innocence.
24. My purpose in using quote marks here is to acknowledge the unstable and problematic nature of these three categories. I have nevertheless used the terms 'First World' and 'Third World' in this paper for want of any more appropriate shorthand terminology for the rich colonising nations and the culturally colonised countries of Africa.
25. Dietrich Berwanger points to both disciplines' mutual neglect of Third World media: 'Third World researchers leave scientific studies on mass media to communication researchers for whom the Third World plays a very minor role' – D. Berwanger, *Television in the Third World: New Technology and Social Change* (Bonn: Freidrich Ebert-Stiftung, 1987), p. 5.
26. Ibid.
27. Ibid., p. 7.
28. Obviously the size of this majority varies from country to country. In countries with large concentrations of the population in an urban area or areas and/or an extensive regional TV network – Egypt and Nigeria are examples of both phenomena – these problems may appear to be alleviated. But it should not be forgotten that even 100 per cent geographical coverage by TV signals – which most countries have not achieved – does

not mean 100 per cent access to television. Though in Nigeria the NTA's 25 regional channels cover 100 per cent of the land area, the NTA estimates its audience at 30 million – out of a total population of 88 million. Government schemes placing battery- or solar-powered TV sets in some villages as an educational aid have been attempted in many African countries, but many of these experiments fell by the wayside due to maintenance difficulties (such as the difficulty of getting spare parts to remote villages), theft of TV sets or batteries, and the like.

29. McLellan, 'Television for Development', p. 6.
30. For instance, his suggestion that government development communicators should 'saturate the target area by plugging the message into as many media as possible. Have the same, co-ordinated message presented on radio, television, newspapers, pamphlets, posters, T-shirts, jingles, spot announcements, etc.' reads a little like a short course in propaganda techniques. Indeed, without the highly centralised relations between government and media which currently exist in many African countries (to the extent that many national TV services are under the direct control of the Ministry of Information), such advice would be difficult to carry out.
31. Quoted in Berwanger, *Television in the Third World*, p. 88.
32. Ibid., p. 90.
33. Ibid., pp. 90–1.
34. Akan, Dagbani, Ewe, Ga, Nzema and Hausa.
35. Paul A. V. Ansah, 'Broadcasting and Multilingualism', in Wedell (ed.), *Making Broadcasting Useful*.
36. Phone conversation with Mohammed Shebl, March 1994. A column in *The Egyptian Gazette* of 24 February 1994, written in the form of a conversation between two friends in a coffee-house, praises *The Family*: 'Watch it, it is worth watching … This serial discusses most of the problems of contemporary Egypt … It is a socio-political serial which has also its entertainment aspect as well … It is an attempt to understand the issues and the causes of these issues.'
37. After *Basi* ceased production, its creator and producer, the novelist Ken Saro-Wiwa, concentrated his energies on environmental and minority rights campaigns, particularly against the environmental effects of Shell's oil operations on the lives of the 500,000 Ogoni people who inhabit the Niger delta. On 23 May 1994 Saro-Wiwa was abducted by the Nigerian military, following two years of military attacks on the Ogoni because of their campaign (K. Bishop, 'Where Trouble Flares', London, *Guardian*, 27 May 1994, p. 15).
38. J. Eboh, '*Basi & Company* battles gutter language on TV', *Concord Entertainment* (Nigeria), 1 February 1986.
39. Fernando Solanas in *CinémAction*, no. 1, 1978, reprinted in *L'Influence du troisième cinéma du monde* (CinémAction, 1979).